THE REVOLUTION OF 1525

THE REVOLUTION OF 1525

THE GERMAN PEASANTS' WAR FROM A NEW PERSPECTIVE

Peter Blickle

Translated by

Thomas A. Brady, Jr.

and

H. C. Erik Midelfort

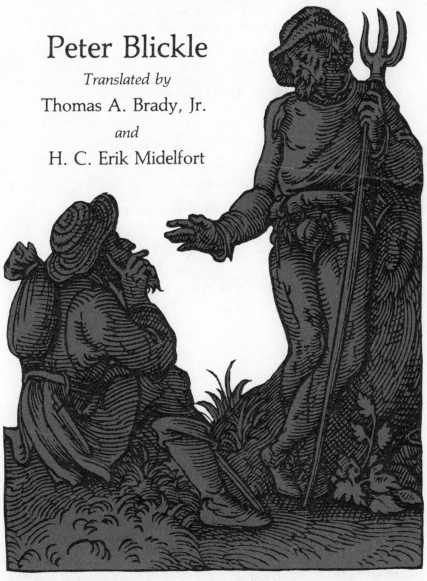

THE JOHNS HOPKINS UNIVERSITY PRESS / BALTIMORE AND LONDON

This book has been brought to publication
with the generous assistance of
the Andrew W. Mellon Foundation.

The original edition appeared under the title
Peter Blickle, *Die Revolution von 1525*, in R. Oldenbourg Verlag, Munich/Vienna,
© 1977 by R. Oldenbourg Verlag GmbH, Munich.
This translation is based on the second, revised and enlarged
edition, copyright © 1981 by R. Oldenbourg Verlag GmbH, Munich.
English translation copyright © 1981 by The Johns Hopkins University Press
Printed in the United States of America
Johns Hopkins Paperbacks edition, 1985

The Johns Hopkins University Press
701 West 40th Street
Baltimore, Maryland 21211
The Johns Hopkins Press Ltd., London

Library of Congress Cataloging in Publication Data

Blickle, Peter.
The Revolution of 1525.

Translation of: Die Revolution von 1525.
Bibliography: pp. 227–33
Includes index.
1. Peasants' War, 1524–1525. I. Title.
DD182.B613   943'.031   81–47603
ISBN 0–8018–2472–9   AACR2
ISBN 0–8018–3162–8 (pbk)

Illustrations on pp. iii, 23, 95, and 163 are from Jost Amman and Hans Sachs,
The Book of Trades (*Ständebuch*), originally published in Frankfort in 1568.

Contents

List of Illustrations

MAPS

FIGURES

A Note on
Money and Measures

Germans of the sixteenth century used a variety of currencies, which fluctuated in exchange value. In 1525 the following equivalents are roughly accurate:

1 gulden (fl.) = 15 batzen = 60 kreuzer
1 pfund heller (lb.) = 20 shillings heller = 240 pfennig (heller)
1 gulden = ca. 1.4 pfund heller

"Heller" designated the origin of this pfennig (Schwäbisch Hall) and differentiated this pound from, e.g., the livre tournois and the pound sterling.

In terms of buying power in 1525 one gulden bought ten geese, or a pair of riding boots, or five bushels of rye, or about thirty-five gallons of common wine. Persons with taxable wealth in excess of 100 gulden were usually householders of moderate means. Families earning less than 50 gulden a year (and having no reserves) were living in poverty.

Land was measured in morgen or jauchert, corresponding roughly to the amount a man could plow in a day:

1 jauchert = 1.5 morgen = 0.47 hectares = ca. 1.2 acres

Grain was measured in barrels called malters, which varied in size from one region to the next. Often the malter was roughly 150 to 180 liters. Sometimes grain was also measured in quarters, which could range in size from 26 to 161 liters. When both malters and quarters were used, an effort was sometimes made to ensure that one malter equalled four quarters.

Translators' Introduction

"Don't bother with this subject unless you read German" is what historians in America commonly say to students who want to learn more about the great German Peasants' War. That the history of this, the mightiest mass movement in European history before 1789, should have remained so long inaccessible to readers of English remains a mystery, one that will soon, we hope, be more a curiosity of historiography than a matter for pedagogical concern.

No single word in the traditional name, "the German Peasants' War of 1525," is now thought to be accurate. Although the heartland of the revolt lay in the southern lands of the German-speaking world, the movement spilled across language lines into the Romance-speaking lands in Lorraine, the Franche-Comté, and the South Tyrol, and into the Slavic world in Carniola and East Prussia. It was not just a movement of peasants but a revolt of "the common man" in the towns and mining districts as well as on the land. It was not simply a war but a failed social revolution. Finally, while the main phase of the movement lasted from February to about June 1525, the revolution began in 1524 and was put down at last only in 1526. Of the more descriptive terms historians have recently applied to this movement, Peter Blickle's has gained some currency: "the Revolution of the Common Man" and "the Revolution of 1525." The former denotes properly the entire tide of unrest among the rural and urban commons of south and central Germany since the mid-fifteenth century, while the latter stands for the properly revolutionary events of 1524–26; and thus the two terms are not rivals but complements.

English-speaking readers of European history between the Middle Ages and the French Revolution have long had cause to lament the lack of an adequate modern treatment of the Revolution of 1525. Indeed, we have been poorly served. In 1897 appeared the English version of *Communism in Central Europe in the Time of the Reformation* by Karl Kautsky, premier theoretician of German Social Democracy. Two years later the English socialist E. Belfort Bax published a long essay, the first extended treatment by a native speaker of English. Then in 1909 appeared the Columbia dissertation of Jacob S. Schapiro, *Social Reform and the Reformation,* which made available for the first time in English some of the chief documents of the revolution and its background. The famous essay by Friedrich Engels, a starting point for all modern debate on the revolution, appeared in English only in 1926, and has been the most widely read account in English ever since. Written in 1850, it was the fruit of Engels's search for a native German revolutionary tradition. These hopeful beginnings in English had almost no successors. Symptomatic of the languishing interest in the Peasants' War is the fact that the best short account in English is still A. F. Pollard's chapter in the old *Cambridge Modern History,* vol. 2, published in 1903.

Until 1975 there was no modern scholarly literature on the Revolution of 1525 in English, apart from occasional articles in learned journals. Most often American and British scholars have been concerned with theological aspects of the insurrection, especially the question of Thomas Müntzer's connections with the Anabaptists and the implications of Luther's violent rejection of the rebellion. Some of the essential German writings on these questions were excerpted by Kyle Sessions in 1968. Three years later Gerald Strauss presented a brilliantly translated anthology of documents of protest and dissent around and before 1525. None of these works, however, dealt directly with the basic contours of the insurrection itself.

In recent years, fortunately, this picture has begun to change. In 1976 Janos Bak edited a collection of studies highlighting the sharp contrasts between Marxist and non-Marxist research, and in 1979 Bob Scribner and Gerhard Benecke published an excellent selection of the best recent studies of the Revolution of 1525, most of them translated from German. It remains true, however, that no extended analysis of the revolution has appeared in English for generations, and no account currently available in English measures up to modern scholarly standards. This translation of Peter Blickle's *The Revolution of 1525* (in the expanded edition of 1981) is meant to fill that gap but also to stimulate interest in a mass movement that should be better known to all students of peasants and of revolution. Blickle's study pulls together huge quantities of information and devotes equal attention to the economic, social, political, and ideological dimensions.* Despite these impressive virtues, it is true that Blickle assumes a basic familiarity with the events of 1525; and so the remainder of this introduction is designed to provide the information the average English-speaking reader will need to draw maximum benefit from this book.

---

*Indeed, Blickle's scrupulous citation of manuscript and printed literature is so voluminous that we have felt compelled to eliminate all but the most essential references from this edition. Scholars seeking full references to the sources will therefore need to consult the German text.

THE COURSE OF EVENTS

The Prelude

The waves of unrest and rebellion in the countryside of South Germany began far back in the fifteenth century. Notable centers of disturbance developed during the half-century before 1525 in Switzerland; in the Black Forest and Alsace on the Upper Rhine; in the monastic territories of Upper Swabia; in Salzburg, Tyrol, Carinthia, Styria, and Carniola; in Württemberg; and in the valleys of the south-bank tributaries of the Main River in Franconia. Of all the major regions of the southern part of the German-speaking world, only Bavaria seems to have been relatively free of serious discontent.

The history of these disturbances on the land conventionally begins in 1476 with *Hans Böheim* of Niklashausen in the Tauber Valley, a shepherd, musician, and lay preacher who is known to history as "the Piper of Niklashausen." His strongly anticlerical but deeply religious movement attracted common folk from all over South Germany before it was suppressed by the bishop of Würzburg. Two years later, in 1478, raids of Turkish cavalry into the Austrian lands provoked peasant uprisings in Styria, Carinthia, and Salzburg.

During the 1490s the center of unrest on the land shifted to the far southwest, where the standard of the *Bundschuh* was raised in the vicinity of Sélestat in Alsace in 1493. The bundschuh, the heavy peasant boot, had been a symbol of peasant solidarity and self-help since the days of the Armagnac invasions in 1439-44, but in 1493 it became a symbol of revolution. The Bundschuh at Sélestat in 1493 failed through premature betrayal, as did its successors in the diocese of Speyer in 1502, at Lehen in Breisgau in 1513, and throughout the Upper Rhine Valley in 1517. The leader of these failed rebellions was the mysterious *Joss Fritz,* a subject of the bishop of Speyer from Untergrombach, who was also to appear in the southern Black Forest in 1524. Fritz first raised the level of demands to a revolutionary level by grounding them on the principle of "godly justice" or "the godly law."

East of the Black Forest, in Württemberg, the year 1514 witnessed a serious revolt. This was the "Poor Conrad" which the spendthrift duke *Ulrich* (reigned 1503-19, 1534-50) provoked through the imposition of new taxes. It began in the Rems Valley, east of Stuttgart, and the peasants were soon joined by urban artisans. The territorial diet of Württemberg, meeting at Tübingen, succeeded in splitting the rebels by redressing urban grievances, and the duke was then able to crush the remaining rebels and execute their leaders.

The Bundschuh on the Upper Rhine and the "Poor Conrad" in Württemberg were only the two most important of a wave of rebellions and other manifestations of discontent in south Germany between 1513 and 1517. In general, the events of this decade were characterized by the growing radicalism of the rebel demands and the growing participation of urban commoners, but also by the spread of the religious principles of godly law as a justification for revolt. This rising tide was accompanied by a series of pamphlets, chiefly from bourgeois sources, which demanded reform in church and state and which often predicted a coming disaster if no fundamental reform were undertaken. Almanacs and astrologers predicted trouble in 1524 with seeming accuracy.

The Beginnings

Most historians have agreed that the great rebellion began with a peasant uprising on the estates of the count of Lupfen at Stühlingen, some miles northwest of Schaffhausen. The rebels found an able leader in *Hans Müller* of Bulgenbach, a former mercenary soldier, who struck an alliance with the nearby Habsburg town of Waldshut, whose inhabitants had refused to hand over the radical preacher *Balthasar Hubmaier*. At the same time, peasants around Nuremberg refused to pay tithes and burned the tithe grain in the fields. In the autumn of 1524 there were new risings all around Lake Constance in Allgäu, Klettgau, Hegau, Thurgau, and near the town of Villingen. As we shall see, Blickle prefers to regard these rebellions of 1524 as the last of the forerunners rather than the start of the actual revolution itself, and it is true that the rebels of 1524 couched their demands in the traditional language of the "old law." As Blickle points out, this was a legal basis on which the peasants could not realistically hope to win. But during the winter months inhabitants of the entire area between the Rhine, the Danube, and the Lech began to join in rent strikes, and soon there were signs of an increasingly radical movement. In contrast to the rather moderate demands of Stühlingen and Hegau, the slogan of the "godly law" now spread from the Upper Rhine Valley, home of the Bundschuh, into the Black Forest. Obviously the rebels were shifting their target from individual grievances and abuses to the entire order of feudal domination—presaging the widening of the rebellion. In the Klettgau, *Thomas Müntzer,* a former Franciscan, former follower of Luther's, and future chief ideologue of the Thuringian rebellion, worked among the peasantry during the winter months.

The lords and princes, for their part, began to prepare a counterstroke, as the Swabian League, the great peace-keeping alliance in south Germany, began to muster its forces. But mercenary troops were scarce in south Germany in the winter of 1524–25, both because the Habsburgs had strained every nerve to throw their forces into the Italian War and because Ulrich, deposed duke of Württemberg, gathered Swiss and other mercenary troops at his fortress of the Hohentwiel in Hegau for a strike to recover his lands. These difficulties meant that when the general rebellion began towards the end of winter, the princes and other rulers were not ready to take immediate action against it.

The Main Phase

The main phase of the Revolution of 1525 unfolded in south and central Germany between February and May 1525. From its centers during the previous year in the southern Black Forest and the lands stretching eastward to Lake Constance, the revolt spread in February and the first half of March into Upper Swabia, the lands along the Upper Danube as far downstream as the borders of Bavaria and southward to the Alps. Between mid-March and mid-April the standard of revolt was raised north of the Danube and onward into central and eastern Franconia, on both sides of the Main River. From mid-April to mid-May, the peasants, miners, and some townsmen rose in Württemberg; in northern Switzerland (Thurgau, St. Gallen, Bern, Zurich, Solothurn, and Basel); in Alsace and the Rhine Valley as far downstream as Mainz; in parts of the Palatinate, Lorraine, and the Franche-Comté; and in Thuringia. Later in the summer the revolution spread easterly into Saxony proper and the Erzgebirge, along the border with Bohemia, and also swept through Salzburg and the Habsburg lands of Tyrol, Styria, and Austria. There were also urban revolts along the Middle Rhine, the region of the confluence of the Main and the Rhine, and as far down the Rhine Valley as Dortmund, plus an isolated but important rural rebellion in East Prussia. To the west in Lorraine, Montbéliard, and Burgundy, and to the south of the South Tyrol, the revolution spilled across the language line into Romance-speaking regions. In the northeast the limits of the affected region (apart from the isolated East Prussian revolt) were marked by a line Hersfeld–Goslar–Halberstadt–Halle–Freiberg–Joachimstal. Of the entire German-speaking south, only the Forest Cantons of central Switzerland and the duchy of Bavaria remained entirely untouched by the revolution.

Regional and local solidarities gave the Revolution of 1525 its coherence and its concrete sense of the possibility of change, but they also proved its downfall. The failure of efforts to build solid ties among rebels across the historic boundaries between the major regions and territories permitted the princes, whose transregional lines of communication were largely unbroken by the revolution, to draw on their resources and to cooperate with one another in crushing the revolution. For this reason the actors who appear in more than one regional theater during the revolution are, with very few exceptions, princes and their soldiers; and for this reason, too, the main phase of the revolution has to be followed region-by-region.

Upper Swabia. A land of scattered Habsburg possessions, powerful imperial abbeys, free nobles, and great political fragmentation, the Upper Danube Valley became the revolution's first major theater. Six rebel armies formed during February and March 1525: the Allgäu army with its core of serfs of the abbey of Kempten, the Lake army from the northern shore of Lake Constance, the Baltringen army from the neighborhood of Biberach (led by *Ulrich Schmid* of Sulmingen, a convinced Lutheran artisan who joined the peasants because he believed in their cause), the Black Forest-Hegau army, the Lower Allgäu army, and the Leipheim army. Largest was the Baltringen army, which may have numbered 10,000 rebels at its height. The capital of the Upper Swabian revolution was the imperial free city of Memmingen, a center of Zwinglian preaching.

United under the slogan of "divine justice," the three main armies— Allgäu, Lake, and Baltringen—united in the so-called Memmingen Peasant Parliament on March 6-7. Their program was the *Twelve Articles of the Peasantry in Swabia,* which was drafted by two men of Memmingen, *Christoph Schappeler* and the journeyman-furrier *Sebastian Lotzer.* Printed immediately in Augsburg, the articles spread like wildfire through Germany and influenced the rebel programs in many other regions. At the same time the leaders of the united Upper Swabian armies negotiated with the council of the Swabian League, then sitting at Ulm. Although the urban members of the league were inclined to negotiate a peace, the princes were not; and on March 25 the talks were broken off.

The league's army, under *Georg Truchsess von Waldburg,* had to defend Württemberg against Duke Ulrich, who with 10,000 Swiss mercenaries took advantage of the revolution to try to regain his duchy. Ulrich actually began a siege of Stuttgart on March 9, but news of the battle of Pavia (February 24) drew his Swiss troops homeward, and Ulrich fled back southward in ignominious retreat. This left the league army free to move southward into Upper Swabia. When, therefore, the Upper Swabian rebels at the end of March went over to open warfare against the monasteries and nobles, Waldburg was already marching against them. He moved first against the Leipheim army in the vicinity of Ulm, which broke and fled with little fight, even though some of Waldburg's troops refused to fight. The Baltringen army, too, gave in without pitched battle (April 13), when the Lake and Allgäu armies refused to march to its aid. On April 15, Waldburg met the large, well-armed Lake army, in whose ranks were hardened mercenary veterans, the only really formidable military force the region produced. At Gaisbeuren near Weingarten, 12,000 faced 7,000 league troops, and so impressed was Waldburg by the strength of the enemy that after a cannonade he offered relatively favorable terms. The Treaty of Weingarten on April 17 offered arbitration of the peasants' grievances if the rebels would surrender captured castles and monasteries, disband their army, and resume payment of rents. Not only did the strongest of all Upper Swabian armies disband without a pitched battle, but the league's army was now free to answer some of the many appeals for help from outside the region. By this time, the end of April, rebel armies had sprung up in Franconia, Alsace, the southern Black Forest, Württemberg, and Thuringia.

Franconia. In this extremely fragmented land along the east-west axis of the Main River, the revolution took a more radical course than in Upper Swabia. Here the main phase began in mid-March as agitation swept in from the Swabian lands to the south. Three of the six Franconian armies gained some real prominence: the Tauber Valley army, the Neckar-Odenwald army, and the Bilhausen army. In the Tauber Valley the revolution began with a simultaneous revolt on the land and in the imperial free city of Rothenburg ob der Tauber, whence it spread through the entire southern part of the prince-bishopric of Würzburg. Although its program resembled that of the "Christian Union" of the three armies of Upper Swabia, the Franconians went further and demanded abolition of feudal dues and the privileges of the nobles and clergy. On March 26 the army of the Odenwald formed up to the westward and soon embraced 6,000 men with numerous cannons. Its leader was *Jäcklein Rohrbach,* a serf from Böckingen, who led the most radical Franconian party. The Odenwalders had the services of *Wendel Hipler,* former chancellor of the counts of Hohenlohe and a university-trained lawyer, and of *Florian Geyer,* a veteran soldier and the most significant of the nobles who joined the revolution out of true sympathy for its aims. They stormed the castle of Weinsberg near Heilbronn on April 16 and massacred its noble garrison the next day, a deed which the revolution's enemies used to good propaganda effect. On the following day the Odenwald army entered the imperial free city of Heilbronn, which became a center of communications among a number of peasant armies and the closest thing to a capital the revolution ever had.

In mid-May the leaders of neighboring rebel armies were summoned to Heilbronn to consider a new constitution in a "Peasant Parliament" under the leadership of Hipler and *Friedrich Weigandt,* an official of the elector of Mainz. By this time the ravages of the rebels in Franconia, especially of the radical group led by Rohrbach, had brought most of the region into rebel hands. Rebel armies took Würzburg, but the bishop fled to his great fortress overlooking the city, and the ensuing siege occupied thousands of Franconian rebels while their enemies both southward and northward were mobilizing against the revolution. Georg Truchsess von Waldburg led the Swabian League's army once more into Württemberg and on May 12 at Böblingen met a rebel army, which he cut to pieces. The news of this defeat was enough to dissolve the Peasant Parliament before it could even get down to work. Moving towards rebel Franconia, Waldburg next retook Weinsberg and captured Rohrbach, who was slowly roasted to death. Many of the rebels at Würzburg, who had failed in their attempt to storm the Marienburg, Würzburg's fortress, now turned to intercept the approaching armies of the league and the electors of Mainz, Trier, and the Palatinate. Waldburg crushed some of them at Königshofen on June 2 and defeated Geyer's "Black Band" at Ingolstadt. On June 8 Waldburg and the princes' commanders rode without opposition into Würzburg, and the Franconian revolution was over.

Thuringia. In Thuringia the revolutionary movement centered in the imperial free city of Mühlhausen, which in 1500 was twice the size of either Leipzig or Dresden. During the winter the city fell under the control of a revolutionary party, whose leadership went to Thomas Müntzer, once he returned to the city in February 1525. Müntzer, a former Franciscan and former disciple of Luther's, was in some ways the most thoughtful theoretician of the whole Revolution of 1525. For several years before the autumn of 1524, in the towns of Thuringia and at Prague, Müntzer had been spreading his doctrine of the coming reign of the poor and downtrodden and the extermination of the rich and the mighty. Expelled from Mühlhausen in September 1524, he and *Heinrich Pfeiffer* began a missionary tour into south Germany, which established the single important ideological link between the Thuringian and south German revolutions. Müntzer and Pfeiffer were back in Mühlhausen in February, and by May 17 they had set up a communistic theocracy and formed alliances with rebellious peasantry in the region. With the publication of the Twelve Articles the rebellion spread far and wide, and numerous towns, including Erfurt and Zwickau, opened their gates to the rebel troops.

Nowhere was the princes' counterstroke swifter or more effective than in Thuringia. *Philip,* the twenty-one-year-old landgrave of Hesse, marched eastward through Fulda; and on May 15 he united with the forces of *Duke George* of Saxony near Frankenhausen, where Thuringian rebels had concentrated their forces. The rebel army broke at the first attack, about 6,000 of them were slain, and Müntzer was taken and later executed. The Thuringian revolution is noteworthy both for the figure of Müntzer, who provided it with an uncommonly articulate leadership, and for the massive participation of townsmen and miners. Its speedy and violent end may partly account for the fact that the revolution did not spread further into the north.

Upper Rhine. While Swabia, Franconia, and Thuringia formed interconnected theaters of the revolution, the Upper Rhine Valley witnessed a quite separate and distinct story. The preliminary risings of 1524 had begun on the southeastern edge of the Black Forest; and *Hans Müller* of Bulgenbach gathered his troops in May 1525 and led them over the mountains to Freiburg, summoning the Breisgau peasants as he went. On May 23 they appeared 12,000 strong before Freiburg; the next day they entered the town without resistance. Here, as generally in the Austrian hereditary lands, the revolution proceeded without military opposition from the Austrian regime or its head, *Archduke Ferdinand.*

When Freiburg fell, Alsace was already in turmoil. Here the risings began around mid-April at Dorlisheim in Lower Alsace and eventually spread southwestward into the francophone Burgundian lands and southern Lorraine. Numerous Alsatian towns and some small cities, notably Wissembourg and Saverne (May 13), fell to the rebel armies. Neither the Austrian regime at Ensisheim nor the bishop of Strasbourg took any measures against the revolt, while the regime of the region's largest city, Strasbourg, worked for a negotiated peace. It was thus left to a neighboring prince, *Duke Antoine* of Lorraine, to march on the Alsatian rebels. On the fifteenth of May he stood before the gates of rebel-held Saverne, and the rebel leader, *Erasmus*

Gerber, sent desperate appeals for aid to the government of Strasbourg. When the rebels evacuated the city, they were cut to pieces, leaving perhaps 18,000 dead on the field. The Battle of Saverne on May 17, 1525, broke the back of the revolution on the west bank of the Rhine.

The Upper Rhine Valley also witnessed some peaceful settlements of the revolution, notably in the lands of the margraves of Baden. The Treaty of Renchen (May 25) between the peasants of the Ortenau in Middle Baden and their lords was the most important adoption of at least part of the program of the Twelve Articles in a large region.

Salzburg and the Austrian House Lands. In the regions which form present-day Austria, the revolution brought together peasants, townsmen, and miners. In the prince-archbishopric of Salzburg, where the unrest was indirectly encouraged by the enmity between Archbishop *Matthew Lang* and the dukes of Bavaria, peasants and miners rose against the prelate and occupied his city of Salzburg in June 1525. This move was prompted partly by the archbishop's persecution of Lutherans and partly by the desires, especially of the citizens of Salzburg, for a new territorial constitution.

From Salzburg the revolution spread over the mountain into the lands of the eastern Alps. In Styria the territorial governor, *Siegmund von Dietrichstein,* gathered an army of knights and mercenary infantry and marched into the Enns Valley, where a rebel army under *Michael Gruber* surprised them near Schladming on June 3, 1525, and took the commander prisoner. It was the greatest rebel military victory of the entire revolution, but Gruber did not exploit it to spread the revolution to the other Austrian lands.

The last great stronghold of the revolution—last to rise and longest to hold out—was the county of Tyrol. For years the province had been disturbed, and the coming of *Archduke Ferdinand* in 1523, with his Spanish adviser, *Gabriel Salamanca,* only irritated an already sensitive situation. In February 1525 emissaries arrived from the Upper Swabian rebels; and Ferdinand sought in April without success to cut the ties between the two regions by occupying the fortress of Füssen. In May a rebellion burst forth in South Tyrol, which, unleashed by local issues, soon spread through the entire province. By now the recognized leader of the rebels was *Michael Gaismair,* a former Habsburg official from a family of peasants and miners around Sterzing whom the rebel army at Bressanone elected their commander on May 13, 1525. After the defeat of the movement, Gaismair drafted in early 1526 the "Tyrolean Constitution," the most profound and comprehensive political program produced by the Revolution of 1525. It sketched a plan for a Tyrolean republic based on the principle of Christian egalitarianism. With its seat at Bressanone in the South Tyrol, the new republic would rest on the common man while abolishing all other social orders, cities, and castles. Gaismair planned an autarchic economy in the hands of elected officials. Gaismair's program was the political high point of the entire revolution, and his vision of a Christian, democratic, peasant republic was the most

sophisticated expression of the revolution's fundamental aims. Gaismair survived the revolution's collapse and took refuge with the Venetians; he later
took part in the Sack of Rome in 1527 and continued to have close relations
with the reformer of Zurich, *Ulrich Zwingli*. He finally fell to an assassin's
dagger in 1532.

The Aftermath

Echoes of the great revolution appeared as far away as East Prussia, where
a revolt broke out on September 2–3, 1525, among the peasants of Samland,
whose leader, the innkeeper *Hans Gericke,* shortly became the commander of
all the rebel bands. The peasants' goal was "to establish a godly regime," but
they were persuaded very soon to keep a truce until *Duke Albrecht,* Grand
Master of the Teutonic Knights, returned to the land. When he did return in
late October, he disarmed the peasants and killed fifty of their leaders.

One of the most significant social characteristics of the Revolution of 1525
was its attractiveness to the urban lower classes, a phenomenon which became
ever more evident as the revolt spread northward. In Upper Swabia and
Switzerland the regimes of the numerous imperial cities (those owing
allegiance to no territorial prince but only to the emperor) failed to join the
popular insurrection, but these urban governments often held their own lower
orders in check only with the greatest difficulty. The territorial towns (those
subject to a territorial prince) were often so similar to villages that cooperation with peasants was easily established. In Alsace, Württemberg, and
especially in Franconia and the Palatinate, rebel leadership often came into
townsmen's hands. In the Rhineland and Westphalia, the movement even
became chiefly an urban revolt which did not spread to the countryside.
Perhaps the most important center for the urban revolts was Frankfurt am
Main, where the events of 1525 reached their climax in a revolt against the
ruling patriciate. Several Alsatian and Rhenish imperial free cities admitted
the revolution voluntarily, as did many territorial towns. The imperial cities
especially were suspected of complicity in the rising, a suspicion which was
not allayed by the urban regimes' policy of seeking a negotiated peace, and
the revolution eventually led to the severe erosion of the imperial cities' power
in the Swabian League.

THE MILITARY BASIS OF THE REVOLUTION'S FAILURE

One of the most important reasons for the revolution's defeat has already
been mentioned, namely, the rebels' failure to establish permanent communications and political solidarity across the historic territorial and regional
divisions. Another reason lay in the rebels' military inferiority. It used to be
fashionable to say that the revolution was doomed to fail because of the

political and military ineptitude of the peasantry, but on these points scholars have recently changed the picture substantially. The contents, shape, and limits of the political vision of the rebels of 1525 are treated very thoroughly in Blickle's text, but something needs to be said here about the military aspect of the revolution.

The Revolution of 1525 occurred just as the mercenary system was unfolding in Germany, a system that gave the German mercenary infantry *(Landsknechte)* tangible advantages over their teachers and rivals, the Swiss. Since they were recruited for limited periods of time, some of these mercenaries returned to their homes, and their skills were available to the rebel armies of 1525. Then, too, in south Germany the peasants were used to bearing arms because they frequently served in territorial military levies. Many peasants must have had some familiarity with a simple defensive weapon, which is not much compared with the skill of a Landsknecht, but it is a far cry from a lack of all military knowledge. Skill with firearms was concentrated in the towns, and every large city employed professional gunners.

Every rising, beginning with that of the Stühlingen peasants in June 1524, commenced with "hoisting the flag" and the election of officers, usually on the day of the rising and always within a few days. This election chose the field commander, lieutenants, drillmasters, and the like, for which the armies normally preferred men with military experience to their own political leaders. At Stühlingen the political leader, Hans Müller of Bulgenbach, was himself a former mercenary soldier, but this was unusual. In the Allgäu army, the chief commander was *Walter Bach,* a veteran of the Landsknecht army of *Georg von Frundsberg.* Such commanders were often difficult to find, and occasionally a nobleman was pressed into service. The most famous example was *Götz von Berlichingen,* whose experience as a brigand and highwayman proved useful in Franconia. Besides the field commanders and lieutenants, the armies had paymasters, victualers and foragers, masters of spoils, provosts, artillery masters, and wagon masters—all the officers found in a normal Landsknecht army.

Each army was divided into companies of varying size, for the men who joined from one town or one district formed their own company, and their commander was normally a local man. Some armies were as small as 2,000–3,000, but others ranged up to more than 15,000 men. But the original recruits often did not see the rebellion through to the end, for many villages and districts organized a rotation pattern which changed the contingent every two to four weeks. In Alsace the rotation was a fourfold one, while in Salzburg miners were sent back to the mines to produce silver with which to hire mercenaries. Such schemes reveal the extreme economic hardship caused by the loss of a quarter or more of the work force from the farms and mines. The severe limits this system imposed on the training of armies constituted one of the greatest military defects of the rebel armies.

Though often ill-trained, the rebel infantry was often decently armed with swords, poled weapons, and farm implements and comprised by far the most effective military arm. The rebel armies also had guns, sometimes quite a few of them. At Böblingen in Württemberg the rebels had eighteen field pieces, and at Königshofen in Franconia forty-seven. They usually lacked enough experienced gunners, however; and they were woefully short of wall-breaking siege guns. What artillery the rebels had came from the towns they captured or which joined them, but it was not enough. Perhaps even more serious was their deficiency in cavalry, a force never in good supply in south Germany. Although cavalry had had its day as a shock force, it was still needed for scouting, foraging, and protecting the flanks of infantry formations in the field; and the chief sources of cavalry—the urban patriciates and the nobility of north Germany—did not come to the aid of rebel armies.

The rebels also experienced grave logistical deficiencies. Their main sources of supplies were plundering and forced contributions laid on towns, and although the problems of food supply were, on the whole, tolerably well solved on a regional basis, they would have been insuperable had the various armies ever united into a single large fighting force.

The rebels' record in the field was none too good. They were generally defeated by the princes' professional troops after a short fight, or they broke after a demonstration of force. In a few cases, however, when the rebels did go over to the attack, as at Herrenberg and above all at Schladming in Styria, they had some real successes against the nobles. The rebels' military record proves, however, that the will to fight and the possession of weapons were not sufficient to guarantee victory. War had become a business of professionals, and untrained bands could rarely expect to hold the day against professional soldiers.

THE REVOLUTION OF 1525 AND THE PROTESTANT REFORMATION

There are two traditional interpretations of the relationship between the Peasants' War and the Protestant Reformation. The older view is that the entire revolt stemmed from the common man's misunderstanding of Martin Luther's doctrine of spiritual freedom and its consequent perversion into a religious sanction for social and political liberty. This was Luther's own opinion, which dispassionate study and wider acquaintance with the sources have shown to be not only self-serving but wrong. The second view is that the Protestant Reformation was the product of Luther's betrayal of the popular movement his agitation had helped to inspire. That Luther tried to sell his movement as preventive medicine against revolution is true enough, but it is simply not true that Luther changed his mind in 1525. His doctrine of the "two kingdoms," the foundation of his political conservatism, was clearly enunciated in his tract *On Secular Authority* in 1523, if not earlier.

The popular movement reached far back into the fifteenth century, and Luther created neither the demand for change nor even its religious expression. He did offer the movement two things. First, his own biblicism strengthened the popular doctrine of "godly law" as the norm for a Christian social order. Second, much more influential than his theology was his personal example as a rebel against the two great authorities of Christendom, the pope and the Holy Roman emperor. Once we free ourselves of the fiction that the doctrine of justification by faith alone was the clear, evident, organizing principle of his appeal from the very start of his career as a reformer, then the catalytic effect of Luther's protest on an already tolerably well-defined popular will to change emerges into the light. The content of that will was already far more radical than Luther's position, for it demanded the transformation of the social order in the light of the idea of Christian equality. This fitted Luther's idea of passive justification of the individual by God far less well than it did Ulrich Zwingli's much more social Christian ideal. Indeed, Zwingli had taught from 1523 onwards that the success of the gospel depended on transforming secular laws according to the law of God, a claim that corresponded closely to peasant desires. It was this spiritual bond between Zwingli's doctrines and the movement of 1525 that lay at the heart of the subsequent Lutheran struggle to eradicate the Swiss reformer's influence in Germany.

It was Luther, not the revolutionaries of 1525, who misunderstood. This son of the colonial borderlands had little or no experience of the idea of Christian freedom which had been spreading in the lands of the southwest and west, even though he lived very near one of its sources, Bohemia. He blithely exploited every possible item of grievance in his early reform tracts, possibly without even knowing with what social dynamite he played. At any rate Luther woke up in 1525 to the fact that if the common people had their way, his reformation was doomed. He had not attacked the power of priests in order to hand it over to the common man. This, as much as his horror over the profanation of religion for mundane ends, formed the basis of his support for princely authority in church and state in 1525 and for the rest of his life. For a little while after 1525, to be sure, the Catholics were able to dampen the progress of the Protestant Reformation by linking it to the Revolution of 1525, but in the long run it was clear that, regardless of Zwingli's position, the Revolution of the Common Man and the Lutheran Reformation had become two different, largely incompatible movements.

SELECTED READINGS IN ENGLISH

Bak, Janos, ed. *The German Peasant War of 1525*. London, 1976.
Bax, E. Belfort. *The Peasants' War in Germany*. London, 1899; reprinted, New York, 1968.

Blickle, Peter. "Peasant Revolts in the German Empire in the Late Middle Ages." *Social History* 4 (1979): 223–39.

Buck, Lawrence P. "Civil Insurrection in a Reformation City: The *Versicherungsbrief* of Windsheim, March 1525." *Archiv für Reformationsgeschichte* 67 (1976): 100–117.

————. "Opposition to Tithes in the German Peasants' Revolt: A Case Study of Nuremberg in 1524." *Sixteenth-Century Journal* 4 (1973): 11–22.

Cohn, Henry J. "Anticlericalism in the German Peasants' War, 1525." *Past & Present*, no. 83 (May 1979), pp. 3–31.

Cohn, Norman. *The Pursuit of the Millennium: Revolutionary Millenarians and Mystical Anarchists of the Middle Ages*. Rev. ed. Oxford, 1970. Pp. 223–51.

Engels, Friedrich. *The Peasant War in Germany*. Trans. David Riasanov. New York, 1926.

Friesen, Abraham. *Reformation and Utopia: The Marxist Interpretation of the Reformation*. Wiesbaden, 1974.

————. "Thomas Müntzer in Marxist Thought." *Church History* 34 (1965): 306–27.

Grimm, Harold. "Luther, Luther's Critics, and the Peasant Revolt." *Lutheran Church Quarterly* 19 (1946): 115–32.

Gritsch, Eric W. *Reformer without a Church: The Life and Thought of Thomas Muentzer, 1488[?]–1525*. Philadelphia, 1967.

Harvey, A. E. "Economic Self-Interest in the German Anti-Clericalism of the Fifteenth and Sixteenth Centuries." *American Journal of Theology* 19 (1915): 509–28.

Heymann, F. G. "The Hussite Revolution and the German Peasants' War." *Medievalia et Humanistica* n.s. 1 (1970): 141–59.

Hillerbrand, Hans J. "The Reformation and the German Peasants' War." In Lawrence P. Buck and Jonathan W. Zophy, eds., *The Social History of the Reformation*, pp. 106–36. Columbus, 1972.

————. *Thomas Müntzer: A Bibliography*. Sixteenth-Century Bibliography, no. 4. St. Louis, 1976.

Hollaender, A.E.J. " 'Articles of Almayne': An English Version of German Peasants' Gravamina, 1525." In J. C. Davies, ed., *Studies Presented to Sir Hilary Jenkinson*, pp. 164–77. Oxford, 1957.

Kautsky, Karl. *Communism in Central Europe in the Time of the Reformation*. Trans. J. L. Mulliken and E. G. Mulliken. London 1897; reprinted, New York, 1959.

Kirchner, Hubert. *Luther and the Peasants' War*. Trans. Darrell Jodock. Philadelphia, 1972.

Kolb, Robert. "The Theologians and the Peasants: Conservative Evangelical Reactions to the German Peasants' Revolt." *Archiv für Reformationsgeschichte* 69 (1978): 103–31.

Laube, Adolf. "Precursors of the Peasant War: 'Bundschuh' and 'Armer Konrad'— Popular Movements at the Eve of the Reformation." In Bak, *The German Peasant War*, pp. 49–53.

Luther, Martin. "Admonition to Peace: A Reply to the Twelve Articles of the Peasants in Swabia." In *Luther's Works*, vol. 46, ed., Robert C. Schultz, pp. 17–43. Philadelphia, 1967.

———. "Against the Robbing and Murdering Hordes of Peasants." In *Luther's Works*, 46: 45–55.

———. "An Open Letter on the Harsh Book against the Peasants." In *Luther's Works*, 46: 57–85.

Mackensen, Heinz. "Historical Interpretation and Luther's Role in the Peasant Revolt." *Concordia Theological Monthly* 35 (1964): 197–209.

Midelfort, H. C. Erik. "The Revolution of 1525? Recent Studies of the Peasants' War." *Central European History* 11 (1978): 189–206.

Moellering, R. L. "Attitudes toward the Use of Force and Violence in Thomas Müntzer, Menno Simons, and Martin Luther." *Concordia Theological Monthly* 31 (1960): 405–27.

Müntzer, Thomas. "Sermon before the Princes (1524)." In Williams and Mergal, *Spiritual and Anabaptist Writers*, pp. 47–70.

Nipperdey, T. P., "The Peasants' War." In C. D. Kernig, ed., *Marxism, Communism, and Western Society: A Comparative Encyclopedia*, 6: 238–47. New York, 1973.

Oberman, Heiko A. "The Gospel of Social Unrest: 450 Years after the So-Called 'German Peasants' War' of 1525." *Harvard Theological Review* 69 (1976): 103–29. Also in Scribner and Benecke, *The German Peasant War*, pp. 39–51.

Ozment, Steven E. *Mysticism and Dissent: Religious Ideology and Social Protest in the Sixteenth Century*. New Haven and London, 1973.

Peachey, Paul. "Marxist Historiography of the Radical Reformation." *Sixteenth-Century Essays and Studies* (St. Louis), 1970, pp. 1–16.

Pollard, A. F. "Social Revolution and Catholic Reaction in Germany." In *The Cambridge Modern History*, vol. 2, *The Reformation*, pp. 174–205. Cambridge, 1907.

Rupp, E. Gordon. *Patterns of Reformation*. Philadelphia, 1969.

Sabean, David W. "The Communal Basis of Pre-1800 Uprisings in Western Europe." *Comparative Politics* 8 (1976): 355–64.

Schapiro, Jacob Salwyn. *Social Reform and the Reformation*. New York, 1909; reprinted, New York, 1970.

Scott, Tom. "Reformation and Peasants' War in Waldshut and Environs: A Structural Analysis." *Archiv für Reformationsgeschichte* 69 (1978): 82–102; 70 (1979): 140–68.

Scribner, Robert W. "Is There a Social History of the Reformation?" *Social History* 4 (1977): 483–505.

———. "The Reformation as a Social Movement." In Wolfgang J. Mommsen, ed., *Stadtbürgertum und Adel in der Reformation*, pp. 49–79. Veröffentlichungen des Deutschen Historischen Instituts London, no. 5. Stuttgart, 1979.

———, and Gerhard Benecke, eds. and trans. *The German Peasant War of 1525: New Viewpoints*. London, 1979.

Sea, Thomas F. "The Economic Impact of the German Peasants' War: The Question of Reparations." *Sixteenth-Century Journal* 8 (1977): 75–97.

———. "Imperial Cities and the Peasants' War in Germany." *Central European History* 12 (1979): 3–37.

Sessions, Kyle C. "Christian Humanism and Freedom of a Christian: Johann Eberlin von Günzburg to the Peasants." In Lawrence P. Buck and Jonathan W. Zophy, eds., *The Social History of the Reformation*, pp. 137–55. Columbus, 1972.

_____, ed. *Reformation and Authority: The Meaning of the Peasants' Revolt.* Lexington, Mass., 1968.

Stayer, James M. "Terrorism, the Peasants' War and the 'Wiedertäufer.'" *Archiv für Reformationsgeschichte* 56 (1965): 227–29.

_____. "Thomas Müntzer's Theology and Revolution in Recent Non-Marxist Interpretation." *Mennonite Quarterly Review* 43 (1969): 142–52.

Strauss, Gerald. *Manifestations of Discontent in Germany on the Eve of the Reformation.* Bloomington, Ind., 1971.

Williams, George H. *The Radical Reformation.* Philadelphia, 1962.

_____, and Angel M. Mergal, eds. *Spiritual and Anabaptist Writers.* Philadelphia, 1957.

Zins, H. "Aspects of the Peasant Rising in East Prussia in 1525." *Slavonic and East European Review* 38 (1959): 178–87.

Zuck, Lowell H. *Christianity and Revolution: Radical Christian Testimonies, 1520–1650.* Philadelphia, 1975.

_____. "Fecund Problems of Eschatological Hope: Election, Proof, and Social Revolt in Thomas Müntzer." In Franklin H. Littell, ed., *Reformation Studies* pp. 239–50. Richmond, Va., 1962.

THE REVOLUTION OF 1525

MAP 1

The Revolution of 1525

1:6,000,000

0   50   100 km

National boundaries
Region of conflict
Regions of severe conflicts
Cities besieged by peasants
Urban rebellions
Townsmen in league with peasants
Miners' rebellions

INTRODUCTION

Interpretations, Problems, and New Perspectives

The German Peasants' War of 1525 first caught the attention of scholars and the general public just before and during the explosive revolutions of 1848; the war was therefore seen in the context of political tensions dominated by the national and the social questions in Germany. Leopold von Ranke called it "the greatest natural event in the history of the German nation."[1] Friedrich Engels wrote that it was "the grandest revolutionary effort of the German people."[2] And to Wilhelm Zimmermann, its first modern historian, the Peasants' War was "a battle of freedom against inhuman oppression, of light against darkness."[3] These quotations testify to the great significance the Peasants' War acquired, a significance it has retained to the present day in both West German and Marxist-Leninist historical scholarship. Stephan Skalweit, for example, writes that the Peasants' War "is even today shrouded in an aura of inexplicability, like a natural catastrophe";[4] while for Max Steinmetz it was "the most important revolutionary mass movement of the German people until the November Revolution of 1918."[5]

Ranke, Engels, Zimmermann—these names became symbols for widely divergent views of the Peasants' War. In 1848 the first efforts at a scholarly approach to the Peasants' War were frequently distorted and sometimes strangled in the welter of political events. In the wake of the reaction that began when King Wilhelm of Württemberg forcibly dispersed the rump Frankfurt Parliament meeting in Stuttgart, public opinion would no longer tolerate the view that the Peasants' War had been a revolution. What had been basically the declaration of faith of a radical democrat, Wilhelm Zimmermann, now fell into disrepute. Friedrich Engels's effort to explain the Peasants' War according to the principles of class conflict and the rise of the national state also attracted little further notice once the social and national questions had been "resolved from above." Instead, historical scholarship now turned to the path blazed by Ranke, who had labeled the Peasants' War

3

a "natural event" because he could find no properly historical place for it in the web of politics and religion that he examined in his *History of the Reformation*. He believed that the revolt occurred because of "the growing oppression of the peasantry," but only during the "last years" before 1525, and that it was partly a reaction to Counter-reformation tendencies and partly the work of preachers who had betrayed Luther. Ranke turned the Peasants' War into a topic peripheral to the main lines of Reformation history, and he prevented scholars from seeing it as motivated by anything but religion.

That research on the Peasants' War did not altogether cease during the second half of the nineteenth century we owe to the burgeoning field of regional history. What research was done, however, was largely descriptive and limited to the accumulation of facts and the publishing of sources. Ideologically neutral historians, such as Hermann Wopfner of Innsbruck and Franz Ludwig Baumann of Leutkirch, published many new sources and made possible a more intensive study of the Peasants' War. But it was only with the broad empirical research of Günther Franz and the Marxist scholar M. M. Smirin (who both reached back conceptually to the work of the mid-nineteenth century) that we find a renewed concern for explaining the Peasants' War and setting it in a larger historical context.

At the beginning Franz stood in the tradition of Reformation historiography, and his original goal was to approach the Reformation through the Peasants' War. His comparative study of late medieval European peasant revolts convinced him that the German revolt was the last and greatest event in a broad stream of peasant rebellions. As this discovery loosened the connection between Peasants' War and Reformation, Franz moved ever further from his predecessors' views. His research into the prehistory of the German revolt showed that the rebellions incorporated Wycliffite and Hussite ideas, which gained increasing influence in the *Bundschuh* revolts and the "movements for the godly law." Franz came to believe that the Peasants' War arose out of the tension between the peasants' partial autonomy in judicial and administrative affairs and the territorial state, just then in the stage of consolidation. He defined the territorial state as one which abandoned the medieval idea of law and claimed for itself the right to make law, whereas previously law could be discovered and modified only through the consent of all those subject to the law. Franz's efforts had far-reaching consequences for the interpretation of the Peasants' War, first because he loosened the connection between it and the Reformation, and thereby greatly reduced the causal role of the Reformation; and secondly because he derived the Peasants' War from the clash between the political principles of lordship and community in Germany, and thereby allowed only peripheral significance to urban participants and socioeconomic factors.

The approach of the Russian school of M. M. Smirin was entirely different. Given the canonical status of Engels's theses, the acceptance of his assumptions had the predictable consequence that Smirin saw the Peasants'

War in a much wider context, in both subject matter and time, than Franz
had done. For Smirin the Peasants' War was neither socially limited to
peasants nor temporally limited to 1525; but it was intimately connected to
the role of the bourgeoisie and to the Reformation. The Reformation was the
inevitable antifeudal reaction against the papal church, aiming as it did at a
national unification that could have lowered the barriers to developing
capitalistic forces and thus to the bourgeoisie as well. These barriers, hitherto
preserved by petty territorial constrictions, had resulted from the contradiction between the existing feudal social order and nascent capitalist relations of
production. From this overall position it is understandable that Smirin gave
much less attention than Franz had to political developments in general and
to the territorial political structures and their transformations in particular.

The divergent interpretations of the "bourgeois" and the Marxist-Leninist
conceptions of history, so clearly visible in the works of Franz and Smirin,
have in recent decades been debated on both sides—more in the West than in
the East—though not much *across* the ideological barriers. On the other
hand, a convergence of East and West has taken place in recent years, beginning specifically with Thomas Nipperdey's article on the Peasants' War in
1966, although this turn has as yet little influenced empirical research on the
revolution. The heavy dependence of Western research on Franz and of
Marxist-Leninist research on Smirin allows us to treat the two approaches
comparatively. It will be easier to survey the terrain if we treat separately the
revolution's (1) causes, (2) goals, and (3) consequences.

1. *Causes.* Recently Günther Franz once again reinforced his old notion,
"that the Peasants' War was not begun primarily for economic or religious
reasons" [6] but was provoked by the rise of territorial sovereignty. Western
historians by and large accepted Franz's views on this point; and until recently
no one has given serious attention to the connection between the Peasants'
War and the Reformation—perhaps because the older literature seemed to
have exhausted the issue. The only debate, and that not very vigorous, has
occurred over the socioeconomic preconditions of 1525. Franz did not simply
invent his low estimation of economic factors, for contemporary chronicles
commonly portrayed the peasants as wealthy, and wealthy peasants were
apparently the leaders of revolution. Waas, followed by Lütge and Lutz,
pushed this idea farther and made peasant prosperity a cause of the revolution, which they have seen as an effort to bring the peasants' political position
into line with their economic position. Among recent writers, only Treue
doubts that the early-sixteenth-century peasant was as rich as commonly portrayed, though Endres has shown for Franconia that this doubt is well-
founded. Here is a connection to the older historiography, for the last non-
Marxist historians to stress the economic causes of the Peasants' War were
Karl Lamprecht and his supporter, Eberhard Gothein.

It is no accident that Lamprecht's advocacy of the socioeconomic causation of the Peasants' War also doomed this line of interpretation, for his entire achievement fell victim to the German "war over method," that bitter struggle between Lamprecht and the established university historians. Two generations of historians have relied on the authority of such academicians as Max Lenz and Georg von Below, who branded Lamprecht's work as lacking in all rigor and have thus lost sight of the whole question of socioeconomic preconditions of the Peasants' War. Günther Franz also evaded the obligation to study economic conditions with an unequivocal pronouncement in the preface to his book: "We will never be able to make clear, indisputable statements about the economic situation of the peasants in earlier centuries." [7] Hermann Wopfner had already criticized this sort of apodictic pronouncement and, in contrast to Franz, believed that careful interpretation of the sources could produce useful results. In fact, however, none of the regionally based studies produced a new outlook, nor did they force even a partial revision of the established interpretation. Thus there was little response to Kelter's attempt (1941), in studying the economic situation, to grasp the Peasants' War as the revolt of "the poor, the poor Conrad" [8] both on the land and in the city.

This dispute, which proved fruitless because it was conducted with inadequate means, necessarily led to a dead end; and the only way out was a new type of economic history, which could test economic theories with the historical facts and thus develop a new approach to the sources. In Germany this was the achievement of Wilhelm Abel and his school, whose work was to a large degree concerned with the later Middle Ages, although they did not apply their findings directly to the regions of the 1525 rebellion. It was David Sabean who applied this approach to the Peasants' War and showed, in a study which is methodologically convincing though geographically quite limited in scope, that the Peasants' War simply cannot be grasped if socioeconomic factors are omitted. Sabean attributed a causative role to internal village conflicts, which were economic conflicts inasmuch as servile dues, military taxes, and the loss of usage rights fell upon an agriculture that had already been pushed to its limits—at least its perceived limits—by a disruptive growth of population.

Smirin (summarizing here only his analysis of the relationship between lord and peasants) believed that the socioeconomic causes had been shaped to some degree by the development of money rents and of exploitation of the demesne by the lords themselves. "In order to appropriate the surplus of peasant agriculture to the maximum degree possible" (to use his own words), the feudal lord expanded his rights over the commons, raised dues and services, and weakened the peasants' property rights. [9] One instrument of this policy was serfdom, with the aid of which exploitation of the peasantry had been growing since the fifteenth century. The peasants' economic position was poor and by 1525 was certainly becoming worse. Since Smirin's work no one has analyzed the relationship between lord and peasant thoughtfully, probably because in both the Soviet Union and East Germany discussion has centered more and more on the "bourgeois" or "early bourgeois" character of the Peasants' War and the Reformation; and the question of early capitalism has also come to dominate empirical research. We may find a connecting link between the older and newer interpretations in the theses formulated by Max Steinmetz in 1960: the invasion of capital in production led to the formation of industrial capital (mining and textile sectors), capitalist relations of production (the putting-out system), and capitalist expropriation (proto-proletariat). On the other hand, the invasion of the cash-goods nexus into the area of agrarian (also artisan) production intensified the feudal exploitation of the peasants through the commutation of rents in kind into money rents and the formation of a "second serfdom." "The progressive fragmentation of the country . . . into ever more numerous . . . temporal and ecclesiastical territories" made Germany in the end an easy prey of the papal church. Steinmetz makes these three focal points of crisis, which were only mutually supporting aspects of one "total national crisis," responsible for the ensuing revolution.[10]

Günther Vogler has recently summarized East German research on the Peasants' War, which has become more comparative, by arguing that the precondition of all preindustrial, bourgeois revolutions was "the development of capitalist relations of production and a corresponding class structure," which conflicted with the feudal relations of production. With the Reformation, this contradiction acquired a "national dimension" in Germany, which "in the form of a socially revolutionary interpretation of the Gospel" provided the general ideology for class struggle. Vogler has clarified this view in two more broadly conceived studies, one on the prerevolts and the other on urban development. The Peasants' War became possible, according to Vogler, because, in contrast to France and England, the agrarian class conflicts in Germany in the fifteenth century brought no relief from feudal exploitation. Instead, feudal exploitation was intensified by the actual inclusion of capitalist forms of production, which were more highly developed in Germany than elsewhere, as the cooperation of peasants and miners in 1525 proves. Moreover, the monarchy could not develop into a "centralized feudal monarchy" because of the rise of petty autonomous territories, which led to increasing dependency on the papacy.[11]

2. *Goals.* If we turn directly to the goals of the revolution as seen by Marxist-Leninist scholarship, we will grasp the coherence of the whole picture more easily. Views on this question are controversial within the Marxist camp, however, and we must limit ourselves here to a few important points instead of presenting all of the various positions. Following Smirin, Steinmetz understood the direct goal of the early bourgeois revolution as "the creation of a unified national state from below." [12] Günther Vogler has recently summarized the criticisms which have been posed from many sides against

Steinmetz's position. His balance sheet does support Steinmetz by conceding that the overcoming of particularism was "objectively" necessary and was "subjectively" favored by some. His own view, however, and that of the majority of the East German historians, was framed as a question: "Whether the overcoming of the limitations laid upon private property by the feudal mode of production, the feudal restrictions on the accumulation of capital, and the ideological barriers deriving from religious ideology" were not even more essential than national unification.[13] This is the basic issue among East German scholars concerning the goals of the revolution: the liberation of capitalism through the overthrow of feudalism, including feudal ideology.

There is little agreement between Marxist and bourgeois conceptions of the goals of the Peasants' War, unless one agrees with Heinz Angermeier that peasant tendencies toward centralization constituted a program of national unification. Günther Franz has indeed sought the peasant program in the political realm, but until recently he has preferred to give primary weight to regional variations, "because the peasants had no uniform goal."[14] From this perspective, however, the Peasants' War threatens to dissolve into a mere collection of local skirmishes; and it means that Franz, whether intentionally or not, has placed himself above criticism. In a 1974 assessment of his own book, Franz for the first time did see as one goal of the revolution "the construction and shaping of the empire by village and urban communes rather than by the state."[15] If one holds Franz to this statement, which remained unproved in his book, the goal of the Peasants' War would have been the transformation of the empire on the basis of rural and urban communities, possibly even excluding the territorial state. Yet, it is still true that for Franz economic, social, and religious concerns remain in the background. On the basis of Horst Buszello's work, we can also challenge the emphasis on the particular at the expense of the general which is common in Franz and his followers, Walter Peter Fuchs and Adolf Waas. While accepting the political priorities established by Franz, Buszello found that the peasant and urban movements were united in a common goal of greater communal autonomy. Beyond this unifying fundamental purpose, rebels constructed two basic kinds of "constitutional programs," depending on whether their revolt remained restricted to a single territory or moved on to organize in some supraterritorial fashion. In the latter case, rebels aimed at free imperial status and a confederation; in the former, rebels (chiefly townsmen) sought stronger "supervision" of princely power through government by estates. In this way the apparent multiplicity of goals was reduced to a few supraregional, unifying programs.

3. *Consequences.* Although the causes of the Peasants' War have been understood in many different ways, there is extraordinary agreement about its consequences. Besides the short-term effects, such as population losses and

the financial burden of reparations, Franz identified the main result of the lost Peasants' War as the victory of the territorial state—that is, the strengthening of the territorial rulers at the expense of the empire, the territorial nobles, and the monasteries. For Franz it was of great moment that "the peasant disappeared from the life of our people for nearly three centuries. He no longer filled any political role. Although his economic and legal status had not changed much, the peasant was now reduced to a beast of burden." [16]

For Adolf Waas, whose books often simply repeat at length Franz's conclusions for long passages, the peasant lost "all active influence in German social and political life from the Peasants' War until the nineteenth century." [17] Fuchs cautiously accepted this thesis for Thuringia; and Hassinger, Ritter, Skalweit, and Oestreich have adopted the interpretation of Franz and Waas. The only one to question this judgment has been Helmuth Rössler, who posed an amiable question in a relativist manner reminiscent of Oswald Spengler: "Why hasn't the peasant ever, anywhere, exercised an effective influence on political development?" [18]

The close connection or even interdependence of Peasants' War and Reformation in Marxist-Leninist scholarship meant that Steinmetz could argue that the lost revolution actually strengthened territorial principalities, for the events of 1525, in his view, helped to establish territorial churches and to secularize church property. Because of the princes' military victory, "the bourgeois Reformation got just the right amount of support to become the perfect ideological expression of petty states run by Lutheran princes." [19] Yet this is surely not the last word on the subject, for Vogler has pointedly reopened many basic questions, including this one: "How did the early bourgeois revolution in Germany affect the entire European development?" [20]

The various positions may now be summed up:

1. To one side it seems that the antagonism between feudalism and capitalism, also mirrored on the ideological level (religion), *caused* the closely intertwined phenomena of the Reformation and the Peasants' War. To the other side it seems that antagonism between territorial sovereignty and communal association *caused* the Peasants' War, inspired by the law of God, a rallying cry which the Reformation fostered even though it was not a basic Reformation principle.

2. To one side it seems that the uniform and progressive *goal* was the abolition of all barriers to the unfolding of capitalism. To the other side it seems that the *goals* aimed at the preservation and strengthening of associative rights and were therefore defensive; and since they were not uniform, they were only potentially progressive (Franz) or restorative (Buszello).

3. The *consequences* of the Revolution of 1525 were the bolstering of the territorial principality at the expense of the empire and lesser powers (Steinmetz, Franz) and the political disfranchisement of the peasantry (Franz).

Although the Marxist theory of revolution has been tested and developed on the basis of the early bourgeois revolution, it is clear (and no one in East Germany now disputes it) that many parts of it still lack empirically verifiable proofs. But the theory can claim to have at the very least set the Peasants' War in a conceptual framework, something which can hardly be said for "bourgeois" scholarship. Whether the Peasants' War is thus correctly conceptualized remains to be proved. Specifically, this means that Marxist-Leninist theory can be put to use to break through and critically examine the encrusted and petrified ideas which have been canonized by general histories and textbooks.

If research in West Germany on the Peasants' War has largely stagnated and for forty years merely repeated Franz's formulae (except for the works of Sabean and Buszello), this is undoubtedly because scholars were sure that by abandoning traditional intellectual history and by using an often neglected type of source, the grievance lists, they could obtain a fairly complete picture of the Peasants' War. Yet in doing so they have failed to exploit forty years' scholarship in economic and regional history for understanding the Peasants' War. If the works of Abel and Lütge—to mention only two names—have taught us anything, it is that the political sphere is not autonomous. What we have learned from the works of Brunner, Mayer, Bosl, and Schlesinger (again, a few names suffice) is at the very least the insight that the structural approach to a geographically limited entity can explain complex historical phenomena. The purpose of my study is to pose questions in new ways and to bring the results of others to bear upon the Peasants' War. The following questions seem to me to take priority:

1. Can the Peasants' War be adequately explained by the rise of territorial state as a sovereign power? Or, to put it differently, does it suffice simply to follow Franz in interpreting the concrete economic grievances as expressions of subjective consciousness?
2. Were the goals of the Peasants' War regionally so varied that, beyond the desire for local communal autonomy, no generalization is valid? And if the goals did not give the Peasants' War its inner coherence, then what did?
3. Recent research in territorial history has demonstrated the progressive maturation of the territorial state from high medieval beginnings to the age of absolutism, without seeing any turning point in 1525. Shouldn't we therefore question the traditional thesis that the peasantry were politically disfranchised in that year?

These questions are and will remain central even though the literature published since the first edition of this book in 1975 has also opened up new perspectives.

New perspectives—they must first be recognized in the ocean of published works that greeted the 450th anniversary of the Peasants' War in 1975,[21] and then they must be conscientiously evaluated for their usefulness and for the possible changes that they may require in general studies, such as this interpretation of the Peasants' War as the "revolution of the common man." Aside from relatively popular works of general narrative (a genre in which the East Germans have accomplished much more than West Germans),[22] and aside from the astonishingly wide research on the Peasants' War in art and literature, historical scholarship in the narrower sense has opened up two new problems or perspectives. On the one hand scholars have sought an entirely new approach to the structures of rural society and to their potential for conflict by employing the theoretical models of "peasant society' and "peasant economy." On the other hand, scholars have reopened the question of the interaction between the Reformation and the Peasants' War, starting from a base in church history or the history of theology.

In his helpful discussion of the idea of the "early bourgeois revolution," Rainer Wohlfeil has brought into use a concept of the Peasants' War as a "social system-conflict." Although the various versions of this phrase remain suggestive and unclear, Wohlfeil has tried to explain the idea of system-conflict this way: it was "a combination of ideas, goals, and actions that were sometimes part of the system and sometimes destructive of the system, in which obviously the phenomena that were part of the system prevailed." [23] Even in works that have seized on this term as a title, there has been no further clarification, which may be the reason why Sabean relegated it to the class of "rather loose, poorly defined theories." [24]

Hans Rosenberg has recently undertaken to give some real content to the concept of social system-conflict. He begins by vehemently rejecting the idea of revolution, whether used by Westerners or Marxists. With this word, Rosenberg claims, historians have "verbally united" in "understanding the Peasants' War as a basically political movement, subsuming it melodramatically under the key concept of 'revolution,' which they never examine closely and never explain. . . . Thus, despite their passionate zeal for work and despite often seductive theoretical foundations, they land in a cul-de-sac of historical knowledge, trapped with grandiose abstractions in a nominalistic game of glass beads." [25]

Rosenberg comes closer to explaining why he rejects the concept of revolution when he turns to what he regards as the "elementary and basic facts" concerning the movement of 1525, aiming to replace "legend-building" with "sobriety." He discovers three "basic facts": the rural insurgents were illiterate; they were primarily concerned with "lowering their rents and dues and improving their own material existence and opportunities in life"; grander ideas, such as "chiliastic notions," were "not part of their purpose, and were also mainly beyond the narrow, local range of their experience and imagination." [26]

What then made the Peasants' War a "social system-conflict"? Rosenberg understands the term as including the tensions among conflicting parties over maintaining the system, changing the system, and overthrowing the system. The system itself is understood as a fluid structure, whose related elements are the "economic and social complex of conditions," the "political and institutional area of action," and the "legal and ethical system of recognized rules for human behavior." [27] Change, which is obviously part of this concept of system, can occur through a dynamic that is "part of the system" itself (a *systemimmanente Dynamik* that preserves the system as it changes); through a "conflict within the system" (an *Intra-Systemkonflikt* in which the system is transformed by essential structural changes); or, finally, through "conflict against the system" (an *Anti-Systemkonflikt* that destroys the existing system). Within these categories the Peasants' War was a "conflict within the system," for several reasons. The primarily material interests of the rebels were aimed at substantially reducing the share that landlords and judicial lords collected of the rural social product. This, Rosenberg argues, would have necessarily "undercut their position as the basic political force in the countryside." [28] The Peasants' War "aimed at a forced reformation, grounded in religion but basically secular and fundamentally materialistic; this 'reformatio' would have brought a relatively radical change in the existing basic socioeconomic order." [29] To keep the argument symmetrical, Rosenberg adds that peasants also "wanted to win the greatest possible autonomy within the village along with rights of communal self-government," or they wanted to be integrated into the corporate estates of their territory.[30] They threatened the current system by using military force; the only feature that could have exploded the current system was the extreme anticlericalism of those who demanded the expropriation of the church—an idea that Rosenberg does not really pursue. Thus, the movement of 1525 was not basically destructive of the whole system, especially since territorial sovereignty was not challenged and the corporate order of estates was not denied. Instead, Rosenberg describes the movement as "mainly regressive," since it aimed "not at radical overthrow of the existing governmental structure of authority, but at a new order that would merely change the system by giving political recognition to the 'poor man' who had been pushed into the background by nobles, clergy, and burghers." [31]

Despite the broad range of his own essay, Rosenberg does not think that the time is right for "creating a general picture that is at once coherent, detailed, and judicious" and urges instead that researchers should take up "detailed studies of local and regional problems, using precise analysis and quantitative methods." Clarity will also come when "historically trained political scientists, sociologists, social psychologists, and anthropologists'' take up the topic.[32]

These strategies for research describe well the latest directions of research on the Peasants' War. Recent work has, however, tended to divide in two directions or approaches: (1) regional and local studies and (2) works more closely connected to theory and to the disciplines of sociology and anthropology. In terms of their methods the regional and local studies are basically traditional history and do not meet the standards that Rosenberg would apply to them. Still everyone agrees that this work has brought to light a mass of detailed information concerning the burdens on the peasant economy, changes in the population, the rural structure of wealth, the village lower classes, and much else, all of which contributes to a more discriminating picture of the Peasants' War. Even so, the wealth of new information is not yet so great as to require a fundamental revision of the existing general interpretations of the event. Moreover, the thoroughness and quality of the new research is too varied. Franconia now has a fair claim to being the best-studied region of all, thanks to the work of Rudolf Endres.[33] Studies of similar quality have been made in Thuringia, Saxony, and parts of Alsace;[34] on the other hand, the right bank of the Upper Rhine, Württemberg, and the whole alpine region have received hardly any attention, with the notable exception of Tyrol, where Michael Gaismair has received the most attention. In this context it seems appropriate to stress the high value of this sort of research into the tiny pieces of the mosaic—examining army lists, for example, to learn about demographic change, or looking at land registers for what they say about the burdens on rural society, or analyzing village legal settlements to discover the social groups within a village. I think this praise is necessary because during the 1970s the discussion of the Peasants' War was carried out on such a high theoretical level that traditional historical method was all too often considered old-fashioned. The charge that "empirical" researchers "must miss whatever the sources do not say"[35] amounts ultimately to denying that traditional history has any interpretive power.

New approaches have come primarily from the more theoretical disciplines of sociology, ethnology, and anthropology, "opening up new dimensions in contrast to the traditional kinds of explanation," pushing "the discussion of the Peasants' War out of the familiar track and into unexplored territory," and "aiming at a historical theory" of the Peasants' War.[36]

The ideas of these researchers regarding conflict in peasant society need to be sketched briefly here in order to understand their implications for work on the Peasants' War. They begin with a few basic assumptions and observations. Peasants in traditional societies are almost self-sufficient; their relations with society outside the village (e.g., the market or the government) are relatively weak; and therefore peasants are mainly concerned with their own household economy and with the grouping of household economies within the village.[37] Rural societies organized along these lines are badly disturbed when they are integrated into the market and into units above the level of the village, such as the government or high culture.[38] These changes bring new social distinctions within the village. Groups spring up that either win or lose because of their varying orientations to the market, and it is especially the "middle peasantry" who feel most threatened in this process because their market orientation makes them extremely vulnerable to the economic crises of a city or a nation.

This middle peasantry becomes the leader of opposition to change, guarding local traditions and implicitly aiming to preserve the village social structure. It is evident, therefore, that peasant rebellions as seen in this light seek to maintain the economic, social, and political status quo and that they follow backward-looking goals rather than progressive, let alone utopian, ideals.[39] When the peasant rebels occasionally do go beyond the village fences, they need an intermediate class of brokers to provide the necessary contacts with the market (artisans, innkeepers), or with the state (lesser officials), or with high culture (the lesser clergy).

Since there is no one theory of rural society or of peasant rebellion, scholars have tested various elements of theory in discussions of the Peasants' War in order to achieve results that could be pushed even further. David Sabean, for example, has dramatically interpreted the Peasants' War as the result of increasing village differentiation into two classes (peasants vs. day laborers) which came about because of increasing population and a growing integration in the market. In its first phase the Peasants' War was a movement led by village oligarchs and aimed at preserving village autonomy (over against the laborers). As it spread, the movement lost its character as a "peasant rebellion," and peasants gave up their leadership roles to burghers and nobles.[40]

John C. Stalnaker has taken over the idea of antagonism between peasants and day laborers but calls it only an accelerator of conflict. Basically he interprets the rebellion as the "collision of 'two rising classes': ambitious lords and prosperous, assertive peasants."[41] This hypothesis is based on the assumption of economic expansion after 1450, explaining the conflict as a fight for shares of the market.

Still other elements of theory have been incorporated in the works of Heide Wunder.[42] In agreement with Sabean and Stalnaker, she stresses dependence on the market as a crucial criterion of differentiation for rural society, but she also emphasizes the way that political relations as well as language and dialect shaped rural society. She has also introduced new distinctions between "part culture" and "subculture," but these may be of importance only in the area she has studied—Prussian Samland.

Even a superficial acquaintance with the theories, hypotheses, and interpretations here mentioned will compel one to admit that these really are new directions for research. On the other hand, one may be less impressed by the lack of theoretical flexibility and of empirical evidence in all of these assertions. Sabean's contention that conflict within the village was a crucial cause of the insurrection loses much of its force because he can hardly find it in peasant grievances. Stalnaker's hypothesis regarding the clash of two groups competing for the market will not be acceptable until it can be proved that the upswing in agriculture after 1450 took place—and it has not been proved. Wunder's research has mainly analyzed the various groups involved in the Samland uprising (German peasants, Prussian freemen, and Prussian peasants), but her conclusions mark no real advance beyond Franz's discussion of the rebellion, which took into consideration these three groups.

Although "theorists" like Sabean have charged "empiricists" like Endres and Laube with using methods that cannot analyze the Peasants' War, they should ask themselves how their use of theory has advanced analysis of the events of 1525. As a quick summary one could say that specific observations have either been overgeneralized (as in the work of Sabean and Bücking) or been set within a general framework that has not been documented (Stalnaker). Time and again their theories are proved with historically dubious methods. This does not mean that the theories themselves are worthless as means of stimulating analysis and new questions, but right now the accusation of methodological weaknesses, if it is to be made at all, should be leveled at both sides, the empiricists and the theorists.

The Marxist theory of the early bourgeois revolution, with its ideas of class conflict and of general crisis of society, certainly contributed to the formation of the opposing Western theory of social system-conflict and to an effort to understand the nature of the conflict and the conflicting parties with theories that would supposedly be more potent than Marxist theories because they were based on empirical data from the Third World. But by conceptually joining the Reformation and the Peasants' War, the theory of the early bourgeois revolution also challenged Western historians of theology and the church to reexamine the relationship between the religious Reformation movement and the social protest movement of 1525. It was obvious that this discussion would break out over the figure of Thomas Müntzer, not only because the Marxist-Leninist interpretation places Müntzer at the culmination of the early bourgeois revolution, but also because in the figure of Müntzer the connection between the Reformation and the Peasants' War was clear. Recently, research into Müntzer has become a Western domain, as Marxist scholars have been content to repeat their well-known contentions. The Marxist theory of basis and superstructure is obviously worn out as an analytical tool, and in any event, the Reformation has played almost no role in the recent research of East German scholars. The general result of this research on Müntzer, if one can summarize matters in a single sentence, is that Müntzer's Reformation was "socially conditioned and mediated," to borrow a phrase from Robert Scribner.[43] The work of Richard van Dülmen provides decisive arguments for this conclusion.[44]

To be sure, research on Müntzer is only part of a more general interest of church historians in the Peasants' War. Indeed, two leading church history publications, the *Zeitschrift für Kirchengeschichte* and the *Schriften des Vereins für Reformationsgeschichte,* each devoted a whole issue to the Peasants' War. Both urged more research on the Peasants' War as a religious movement, a point that was strongly echoed in the reviews of the literature that appeared in 1975. Heiko A. Oberman put this claim programmatically when he argued "that the Peasants' War demands its place in church history with the same right as those movements stemming from Wittenberg, Geneva, or Trent." [45] Why this should be, however, cannot be learned in these recent publications. Above all, it is unclear just "what place" the revolt should take next to Wittenberg, Geneva, and Trent.

The real reason theologically interested historians and historically interested theologians are now concerned with the connections between the Reformation and the peasant insurrection lies on an entirely different plane. The works of Henry Cohn, for example, have considered anticlericalism to be the hinge on which the early reform phase swung around into the following revolutionary phase of the Peasants' War.[46] In a sense Cohn sees anticlericalism as a catalyst within the protest movement. In a different area of research the works of Martin Brecht and Gottfried Maron have reopened the old question of Luther and the Peasants' War by explicitly or implicitly (in the case of Maron) emphasizing Luther's ties to the peasants.[47] Scholars have been much impressed with Brecht's hypothesis that Schappeler and Lotzer, and therefore the influential Twelve Articles, and the Federal Ordinance as well were more indebted to Luther than to Zwingli. In general this newer research is making a real effort to integrate the Peasants' War and the Lutheran Reformation, whereas earlier research kept them separate, partly for apologetic reasons.

Even so, scholars have not yet done much to show the interdependence of the Reformation and the Peasants' War. What has been lacking is a model that could explain which elements of Reformation theology and Reformation ethics were effective in rural society and why they were so. There are beginnings of this sort of model of interaction in van Dülmen's work, and such concepts have been developed much more clearly for urban societies in the works of Robert Scribner, which combine high theoretical ambitions with the necessary sharpness of analysis.[48] But no one has yet done this for peasant society.

What conclusions may we draw from these "new perspectives"? Any general interpretation of the events of the Peasants' War must come to terms with the fact that discussion of "peasant society" and "peasant economy" has produced almost no tangible, useful results for 1525. To achieve real results we will need detailed studies of the sources analyzing small regions because problems of integration in the urban market will require recourse to land registers, tax books, and other comparable statistical sources and will also need the help of urban historians. Whether the sources will permit us to generate any reliable data for the period before 1500 may be doubted. But it is more to the point to ask whether the gain in method hasn't actually brought an unfortunate shrinking of our picture of the peasant. I have not yet been persuaded that models based, for example, on the peasants of twentieth-century Latin America can be usefully applied to the empire or to Europe in the sixteenth century. In the theoretical studies of 1525 mentioned above the peasant has been strangely reduced to his economic interests alone.

At least the authors who emphasize connections between Reformation and Peasants' War have not tried to close off discussion of the complexity of rural society and the peasantry. At the moment the only possible way of interpreting the events of 1525 in a more general and conclusive way would seem to be to pursue these connections, using the fruitful points of departure of van Dülmen, Scribner, and Brady.

Therefore it seems sensible to add a fourth question to the three I listed in 1975.* This question was not completely ignored in the first edition of this book, but it should perhaps be stated even more clearly:

4. What was the relationship between the Peasants' War and the Reformation? Can we show a mutual dependence that would go beyond a simple adding up of individual influences?

*See above, p. 10.

CHAPTER 1

The Twelve Articles:
The Manifesto of 1525

You are robbing the government of its power and even of its authority—yea everything it has, for what sustains the government once it has lost its power?—Martin Luther, Admonition to Peace: A Reply to the Twelve Articles of the Peasantry in Swabia

The Peasants' War of 1525 was one of the most extraordinary and spectacular events of German history in the age of the Reformation. The Holy Roman Empire of the German Nation lay helpless as castles, palaces, princely residences, and monasteries were put to the torch, from Thuringia to Tyrol, and from Alsace to the territory of Salzburg. Noble and ecclesiastical lords were forced to flee before their peasants, and the imperial ruling powers had to struggle for survival. Later, it was the villages that lay helpless while peasants were beaten, butchered, and executed by the princes' mercenary troops. As villages and farms went up in flames, hopes and yearnings for a better, Christian world of brotherhood and neighborly love went with them.

Without the Twelve Articles, the Peasants' War would have been very different. The Twelve Articles of the Upper Swabian Peasants were a list of grievances, a reform program, and a political manifesto all in one.[1] These "Just and Fundamental Articles of All the Peasantry and Tenants of Spiritual and Temporal Powers, by Whom They Think Themselves Oppressed" are the conceptual glue that bound the Revolution of 1525 together both in time and in substance. They were formulated at the beginning of the revolt, in late February or early March of 1525, and after the military defeat they stood on the political agenda at the Imperial Diet of Speyer in 1526.[2] In the brief space of two months twenty-five editions appeared, producing a total of perhaps 25,000 copies and reaching large sections of the empire. Those cities, nobles, and clergy who could be persuaded to join particular armies of peasants swore oaths to uphold the Twelve Articles.

What explains the amazing success of the Twelve Articles? In the preamble the peasants vehemently rejected any causal link between the new evangelical doctrine and the revolt, between Reformation and Revolution. Since the main purpose of the gospel as they understood it was the promotion of peace, love, unity, and tolerance, the new teaching could not be the cause of rebellion. The cause of rebellion was, rather, the destruction and suppression of love, peace, and unity—in short, the suppression of the gospel and of God's will. The display of such an aggressive sense of mission was governed by an apparently unshakable belief in God, which did not shrink from bold analogies, and the peasants optimistically compared themselves with the Israelites in Egypt. Liberation of the peasants was God's will and God's judgment. God's will, God's judgment, God's majesty—these were the assumptions behind the concrete demands, which were laid out in eleven points.*

1. The peasants demanded the right of parishes to call and remove their own pastors, for only thus could they assure the pure teaching of the gospel without the interpretation and tradition of the old church. This was essential if man was to reach the ultimate goal of life, a supernatural perfection which could be attained only by the uniting with God who would "instill His faith and grace."
2. The small tithe was to be abolished and the large tithe, administered by elected church wardens, was to be distributed by the whole community, first to the pastor according to his needs, then to the village poor, the rest to be reserved for the territorial defenses, if necessary, in order to lighten the villagers' tax burden as much as possible.** During the late Middle Ages seigneurial rights had become transferable and saleable, and tithes, too, had largely passed into the hands of the nobility, upper clergy, cities, and urban foundations and seldom remained in local parish hands. The peasants thus proposed to indemnify those current titheholders who could document purchases of these rights from the community; but in all other cases they would simply restore the tithe to the local community.
3. Serfdom was to be abolished. This did not mean, however, that the peasants would refuse to be subject to any magistrate or lord.
4. The right to hunt and fish freely was demanded, partly because of the substantial crop damage caused by wild game. To the extent that fishing rights could be shown to have been sold off by villages, a mutually agreeable settlement was to be reached between the village and the current holder of fishing rights. If no documentary proof was forthcoming, fishing rights were to revert to the village.
5. Unless it could be shown that a village had sold off its woods and forests, they were to be restored to the villages in order that the peasants could collect free building timber and firewood—always

---

*See Appendix 1 for a full translation of the Twelve Articles.
**The small tithe was an ecclesiastical tax on livestock. The large tithe was levied on the grain harvest or other principal crop (e.g., wine).

under the supervision of elected community forest wardens. If the sale of wood or forest rights could be documented, amicable agreements were to be made with the forest tenants.

6. Labor services were to be reduced to a tolerable level, using tradition and the gospel as guidelines.

7. The provisions of feudal leases were to be observed. In order that the peasant might properly build up his own farm and obtain an appropriate return for his labor, labor services were not to be arbitrarily raised. If the lord needed services, peasants would provide them in return for proper payment if work on their own farms permitted it.

8. Since landlords' dues on tenant lands were often set so high that the tenant could no longer even retain a subsistence minimum for himself, these dues were to be reassessed by "honorable persons."

9. Because judicial rulers constantly used their legislative powers to raise the fines for serious crimes ("great mischief")[3] and assessed such punishments arbitrarily, the peasants demanded a roll-back of fines to levels set by the older judicial ordinances.

10. Meadows and fields once belonging to a village were to revert to it if no proof of purchase could be presented. Where such lands had legitimately passed to others, a peaceful settlement was to be attempted.

11. Servile death taxes were to be refused in future because they unjustly burdened heirs and were even used to expropriate peasants.

12. The twelfth and last article took up the theme of the preamble again, emphasizing the basic desire of the peasants to harmonize the secular order with the Word of God. If some of their articles could be proved by Scripture to be unjustified, the peasants would drop them. And vice versa, as a logical corollary, they would pass whatever new demands might be found to flow from the Bible.

Except for the programmatic articles on the election of pastors and on tithes, these grievances were the products of a crisis in the agrarian order of the late Middle Ages and early modern period. "Agrarian order" is here taken to mean the structure of relationships between the rights of feudal lords in matters concerning land, serfs, and lower jurisdiction on the one hand, and the communal or corporative rights of the village on the other.[4] The Twelve Articles attacked the feudal lords as landlords when they demanded reduction of dues and services; they attacked feudal lords as masters of serfs when they insisted on the abolition of serfdom and the services and death taxes that flowed from serfdom; they attacked feudal lords as holders of judicial rights when they demanded the use of the common law in legal decisions; and finally, they attacked feudal lords as "territorial sovereigns" when they rejected the governmental authority that had developed out of seigneurial, servile, or judicial rights.

Even in the absence of a profounder analysis, categorizing these grievances according to the elements of the agrarian order helps to understand why they spread so widely. The Twelve Articles opposed the whole feudal social and political order, which survived most completely in those structures of the agrarian sector that were relatively uniform from one region to the next. Because both the agrarian order as a whole and specific revisions of tenurial law relied on the late medieval sense of mutual consent and could never be imposed simply by the command of a lord, peasants could now criticize feudalism more sharply than ever before, for the principle of consent had obviously been violated and even nullified by the lords.

The Twelve Articles did not simply exhaust themselves in negative criticism and defensive efforts to push back seigneurial claims. They were fully revolutionary in two respects: in practice, in the articles on serfdom, tithes, and the election of pastors; and in principle, in adopting the gospel as the norm of society and politics.

The demand for the total abolition of serfdom was revolutionary, at least in many parts of Upper Swabia, because feudal lords, as rulers over villages and hamlets, relied heavily on serfdom, from which rights to taxes, to military muster, and to judicial authority were derived. If serfdom fell, an essential, or in some regions even the crucial, pillar of noble and ecclesiastical lordship would collapse, leaving a political vacuum. The peasants were well aware of the broad implications of this demand, for they explicitly protested that the abolition of serfdom was not intended to destroy every other kind of authority, a claim not voiced in any other article. Yet the Twelve Articles left open the future shape of political authority and allowed room for many kinds of political reconstruction.

Restoring tithes to the community meant an assault on the rights of the feudal upper class because, throughout the area where the Twelve Articles originated, the tithe supplied a third to a half of the income of feudal lords and of urban welfare institutions.[5] Refusing the tithe to a person entitled to it could mean his economic ruin. Here it is clear that the sanctity of property, repeatedly defended in the Twelve Articles, would be only an empty formula if the demands were put into practice, even if the peasants did not so intend. For, in fact, this pamphlet proceeded from the tacit assumption that tithes, forest and fishing rights, and common lands were all originally communal possessions. The only property claims they respected were those based on contracts of sale from the villages. One cannot say with any certainty what these demands would have meant in practice for the finances of the feudal lords, but it is probably not going too far to suspect that some noble and ecclesiastical lordships, such as the noble convent at Lindau, which already had barely enough income to survive,[6] would have disappeared, just as the lower nobility had in the wake of the late medieval agrarian crisis.

Choosing one's own pastor, even if it was only intended to secure pure preaching, would destroy the last vestiges of the noble proprietary churches. In this demand the old church and the feudal lords stood to lose not just an instrument for pastoral care but one which spread political propaganda and increased their economic power.[7]

The demand alluded to in the Introduction and explicitly stated in article 12—that the secular order be deduced from the Bible and legitimated by the Bible (a demand of Luther and Zwingli, too)*—must have had a redemptive message for the peasants of such a religiously turbulent time as the early sixteenth century. As the eleventh article accusingly and in desperation said, the "skinning and trimming" by the lords, which had replaced their "guarding and protecting," must now end. The effort to realize God's will, God's justice, God's majesty, in this world ignited the hope for a world overcome by peace. As a legal norm the Gospel logically overwhelmed older legal norms. To be sure, it was the "custom" that the peasant might not hunt or fish, but this custom was not in accord with "God's Word," to which it therefore had to give way. The peasants did, of course, demand the lowering of services to the levels current in their parents' day, but only if that standard was also in accord with God's Word. The death tax was certainly a "custom," but because it went "against God," it had to be abolished. Even where the text itself did not invalidate long-standing tradition through God's Word, as in the demand for just assessment of fines, biblical references in the margin attempted to bolster the complaint theologically. This urgent appeal of the Twelve Articles to live according to God's Word pointed deliberately at social and political change.[8]

Like a parabolic mirror, the Twelve Articles collected and focused the grievances of individual Upper Swabian villages, and multiple reprintings made the crisis of the agrarian order clear to peasants of the whole empire. To understand the articles in terms of their local economic, social, and political background is actually to lay bare the basic causes of the revolution of the common man. This will be the first step of our analysis. The second step will examine the revolutionary goals. By basing their demands on the Bible, the Twelve Articles constructed an alternate framework and thus pointed a way out of the late medieval crisis, which had become a social and political crisis as well as an agrarian one. The way out was concretely described only in specific examples, remaining flexible in other respects and thus allowing room for further expansion of the revolutionary program.

---

*Many scholars would disagree with this characterization of Luther's thought. —Trans.

I

THE CRISIS
OF FEUDALISM AND
THE CAUSES OF
THE REVOLUTION

We ought to serve the lords because they protect us. But if they don't protect us, we are not obliged to serve them.

—*Der Schwabenspiegel*

CHAPTER 2

The Twelve Articles and Their Economic, Social, and Political Background

The immediate goal of the Twelve Articles was to overcome the crisis of late medieval agriculture and the agrarian order. If we exclude the first two articles—on the election of pastors and the communalization of the tithe—the others may be clustered in three general categories: first, serfdom, death taxes, and servile dues; second, rights to hunting, fishing, lumbering, and the use of the commons; and third, seigneurial lordship with the attendant lower jurisdiction and seigneurial dues. The Twelve Articles were constructed from the grievances of individual peasants, villages, and territories of Upper Swabia; and our task is to see whether and to what degree they were representative of peasant grievances in general and how far they expressed the most general causes of the revolt. Our best approach to this task is to examine and quantify the individual grievances in the local lists.[1] This will also allow us to describe the problems that had priority in the peasants' own minds.[2] By investigating the extent to which this consciousness reflected actual conditions, we can begin a much-needed analysis of the factors that caused the Revolution of 1525.

We are sure that the anonymous Twelve Articles came from Upper Swabia, although we cannot determine precisely whether they simply summarized the particular grievances of the Baltringen peasant army. It is nearly certain, however, that they were drafted by a journeyman furrier of Memmingen, Sebastian Lotzer, whose experience was limited to Upper Swabian conditions; and he may well have had help from a Memmingen preacher named Christoph Schappeler. Lotzer did have very close relations with the peasants of Memmingen's urban territory as well as with the Baltringen peasant army. Even if they did grow directly out of this army's grievances, the Twelve Articles were actually representative of the entire region of Upper Swabia, for a quantitative analysis of all the Upper Swabian grievances shows that the frequencies of individual grievances are nearly the same for the entire region as for the grievances from the Baltringen army's home district.[3] If, however, an

MAP 2.   GRIEVANCE LISTS FROM UPPER SWABIA

analysis of the local articles is to convey more than a general impression, they must be quantified. A statistical analysis of local and regional grievance lists, and thus a "hierarchy of grievances," can show the weight of individual items in the entire complex of grievances—something the Twelve Articles reveal only in a very limited way.

Serfdom was the most important grievance, both quantitatively and qualitatively. Seventy percent of the villages and seigneuries demanded its unconditional abolition, and if we add to this the individual complaints against confirmation fines, death taxes, and restrictions on the freedom to marry, then 90 percent of all peasant lists attacked serfdom. Further, in twenty-four of thirty-five lists, the article against serfdom stood in first or second place. Among the grievances against particular economic and legal consequences of serfdom, those against the death tax (37 percent) clearly took first place, followed by confirmation fines (27 percent) and marriage restrictions (24 percent). Demands for the abolition of the servile labor obligations deriving from serfdom were, however, relatively rare (11 percent).[4] The relative weights of the individual demands partly explain why the Twelve Articles gave a separate place to complaints against the death tax in addition to the general demand for the abolition of serfdom.

Eighty-one percent of the lists contain particular grievances about hunting and fishing rights, the wood supply, and the commons. Most important of these were the protection and expansion of lumbering rights (61 percent) and the usage of the commons and pastures (46 percent). The Twelve Articles' broad demand for the restitution of common fishing rights corresponded to demands in local lists for complete (27 percent) or limited (4 percent) freedom to fish and to use the waters (26 percent), two closely related, if not identical, demands, which taken together occur in more than half (52 percent) of the lists. Hunting rights seem to have been less important, as only 20 percent of the peasants demanded them; and the figure climbs only to 22 percent if we include complaints about crop damages by wild game.

A survey of the detailed grievances against landlordship reveals another focal point of crisis: 83 percent of the lists mention it. Many articles demanded a reduction of rents (72 percent) and the transfer fines paid when farms changed hands (61 percent), though there is a suggestion that such demands did not reflect arbitrary increases by the landlords. A majority of the peasants claimed that the rents were too high (39 percent) or, less often, that they had been raised (17 percent), which fits the fact that relatively few articles (15 percent) alleged a deterioration of property rights. Finally, grievances against services owed to seigneurs in their role as landlord were insignificant (5 percent), although we must concede that in most cases we cannot tell which specific rights of dominion prompted the demand for abolition of services.[5] Such difficulties in identification may be responsible for the divergence between the local lists and the Twelve Articles, because the latter place the attack on seigneurial services just after that against the high level of rents.

If we may draw inferences about the relative weights of individual grievances expressed in the Twelve Articles from their scope and urgency of tone, then these supraregional articles agreed thoroughly with the local lists in all three groups—serfdom; rights to hunting, fishing, timber, and the commons; and seigneurial obligations. When it came to seigneurial justice and ecclesiastical tithes, however, there were important differences.

With regard to the administration of justice, the Twelve Articles were relatively restrained, laconically criticizing only the high level of fines for "major crimes" and novel criminal laws. The local and regional lists gave much greater weight to the whole judicial sphere (67 percent). Relatively infrequent (10 percent) were direct complaints against increases in fines; somewhat commoner (22 percent), those against legislative practices; and allegations against maladministration of justice dominated (41 percent) this sector. Complaints against refusal of justice (13 percent) and illegal citations before alien courts (24 percent) have no counterparts in the Twelve Articles, unless we give a very broad interpretation to the complaint that "we are not punished according to the severity of the case but sometimes out of great ill will and sometimes out of favoritism." One might see in this a protest against refusal of justice and against circumvention of the prescribed legal channels.

The Twelve Articles' demand for the election of pastors clearly did not derive from local grievances but was rather the product of a development within the peasant armies during February 1525. Only 13 percent of the local lists mentioned this item, a figure which falls if we include only the lists which were certainly drafted before the Twelve Articles. More widespread (20 percent) was the demand for the proclamation of the pure gospel, though this did not always imply the local election of pastors.

Whereas the Twelve Articles and the local grievance lists agreed about tithes, demanding the abolition of the small tithe (44 percent) and the abolition or redeployment of the large tithe (41 percent), they differed on taxes. A matter of some real importance in the local lists (30 percent), taxes received only one very obscure mention in the Twelve Articles, and this in the article on tithes: the surplus tithe money, beyond what was needed to pay the pastor and care for the poor, was to be reserved for territorial defense. This redeployment would tend to relieve the peasants from defense taxes, an item frequently attacked (28 percent), along with unspecified taxes (13 percent) and the excise (2 percent), in the local lists.

Wherever the local and regional grievance lists incorporated other demands, complaints were so tailored to local conditions that they cannot be subsumed under more general categories.[6] In this respect the Twelve Articles appear to be a generalization of peasant grievances in the entire land between the Black Forest and the Lech River, and between Lake Constance and the Danube. In presenting a uniform principle of legitimacy, of course, they went far beyond the local lists, which sometimes appealed to the old law and sometimes to godly law. The Twelve Articles also presented political goals meant to promote the long-range security of a reformed agrarian order with the structure of the territorial state in Upper Swabia—a reformed political and social system. The instrument of this reform was to be the communalization of the offices and duties which had previously been the rulers' exclusive domain. Taken together this implied a real even though vague alternative to feudalism, which is hardly to be found in local lists.[7] The broad, solid foundation on which the Twelve Articles were erected and their close connection to real life, far from any utopian speculation, emphasize the unmistakable relevance of this program, produced basically by the broad mass of peasants—even if they needed the editorial assistance of men like Lotzer, who could think logically and abstractly.

Although the Twelve Articles could lead one to conclude that the revolt's various causes were all of equal weight,[8] this was not true for Upper Swabia. With our quantitative analysis of individual articles of grievance, we are now in a position to treat the whole question with greater precision. In the first section below, we will treat serfdom, which undoubtedly provoked the most conflict, imposing as it did the burdens of death taxes and labor services on the peasant economy and creating social problems by the imposition of marriage restrictions. Serfdom reduced the net yield of peasants' farms because the peasants had to pay their servile obligations from their own produce; and the demand that rents be lowered meant that they found the economic burdens excessive. Landlordship to be sure, was attacked as frequently as was serfdom, but never with the same passion. We should therefore not speak simply of a crisis in landlordship but—and this is our second section—of a *crisis in agriculture.* The massive appearance of demands about woods and commons, fishing and hunting rights, plus the complaints against labor service (which ranked just behind serfdom), show that agricultural problems formed a real focal point of crisis, one which could be aggravated by even small increases in taxes, for example. Our third section will examine the lords' tendency to transform the old-fashioned lordship into a petty state and the tenants into subjects. Complaints against the lords as holders of legislative and high and low judicial powers were in fact of about equal weight with complaints against the economic burdens we have identified with the agrarian crisis. Finally, in a fourth section, we will try to clarify the structural problems concealed by the individual grievances and to determine how strongly the individual areas of grievance affected the entire complex of economic, social, and political relations.

SERFDOM VERSUS FREEDOM

Serfdom, although it had declined by the later Middle Ages in many territories and lordships of the Holy Roman Empire, remained an important economic and legal burden for the subjects of monasteries, nobles, and even some urban hospitals throughout southwestern Germany but especially in Upper Swabia.[9] If we list just the master's rights over his serfs, we get a merely one-dimensional picture of serfdom in the early modern era. The annual confirmation fine paid as "bond-penny" or "bond-chicken," plus the various forms of death taxes (best animal, best garment), seem modest when compared with the rents due the landlord; and restrictions on mobility and on "exogamous marriage" (marriage to other lords' serfs) seem none too serious for an agrarian society normally considered to have been quite static. Thus, we can understand the peasants' vehement opposition to serfdom only if we probe more deeply into the condition of serfdom during the fifteenth century.

The serfdom we find in substantially the same form all over Upper Swabia around 1525 was mainly the product of an intensified lordship within the past century. We can show that in the lands of the abbey of Schussenried, for example, serfdom proper first developed around 1400, replacing what were clearly looser, earlier forms of dependence, in which the peasants had had de facto rights to mobility, free choice of lord, and free choice of a marriage partner. Here and there the language of the sources testifies to looser forms of personal dependence. At Weingarten, for example, the peasants' personal ties to abbot and chapter during the fifteenth century were not yet described as "servility" or "serfdom"; rather, the legal sources of that age speak indifferently of "poor folk" or "poor folk who belong to the abbey." The concept of servility was regularly applied to Weingarten dependents for the first time in the sixteenth century. To take another example, Ochsenhausen's dependents in 1500 were still called "dependents" or "those belonging to our jurisdiction." The peasants in the lordship of Staufen in Allgäu denied to their lord, the count of Montfort, that they were serfs; and in fact they were first designated as "serfs" of the Montforts by the ruling of an imperial commission in 1467.

These examples should not be taken to imply that there was no serfdom in Upper Swabia before 1400. Domanial customaries, such as those extant for the domanial farms of St. Gallen and Allerheiligen, document the development of serfdom out of an old domanial bondage. On the other hand, the lack of conceptual precision in many of the documents that did deal with servile relations betrays a great uncertainty surrounding the legal institution of serfdom between the end of the fourteenth and the middle of the fifteenth century. In the second half of the fifteenth century, imprecise terms such as "a person belonging to God's house" (i.e., a monastery), "a poor man," and "the common man" give way to more precise terms such as "personal dependent" and "serf."

This conceptual transformation signals structural changes in the agrarian order which were relevant both to the peasants' legal status and to peasant agriculture. During the first half of the fifteenth century, lords used every possible opportunity to bind "their" peasants more closely to themselves by intensifying the forms of personal dependence, regardless of whether the peasants were serfs bound to the land or "subjects" under their jurisdiction. To implement this restrictive policy they prohibited the free choice of lords, abolished the right of free movement, and punished subjects who married other lords' serfs. The abbey of Schussenried for half a century around 1400 made its male subjects agree by oath and in writing that they would take no other lord for themselves, their wives and children, or for their property, which was tantamount to the loss of the right of mobility and of the right of choosing one's lord. Violators were punished with confiscation of goods, thus depriving the peasants of the very basis of their existence, while those who fled could not claim legal protection from lay lords, cities, or other monasteries. The abbot and chapter of Rot an der Rot made the leasing of tenancies contingent on the tenants' willingness to renounce rights of free movement and choice of lord. Far from being unique, this procedure was characteristic of many Upper Swabian monasteries; and such efforts to prevent their peasants' mobility and to reinforce the material dependence of their tenants by adding personal dependence in the form of serfdom occurred also in the lay lordships of Upper Swabia [10] and were often aided by the German kings and emperors.[11] The cities of Upper Swabia, on the other hand, were hardly interested in the institution of serfdom at all.

Peasant mobility was also increasingly limited by the efforts made to punish those who married outsiders.[12] Freedom to move and freedom to marry were so interdependent that the latter naturally followed the former, and exogamous marriages usually had far-reaching consequences for inheritance rights as well. Since according to the laws of Swabia, children inherited their status from their mother, the husband's master stood to lose control of his serf's property, which he could otherwise claim on the basis of serfdom and sometimes even burden with taxes. If the serf had a heritable tenancy from his master, the master legally had to lease the land to the legitimate heirs, children who were no longer the master's serfs. This necessarily led to complications with neighboring lordships because seigneurial rights were derived partly from dominion over serfs and partly from dominion over land.

Serfs who contracted exogamous marriages were increasingly punished by the confiscation of their real and personal property. In 1432 the abbey of Weingarten and its serfs signed a treaty which allowed the monastery to collect one-half to two-thirds of the estates, plus the usual death tax of best animal and best garment, when a male or female serf died. The penalties in the Schussenried territory were even more severe, for here after 1439 a death tax of two-thirds of the property was collected from male serfs who made exogamous marriages, and such serfs were forbidden to inherit from their parents. As at Weingarten, the female serfs of Schussenried had to give up a third of their property to the monastery in such cases. The abbey of Rot demanded that its serfs buy their foreign spouses free and then bind them into the bondage of Rot. If this was not possible, special fines had to be paid annually.

The high level of fines for exogamous marriages, which sometimes led to complete disinheritance of children when both parents were punished by their respective masters, not only sharpened conflicts between lord and peasant but also created conflicts within villages and within families. In the political structure of fifteenth-century Upper Swabia only the beginnings of consolidated territories existed, and scattered lordships were the rule. This meant that serfs of the most varied masters lived together in the same village, and there were very few Upper Swabian villages whose inhabitants all belonged to one lord.

To marry an outsider was to produce the stuff of intrafamilial conflict, because each lord pressed his serf year after year to procure the spouse's freedom from the other lord. Families, too, disliked such marriages, because they created a danger that inherited familial property would be confiscated by the ruler, who claimed compensation from both personal and real property. This kind of massive invasion of the private sphere, which was especially common in ecclesiastical territories, preserved freedom of marriage only de jure, while de facto the penalties formed a marriage prohibition. Such practices must have seemed highly suspect to peasants and must have provoked much resentment. Marriage to outsiders ceased to be a problem only when exchanges of serfs by noble and clerical masters created consolidated areas of serfdom while allowing the peasant to retain his holding and residence. This process, arising from a desire to round out the territorial state, began around the middle of the fifteenth century.

From the early fifteenth century onwards abundant evidence suddenly appears in almost every Upper Swabian lordship of a prohibition against the right of free movement, the freedom to choose one's lord, and the right of free marriage. We may conclude that previously such "infractions" were not prosecuted by the seigneurs. The legal problem behind this fact—was mobility actually licit in the earlier period, or were lords only reactivating an old right?—is irrelevant to the peasants' consciousness of the situation. For them the addition of serfdom to seigneurial burdens meant increased pressure from above; and as the pressure grew, it became impossible to avoid. Thus was born a truly dramatic conflict, for the Upper Swabian seigneurs were struggling against an economic and political catastrophe whose entirely external causes could be mastered only if they adopted a policy of enserfment. In the wake of the late medieval agrarian crisis, enormously accelerated (if not unleashed) by the fourteenth-century epidemics, agricultural prices fell so far that seigneurs, whose incomes derived almost exclusively from rents in kind, suffered grave losses. Much greater population losses in the towns both sharply reduced the ranks of consumers of agricultural products and led to urban labor shortages, a development which drove wages and prices of manufactures sky-high. Opportunities for wage-earning in the cities must have been so attractive to peasants that by the end of the fourteenth century they fled from the land in unprecedented numbers. The lords were led to fear even greater losses of income, because not only were incomes depressed by low grain prices, but there was a danger of insufficient labor to work the fields. They could only try to stem this flight from the land by expanding their powers over the peasants so as to make flight impossible. Their instrument was serfdom.

Against this background of agrarian crisis, the massive emigration of peasant "subjects" also threatened to destroy the political power of noble and clerical lords. Hence the double function of the establishment or intensification of serfdom: to preserve as much as possible of the economic basis of feudal lordship, and to sustain the lord's political dominion. The loss of mobility robbed the peasants of the opportunity for economic improvement. And just as the abolition of the right to move about freely, to choose one's lord, and to marry freely all increased seigneurial pressure on the peasantry, so the exclusive dependence on a single lord was strengthened by the Upper Swabian lords' success in developing landlordship and serfdom into an exclusive claim to sovereignty over their "subjects" (a term which is now entirely appropriate). In a treaty with its subjects made in 1448, the abbey of

Weissenau confirmed that on the basis of serfdom the abbot could demand services, exact obedience, and hand down punishments. The peasants of the abbey of Rot swore in 1456 that as serfs they would be "useful, willing, and obedient" to the abbot and chapter.[13] Weingarten's subjects at Hagnau accepted in 1523 a nearly unlimited sovereignty of the monastery, based on their dependence as serfs. In Allgäu lords secured their titles of ownership and their incomes chiefly through serfdom, since their direct controls over the land itself were limited. In the county of Kempten, for example, peasant allods were being taxed as early as the fifteenth century, which was unusual in the rest of Upper Swabia; throughout Allgäu masters of serfs possessed unchallenged rights to fiscal, military, and judicial powers.

The close connection between mastery over serfs and political authority, or (more precisely) the sovereignty which lords claimed along with serfdom in order to protect their economic and political interests, was widespread all over upper Swabia. Even here, however, there were lordships in which local sovereignty developed more out of dominion over land than dominion over serfs. The common connection of mastery over serfs with political rule was well known to the peasants in 1525, and feudal lords could not understand the peasant demand for the abolition of serfdom as anything less than an attack on the very foundations of their world. This is the reason for the intentionally soothing words of the third of the Twelve Articles, which insisted that the aboliton of serfdom intended no abolition of government.

The intensified forms of personal dependence not only invaded the private sphere to an alarming degree; they also became the lords' instrument for claiming a larger share of agricultural production. The economic exploitation of serfdom became attractive because it offered some compensation for the losses occasioned by the agrarian crisis, although pushing the economic burdens beyond tolerable limits necessarily drove peasants from the land. And when it came to death taxes, the lords went way beyond these limits.

In the wake of the agrarian crisis, lords very likely extended their demands for the servile death tax to subjects whose legal position did not oblige them to pay it. In Weingarten, whose inhabitants were not explicitly serfs during the fifteenth century, when a peasant left no children or only married children, a death tax was collected according to the old domanial principle: the best animal and best garment, plus one-third of the estate. In Hagnau under the same conditions the death tax devoured one-half the estate; and even grimmer were the regulations in the Montforts' lordship of Argen and the monastic lordships of Rot and Ochsenhausen, where the entire estates of childless subjects were confiscated if the subjects could not be shown to have had the higher status of leaseholders. It must have been even worse for peasants when these exorbitant death taxes were collected before the children had received their marriage portions, as occurred in Schussenried and Kempten. In the monastic lordship of Weissenau and apparently also in part of the Waldburg lands, an unspecified portion of the estate was demanded without any consideration for the children. Thus, the peasants' personal property—including allods, where they could not be redeemed for cash—shrank from generation to generation.

The example of Ochsenhausen suggests that these practices were mostly recent innovations. Here a papal privilege of 1453 first sanctioned the confiscation of the real and personal property of serfs who left no legitimate children or whose legitimate children were already married. The legal status of the Ochsenhausen subjects was clearly a disputed matter, because such a privilege would not have been necessary if the serfdom there had been uncontested. Peasants expressed their reaction to this legal change in this laconic verse: "Law arises not from innovation but from custom." They explained to their clerical lord that it would be better for their children to live in concubinage and have bastards by their mistresses because single children could inherit, but married ones could not.

The Ochsenhausen peasants' arguments disarmingly exposed the incompatibility of their clerical lord's spiritual claims with his strivings for temporal power. And they did not make do with words only. The intensification of the forms of personal dependence led to documented revolts in Weingarten, Schussenried, Rot, Kempten, Staufen, and Ochsenhausen, and probably also at Weissenau. These were all motivated, as we can tell from the peace negotiations, by the lords' practices in the area of serfdom. Given that the peasants were little inclined to settle conflicts by resorting to rebellion, and that their regular acts of obeisance created almost insurmountable psychological barriers to any attempt at passive or active resistance, the Upper Swabian revolts of the fifteenth century provide an index of the tremendous intensification of the forms of personal dependence. The revolts' primary target was the servile death tax. In 1439 the monastery of Schussenried gave up its claims to one-half of the peasant's estate and thereafter collected only the best animal and best garment. In 1448 Weissenau relinquished its previous claims on "some of the estate and goods" to the closest heirs and, like Schussenried, had to be content with the best animal and best garment. Reductions of the death tax to the same level occurred at Rot in 1456, Ochsenhausen in 1502, Weingarten (for its Hagnau serfs) in 1523, and Langnau in 1524. In 1496 the counts of Montfort surrendered their claim to the entire real and personal property in favor of the next of kin. Throughout Upper Swabia it was only in Kempten and Weingarten (minus the Hagnau district) that half the estate was still seized as a death tax in 1525.

By 1525, therefore, the real burden of death taxes on the peasant economy varied enormously. In some places peasants and ruler reached a practical solution, as at Schussenried, where serfdom was not even mentioned in the grievances of 1525; but elsewhere the economic burden remained terribly high, as at Kempten, where the grievances against the intensification of personal bondage dominated the peasants' statement of grievances.

On the whole, the treaties concluded between monasteries and nobles on one side and entire bodies of subjects on the other brought real relief to the peasants, although not enough relief to eliminate serfdom as a target of grievance. Where such treaties had been concluded, the death tax in 1525 normally consisted of the best horse or cow, the best garment, and, less frequently, some cash as well. Even these payments weighed heavily enough on the peasant household, because they often coincided with transfer fines and payments to buy out the siblings' interest in the estate. But death taxes were probably even higher in areas where no such agreements existed to regulate them. This could explain the remarkable vehemence of the eleventh of the Twelve Articles, which charges that "against God and all that is honorable" widows and orphans are shamefully robbed by "the very ones who should be guarding and protecting our goods [but] have skinned and trimmed us of them instead. Had they the slightest legal pretext, they would have grabbed everything."

It is thus understandable that the Twelve Articles demanded not only the abolition of serfdom but explicitly the elimination of the death tax, because the economic burdens arising from that tax were high, and because it was so often collected from peasants who denied that they were serfs.[14]

PROBLEMS OF THE AGRARIAN ECONOMY

Landlordship and Peasant Property

When noble and ecclesiastical lords used serfdom to pay themselves back for the losses of income they suffered because of the agrarian crisis, their actions had slow but sure effects on the whole structure of property. This was so because the lords seized a major portion of estates when their serfs died. Although an industrious peasant in 1400 could still count on accumulating a modest estate to pass on to his children, during the fifteenth century such family estates were very likely destroyed by death taxes. When lords demanded a third or a half of a serf's estate, they did not exempt whatever land a peasant might own outright, an abuse that serfs found especially grievous, since this loss of land was irreversible. Conceivably a serf with sufficient cash could have paid off the lord instead of allowing his lands to be seized; but there were natural obstacles to such a course because the late medieval agrarian crisis necessarily reduced the cash income of even the market-oriented farms, and in any event the vast majority of peasants were excluded from the marketplace by their farms' meager yields.[15] Thus only rarely could a serf raise the cash required to ward off his lord's inheritance claim to the land.

Our image of the late medieval agrarian order has been largely determined by the belief that all of the land used in agriculture was subject to seigneurial controls, a view which is badly in need of revision.[16] Even in the late Middle Ages peasants doubtless owned a substantial amount of land outright, although of course there were variations from one lordship to the next. Just looking at the surviving records from the sixteenth to the eighteenth centuries suggests that peasants owned 33 percent of the lands in the Tettnang region, 40 percent around Mindelheim, and between 60 and 70 percent in Allgäu. If anything, these figures were probably even higher in the fourteenth and fifteenth centuries, for we know of almost no cases of seigneurial lands being converted to allods.

These high percentages come from regions where serfdom—or the appropriation of peasant land, to be more exact—played a comparatively small role. Although there was probably almost no allodial property in the territories of the abbeys of Schussenried, Weingarten, Weissenau, Ochsenhausen, and Rot during the early modern era (an hypothesis which remains to be proven), [17] this situation may well have resulted from great tracts of allodial peasant property being brought under the landlords' control during the late Middle Ages. Such a development may have caused a substantial expansion of landlordship and of peasant dependence as well, even though by the mid-fifteenth century contracts between lords and serfs were generally eliminating the death tax on cattle and clothing. This means that the lords' seizure of lands may have gone on for little more than fifty years. Its economic consequences lasted longer, of course, because peasants now controlled less of the unencumbered (and therefore more productive) land which could have been planted in specialized crops for the nearby urban markets.[18] Instead, the peasants had to farm lands controlled by the seigneurs and subject to seigneurial dues. The fact that the individual family's average acreage was reduced made conditions even worse. Quite possibly these lands appropriated by the landlords formed the reserve on which the rapidly growing class of day laborers was employed around 1500.

The Twelve Articles referred to landlordship in the strict sense in only two places: where they described seigneurial dues as unreasonable and insufferable (article 8), and where they demanded a return to the services specified in their leases (article 7). In fact, one finds that farm tenants were repeatedly[19] compelled to give up their farms because they were not able to pay the seigneurial dues in full.[20] Starting after 1450 and with increasing regularity by 1525, peasants gave up their farms because their outstanding debts for dues and interest had increased up to 39 malters of rye (ca. 5,850 liters) and 116 pfund heller.* We also find occasional evidence of the conversion of land transfer fines (only rarely collected in the fifteenth century) into annual rents in kind or in cash. Such conversions demonstrate that the ordinary burdens on agriculture were quite heavy, and this is confirmed by the provisions in village and judicial ordinances for handling arrears in interest and rent payments. The abbey of Weingarten skimmed off an average of 20 percent of the agricultural product through these rents, but the burden was not shared at all evenly; usually the smaller farms paid proportionally higher rents, up to 40

*See "Note on Money and Measures," p. ix. These are very large sums.

percent in some cases. Elsewhere, as in the monastic lordship of Heggbach, at least the amount of grain due was reckoned only by the size of the farm, so that here all the peasants were taxed equally; even so, the grain tax alone came to 30 percent of the harvest without even considering tithes and lesser dues.[21]

If farms were overburdened in 1525, we need to find out whether this was because the lords had raised the rents or because of other factors which lay hidden behind the complaints in the grievance lists. As a matter of fact, down into the eighteenth century the law forbade arbitrary increases in rent. Heritable tenancies, which the lord had to lease to a particular family, usually could not be taxed more heavily. Only farms let out for the life of the tenant or for a set number of years could have new conditions imposed with every change of tenant.[22] There is, in fact, no evidence of rising rents on heritable tenancies. Payments stayed constant for centuries although the landlord could exploit land transfer fines to benefit from changes in the land market, a practice that only really took hold in the sixteenth century.

Even on tenancies leased for life or for a set term, rents in most cases stayed the same or rose only a little.[23] And even where at first sight rents appear to have risen substantially, as on a farm in Frickenhausen whose dues in 1495 were twice what they had been in 1474, these higher rents could have been due to increases in the size of the farm.[24]

Thus landlords before 1525 did not benefit from any tangible or substantial increase in burdens on peasant farms. The justified complaint against too heavy burdens must have had other reasons. Above all, farms might have seemed to be taxed beyond endurance if landlords permitted no remissions and forced full payment of dues despite poor harvests, like those during the years before 1525. In any event, 28 percent of the local lists of grievances from around Baltringen and 24 percent of the grievance articles from all the Upper Swabian peasants contain the demand for a reduction in dues when crops failed or were damaged in storms.[25] A closer examination of estate documents and agricultural records also clarifies two developments that could explain the article on seigneurial rents: a rapid increase of day laborers and the clearing of new fields which continued on into the sixteenth century.

These developments, plus occasional divisions of farms, whether sanctioned or not, point to a strong peasant demand for land, which obviously could not have been motivated by any hope of profits, because of the heavy burdens on these farms. Instead, it seems much likelier that population growth caused both the increased demand for land and the perception that seigneurial taxes were too high.[26]

Woods and Commons: Hunting and Fishing

The demands in articles 4 and 5 of the Twelve Articles that communal woods be gradually restored in order to assure the peasant economy an adequate supply of wood for fuel, construction, and fencing, and that hunting be open to all (with special mention of the harm done by wild game) had a common basis. Wood, the most important raw material of the Middle Ages and early modern period, had become disturbingly scarce. As a result of the heavy demand in the numerous Upper Swabian imperial cities, wood fetched higher prices, especially for building but also for fuel. This led at first to a raid on the forests, but soon men realized that profits could be maintained only through long-range conservation of the forest. A further stimulus to an improved management of the woods arose from the passion of noble and ecclesiastical lords for hunting, for stocks of game also suffered from reckless attacks on the forest. One easy way of increasing and securing forest yields was to restrict peasant rights to use the woods. In the late Middle Ages Upper Swabian peasants often obtained extra income now and again by making charcoal from beechwood or by selling wood, especially if their own woods or those of their community or those they leased or had a right to use were close to convenient transportation, that is, if their timber could be shipped.[27] By the end of the fifteenth century and the beginning of the sixteenth, such rights could rarely be exercised.[28] Even more difficult for the peasant economy was the fact that timber allotments were fixed or reduced and forest pasture sharply restricted.[29] The wooded sections of leasehold lands were now usually separated from the lease, and rights to forest usage were regulated.[30] In the Altdorf woods from 1531 on, peasants were allowed to cut only alder and hornbeam. According to a contract of 1454 the subjects of the monastery of Schussenried were not entitled to cut oak or beech trees, but timber for construction was to be granted upon the proper petition. In Jungingen near Ulm fees were introduced to reduce consumption.[31] Elsewhere timber allotments were limited to a set amount of wood. The growing scarcity of wood supplies also brought new restrictions on forest pasture. Upper Swabian forests had already been much reduced by the clearings that continued into the sixteenth century, by slash-and-burn agriculture, and by clear-cutting of timber for market to such a degree that even in newly cleared areas limits had to be set on the number of swine that could be driven into the woods. And forest conservation policies reduced forest pasturing even further, because larger areas were now off limits than ever before and the periods in which the woods were off limits were more extended, when forest pasture was not simply forbidden altogether.

The peasants did not dispute the need for a policy to conserve the forests. In the Twelve Articles they gave assurances that the fulfillment of their demands would not "lead to denuding the woods," since officials set up by the communes were to provide for orderly forest management (article 5).[32] The peasants were not pleased, however, that landlords and forest lords enriched themselves at peasant expense, for as a matter of fact seigneurs drew substantial incomes from the sale of wood. Probably every single Upper Swabian monastery in the late fifteenth and early sixteenth centuries increased its revenues significantly by selling wood, and of course, the same was true of the nobility. In the year 1562 alone the small monastery of Gutenzell sold 3,000 gulden worth of wood to the imperial city of Ulm. In 1554 the Fuggers sold 7,000 gulden worth of beechwood from their lordship of Boos to Ulm (this was the same lordship they had bought just three years earlier from some citizens of Memmingen for the comparatively ridiculous sum of 29,000 gulden). We can point up the economic importance of wood, finally, by noting that towns tried to make themselves independent from their suppliers by buying up woodlands, while landlords also struggled to extend their woods and forests.

Another motive for keeping the peasants out of the woods as much as possible was the lords' passion for hunting. The Innsbruck government put it bluntly when it told the forester for the margraviate of Burgau that oak and beech forests were to be especially protected, because they provided fodder for wild boars and deer.

Even a brief survey should also note that restrictions on the use and exploitation of woodlands varied according to region and lord. In Allgäu, certainly the most densely wooded area of Upper Swabia in 1500, complaints about restrictions on forest rights were rare, whereas they were common among the peasants of the Baltringen army. It is also noteworthy that complaints about inadequate wood supplies and pasture rights were much more frequent in noble and monastic lordships than in areas controlled by towns.[33] And even before 1525 peasants were securing their long-term wood supplies through contracts between the lord and whole bodies of subjects.

Oddly enough, hunting rights were demanded only sporadically by the subjects of the nobility (26.66 percent), while the peasants of monasteries and hospitals did not make this demand at all. This does not mean that the latter had more extensive hunting rights than the subjects of nobles, but rather that prelates and burghers hunted little or not at all and therefore did nothing special to preserve wild game in their forests. As a result field crops were less often destroyed by game and by hunters. In the Twelve Articles, apart from the complaints about wood supply and forest pasturage, the peasants demanded use of the common only once: when they insisted on the return of alienated communal meadows and cropland (article 10). An examination of local grievances proves that common lands actually provided very little ground for conflict, at least between the peasant and his lord. Complaints about injuries to rights to the commons were infrequent among both the armies of Baltringen (12.82 percent) and the peasants of Upper Swabia as a whole (11.11 percent), but were more common among subjects of monasteries (23.32 percent), who clearly had reason to object to restrictions on their usage rights. Subjects of Ochsenhausen protested in 1502 that the abbot was charging a ground rent for use of the common and excluding peasants' cattle from the fallow of his demesne fields. Under pressure from the Swabian League the abbey had to agree to rent out the commons only if the peasants approved and to permit cattle on the fallow fields of the monastery.

Wherever day laborers and small peasant holdings demonstrably increased, the livestock holdings of large farms must have dwindled. The local village ordinances of around 1500 provide evidence for a growing regulation of cattle stocks. Prior to 1500 each farm could generally keep as many cattle as it could maintain through the winter. If the farmer's rights to use the commons were restricted, some hay from his meadows would have to be used up in the summertime. Hence cattle stocks had to be cut back, and with them personal wealth. When local grazing customs were set down in writing, the lords also saw to it that grazing rights were further restricted.

In contrast with the occasional demands for freedom to hunt, demands for unrestricted fishing were much more frequent. If one assumes that the request for fishing and for "deregulation of the waters" had basically the same content, then more than half of the Baltringen villages belonging to nobles or monasteries complained of fishing restrictions.[34] It is possible, however, that peasants demanded the deregulation of rivers and streams or the restoration of communal waters in order to secure the irrigation of their meadows. We must draw inferences with caution here, because the subject has not yet been studied in detail, and the sources we do know have emerged unsystematically; but it seems that the peasants were forbidden to irrigate their meadows or water their cattle, and sometimes they were put off with the scornful argument that these practices would harm the fishing.[35] Such arbitrary and frivolous decisions were based on the so-called fisheries' law, even though lords could not claim any exclusive right to fish in all waters. We get some sense of how strictly violations of these rules were punished in an example from Rot, where the abbot threatened his subjects with excommunication if they did not obey regulations.

Even if one keeps these two kinds of complaints strictly separate, demands for the deregulation of fishing were frequent. At the end of the fifteenth century there was a notable rise in prohibitions of fishing, although we cannot say in every case that these regulations were new. Yet village ordinances and rural collections of laws suggest that they were indeed new because, at least in the fifteenth century, such formulations usually recorded only those rules that were not regarded as self-evident. Legal uncertainties among the lords point in the same direction, as in the case of the abbey of Rot, which obtained Emperor Maximilian's explicit confirmation of its exclusive fishing rights throughout its whole territory and at the same time, with imperial approval, raised the penalties for poaching fish to twenty times their previous level. These high fines attached to fish poaching suggest that it was difficult to implement such regulations. Would a peasant run the risk of high penalties, all the way up to excommunication, if he had not been used to eating fish and if he had not believed that he was protecting an old right?

It is tempting to regard the demand for free hunting and fishing as a revolutionary symbol because meat and fish were the food of lords. Yet the background of the Twelve Articles shows that hunting complaints were restricted to nobles' villages and that they fell far behind fishing demands in sheer numbers. In the real world these two demands were linked only in that they were rooted in the economic problems of the peasant: both the damages from wild game and the prohibition of fishing were oppressive to the peasant household. And both demands were also linked symbolically since both found their legitimation in the book of Genesis (Gen. 1:26–28).

Services and Compulsory Labor

"Service" and "forced labor" are synonyms and do not help us categorize the various kinds of labor services, especially since by 1500 a distinction was no longer recognized between forced labor as working for the lord and a more general service, which could be required for the needs of the village community. We can see this in the linguistically meaningless term "community forced labor." The authors of the Twelve Articles and of the local grievances were no longer able to align services and forced labor with precisely determined seigneurial rights, so that it is extremely difficult for us to tell what kind of forced labor the peasants were complaining about.

The landlord, the master of serfs, and the judicial lord (or bailiff) all had the right to demand labor services from the peasants in order to cultivate the lord's fields, to provide firewood for castles and monasteries, and to build and maintain castles and roads. Sometimes the forced labor owed was limited, that is, the number of days of labor and the specific jobs to be done annually were firmly fixed for each farm; but sometimes the services were not set and could be claimed by the lords at need. Because lordship over land, person, and justice already largely overlapped by 1500, it is extraordinarily difficult to say which right of lordship legitimated a specific claim for forced labor. With a great deal of caution, however, we may probably assume that the forced labor owed to landlords was relatively most fixed. This seems warranted by the feudal grants and contracts that spelled out the duties of the tenant to his landlord. It is noteworthy that the Twelve Articles complained about landlords who did not abide by leases when it came to establishing labor services (article 7). Examination of feudal contracts shows that only a very few contained provisions for labor services, and if actual services were mentioned, they were only the set days of forced labor. The hospital at Memmingen, for example, required two to three days' work on its lands; the abbey of Marchtal established two to four days; the abbey of Rot, four days; the prince-abbey of Kempten and the Montfort lordship of Argen, four to six days; and the monastery of Ochsenhausen, sixteen days per annum.[36] Less often, one finds a clause that in addition to fixed services, an unspecified amount of forced labor could be required according to local and seigneurial custom. Complaints must have been aimed only at these unspecified forced labor services, which must have gradually become the focus of a burning resentment, as for example when a formula was inserted into feudal leases according to which a farm tenant owed his landlord "obedience, judicial counsel, labor service, taxes, and military service." Here was a decisive development for the history of lordship and for the peasant uprising: the transformation of landlordship into true government. A government could claim labor services, such as unspecified compulsory labor, even where the landlord had not had the right to them. Because late medieval sources are so scanty, we cannot really tell whether the unspecified compulsory labor services were greater or lesser than the specified ones. Since lords did not commonly cultivate their own demesne to any extent, the demand for forced labor was certainly low. And yet demands for assistance with the hunt could be oppressive; in 1500 such services were probably performed only by subjects of the nobility, inasmuch as demands for freedom to hunt cropped up only in noble lordships. Cartage services could also be oppressive, especially for monastic subjects who had to transport wine from Lake Constance to the wine cellars of Upper Swabian monasteries. And forced transport and construction services for castles, palaces, and monasteries could also be oppressive if they had to be performed "as much and as often as demanded," as the subjects of the monastery of Rot complained.

We know few concrete details about the actual burdens on agriculture, including labor services, because the use of such services could vary from year to year and from place to place according to need. In village ordinances there was a distinct tendency as early as the fifteenth century to leave the actual number of labor services open and simply to emphasize a general obligation to provide services. Uprisings against increases in labor services, as in the lordship of Söflingen, did not induce the monastery to set down exactly what services it would require each year. We cannot say for sure whether a legal opinion for the town of Memmingen portrayed conditions in Upper Swabia accurately when it replied angrily to a complaint by Memmingen peasants that the surrounding seigneuries sometimes required services twice a week.

Even if the burden had been substantially smaller, it is not hard to understand why peasants complained about unspecified forced labor services because the strong demand for land (even in the form of mere cottage holdings) and the heavy load on tenancies (sometimes pushing them to the limit of endurance) probably often induced peasants to supplement their incomes through wage labor, which arbitrary services made impossible.

Territorial Taxes and Military Taxes

The tax burden of peasants was composed of excises, territorial taxes, and military taxes, levied at widely different rates in different regions. The excise was a common consumption tax in cities, but it was seldom imposed in the countryside and apparently provoked no complaints there.[37] More serious were the territorial taxes, although they were levied only in certain districts. They were quite common throughout Allgäu but were absent from the majority of Upper Swabian districts. This may be explained by the fact that Allgäu had few farms owned by landlords, and lords made up their income through personal taxes levied on peasant private holdings. In 1467 the Montfort district of Staufen replaced the usual lump sum tax levied on the whole body of subjects with an individual property tax of 0.5 percent, and the counts of Montfort extended this system to their district of Argen in 1496. We also find this kind of territorial tax in Augsburg's rural districts of Marktoberdorf and Rettenberg-Sonthofen; and it was introduced only after 1525 in the county of Kempten, where the territorial property tax was levied at 0.5 percent based on sworn self-appraisals. Taxation in the fifteenth century had clearly been very arbitrary. At first sight the tax rate seems low, and yet in some circumstances it could amount to 40 percent of the cash value of seigneurial dues. Here again we must emphasize that farms in Allgäu were mainly the private property of the peasants, and so it is understandable that in Allgäu only the peasants of Kempten complained about territorial taxes, obviously because of their arbitrary nature and constant increase.

Although such territorial taxes were to be found only in certain regions, military taxes were levied throughout Upper Swabia, against fierce opposition. Collecting military taxes involved legal complications, since the military duties of subjects were limited to a specific time, place, and cause: to one day, to the area of the lordship, and to the cause of territorial defense. By the late fifteenth century, however, the demands of the empire and of the Swabian League had so grown, with the Turkish threat and the problems of disorder in Upper Germany, that the estates voted new taxes, which they immediately tried to transfer to their subjects. Since taxes for the empire or for the league were only a substitute for unperformed personal military service, it would have been legally correct to finance these taxes from the ruler's household revenues, and not from new taxes.

Both lords and peasants seem to have understood this legal situation. In 1488 peasants from the abbey of Rot rebelled against a tax for the Swabian League. After the peasant ringleaders were captured, a court of arbitration run by the noble Society of St. George ruled that the peasants were now obliged to pay taxes to the league. It was probably to prevent a recurrence that the abbot of Rot secured a privilege from King Maximilian in 1497 which allowed him to shift imperial taxes to his subjects. This step clearly shows that the abbot was uncertain about his legal rights. Elsewhere, too, peasants protested having to pay imperial and league taxes; when lords lumped the taxes together as a "military tax," they wiped out the terminological distinctions that had differentiated the legal origins of these taxes. The serfs of Weingarten maintained that their payments of dues and rents obligated their lords to protect them without further taxation. In Ochsenhausen peasants agreed to pay military taxes only on condition that their farms held in servile tenure be transformed into hereditary leases. Only then would they have been part of the feudal pyramid and obligated to share the burdens of the empire. Surely

here we can hear echoes of older legal ideas like the one formulated in the *Schwabenspiegel:* "We ought to serve the lords because they protect us."*
The compromises struck between lords and subjects in the sixteenth century also clarify the legal situation. Such compromises obligated the ruler to assume one-third or one-quarter of imperial and Swabian League taxes in Ochsenhausen, Kempten, Rothenfels, and in the Habsburg province of Swabia.

Peasants such as those in Rot and Ochsenhausen did not rebel against military taxes simply to establish legal claims that were economically insignificant. It is difficult, however, to discover just how heavily these taxes burdened the peasant economy. According to estimates from 1519, when the Swabian League took military action against Duke Ulrich of Württemberg, the military tax would cost a farm about half a gulden monthly. Even though such taxes were not regular, this would have been an enormous load. In the lands of Rot we know from imperial edicts that military taxes were raised in 1507, 1510, 1522, and 1524. Data are missing regarding the demands of the Swabian League, so that taxes were doubtless levied in other years as well. A very conservative estimate would place the tax burden for an average farm for a single military levy at around one gulden.

Wherever farms were already teetering on the brink of survival, military taxes could overload them seriously; and peasants opposed this tax all the more strenuously because it had obviously become common only at the end of the fifteenth century, and because the legal basis for its introduction was extremely shaky. Yet one should also note that the military tax caused real problems only between prelates and peasants. In noble and urban areas the military tax rarely appeared among the local articles of grievance.[38] The Upper Swabian nobility obviously met its imperial and league obligations with troops, while cities may have financed their military tax from their own budgets or from their hospital revenues.

FROM LORDSHIP TO PETTY STATE, FROM TENANT TO SUBJECT

The Twelve Articles attacked the administration of justice and of government by explicitly denouncing injustices, especially arbitrary penances and punishments, and by demanding an expansion of communal self-government in questions relating to forests, common lands, the church, and property relations. Once we understand something of the problems of the agrarian economy, these two demands are easily explained. An invasion of the common lands and forests by feudal lords became possible only where communal institutions had already been replaced by seigneurial ones or degraded to

---

*The *Schwabenspiegel* was a south German legal code of the late thirteenth century.

instruments of seigneurial power. Just as with the development of serfdom, here too, new laws were introduced to rob the village courts of some of their power to make law.

If the assertions of the Twelve Articles are checked against the local complaints, the demands aimed directly at the feudal lords as "lawgivers," as "judges," and as "the government" stand out much more sharply. At the village level throughout Upper Swabia the problem of full communal autonomy was a much smaller area of irritation than was the administration of justice.[39] These two concerns were related, of course, since a demand that justice be rendered according to older customs could imply the desire to restore village courts to all their original powers. Nonetheless it is understandable that the local complaints, echoing immediate concerns, would stress concrete difficulties and that the Twelve Articles, with their general program, should go on to consider how specific demands, once granted, might be secured for the long term.

In the area of administration of justice, objections to judicial practice were by far the most numerous (40.74 percent), while being summoned before "foreign" courts (24.07 percent) and refusal of justice (12.96 percent) were less common complaints. If we differentiate these complaints according to what sort of lordship they came from, we find that in the Baltringen army, grievances concerning legal procedure were much more common in noble (40 percent) and monastic (47.05 percent) domains than in villages belonging to urban hospitals (14.28 percent), but that it was mainly urban subjects who complained of being summoned before foreign courts (42.85 percent).[40] This makes sense because most urban regimes had not yet established court systems throughout their territories,[41] and therefore jurisdictional disputes could arise with neighboring noble and monastic lords. Since peasants in the territories of imperial cities only rarely attacked the judicial activities of burgomasters and councillors (14.28 percent), it is not surprising that these villagers never complained about invasions of their communal rights.

Those grievances which were aimed mainly at the noble and clerical lords in their role as rulers reflected (imperfectly) governmental changes of the century or so before 1525. At the beginning of the fifteenth century the government, legal administration, and continuing evolution of the law were still probably much more in the hands of the community than in 1525. The lax attitude of the nobles and monasteries toward their rights of dominion made possible the delegation of these rights to the community. The numerous reformed monasteries in Upper Swabia were chiefly interested in religious affairs; and they performed their governmental duties indifferently, so long as they drew sufficient income from their lands and from the endowments for masses for the dead. The Upper Swabian nobility, most of whom were descended from the imperial *ministeriales,** saw their main function as royal

---

*Originally, unfree servants of the German emperor; during the twelfth and thirteenth centuries they rose to noble status as imperial knights.

and imperial service. Their evident lack of interest in local government even in the fourteenth century is ultimately understandable in terms of the great importance of the imperial vicegerents of Upper Swabia.* The powers of the fourteenth-century vicegerents included high justice, command of the forests, customs rights, the protectorate over monasteries, and rights within the imperial cities—all powers which remind us that Swabia had had a fundamental importance for the rule of the Hohenstaufen during the twelfth and thirteenth centuries.

The agrarian society of the village took care of the most elementary "state" functions of preserving the peace and law enforcement; noble protection was necessary only for external threats. In practice villagers were governed by peasant officials, judges, councillors, and superintendents. These peasant magistrates controlled the complicated three-field system, grazing rights, irrigation of the meadows, and allocation of wood supplies. Sometimes on their own authority and sometimes on that of the lord, they issued commands and injunctions to assure the cooperation so necessary to the village way of life. In the village court they passed judgment in matters of notarial record and in cases of petty justice. During the fifteenth century, however, the balance of administrative and jurisdictional powers shifted from the village community to the ruling lord. Rulers now exercised an increasing influence over the election of community officials and finally replaced election with outright nomination. It is true that their weak governmental apparatus continued to require peasant help with administrative and judicial tasks; but these members of the community now stood under the firm control of their superiors, whose power to command and to forbid gradually ensured the dominance of new interests in the life of the village—those of the noble and clerical lords. The village woods, waters, and meadow, the communal fire brigade, and the religious cultus suddenly attracted the authorities' attention. Faced with detailed governmental rules on reparation and punishment, village courts withered away as they steadily forfeited their lawmaking role. It is conceivable that social tensions, oligarchical tendencies, and the economic crisis occasionally rendered a village incapable of surviving as a political organism; it is even conceivable that it became necessary to regulate village affairs "for the praise of God Almighty and for the improvement . . . of the subjects . . ., and also for the improvement and increase of their honor and possessions" or simply for the support of the "common good." [42] It is much more likely, however, that the root of such caretaking was a changed conception of government. Since village ordinances are the recorded remains of disputes between competing authorities, their remarkable increase in the fifteenth century is evidence of the attention that was now devoted to administrative tasks. During the same period, ecclesiastical procurators and stewards were replaced by secular officials in monastic lordships. These officials

*The imperial vicegerents (*Reichslandvögte*) were governors appointed for the rule of southwestern Germany after the collapse of Hohenstaufen power in the thirteenth century.

(stewards or bailiffs) usually were descended from imperial city families and behaved all the more energetically and successfully in their judicial, administrative, and police functions. They saw to the collection of fines, regulated weights and measures, inspected mills, carried out surveys of the boundaries, supervised the collection of tithes, and checked the receipts. Occasionally they had their own police force to give a "needed emphasis" to government regulations, intimidating rebellious peasants and arresting stubborn subjects, who then disappeared into jails—another innovation of that age.

Although these administrative changes were still poorly integrated if viewed according to the ideals of the seventeenth century, they nevertheless reveal a new idea among the Upper Swabian lords, one that was connected to a more far-reaching goal, namely, the idea of the territorial state. The governmental topography of Upper Swabia in the early fifteenth century was fragmented; to be sure, farms and serfs were concentrated around some center of dominion, whether a castle, a monastery, or a town, but they also spread far into the spheres of interest of foreign powers. The feudal holdings of the prince-abbot of Kempten were scattered with varying concentration from the Alps to the Swabian Jura, from the Lech to western Allgäu, without territorial bridges between all the pieces. The Truchsesses of Waldburg had individual estates and complexes of estates dispersed throughout Upper Swabia. The possessions of Memmingen citizens pushed into Allgäu, up to the Lech, and into the region around Ulm. In the transition to the sixteenth century, however, the actual area ruled by the abbey of Kempten was restricted to the county of the same name. The Waldburg family successfully asserted its authority in the lordships of Waldburg, Wolfegg, Zeil, Wurzach, and Trauchberg. The imperial city of Memmingen now had a territory that encompassed about twenty villages, all in the city's immediate neighborhood. A hundred years had sufficed to disentangle the overlapping possessions and intertwined rights of landlordship. In short, although in 1400 a village might have had three, four, or even more lords, often with nearly equal shares of the village, a century later the weight had shifted to the advantage of one lord, who was now the dominant landlord and usually the local ruler despite the vestigial claims of other lords.

Something similar happened with serfdom, which provided the major way by which territories were formed in southern Upper Swabia, because here landlordship was not very well suited to serve as the basis for the transformation of seigneurial rights into territorial government. In a broad belt from Lake Constance to the Lech the control of courts, taxes, and military belonged to the master of serfs alone and not to the landlord. The prince-abbot of Kempten quite correctly described the structure of lordship and the basis of his rights in Allgäu in the following terms: "The fields belong to the poor people, and the same poor people in turn belong to the lords, and every serf spreads his lord's jurisdiction over himself and over his land; a serf is subject to the justice, punishments, taxes, and demands for personal service of that

MAP 3.   THE REGIONAL DISTRIBUTION OF THE SERFS OF
OTTOBEUREN, CA. 1450
(Not including locations within the monastic lands of Ottobeuren)

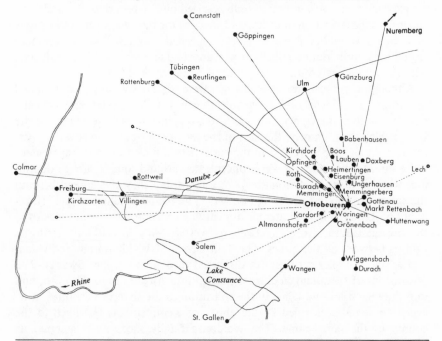

lord alone and no other."[43] Here the territorial state could only be built on serfdom, for no change could be achieved unless the serfs' freedom of movement and marriage options were restricted. In 1450 the serfs of the small domain of Rothenfels did not live only in the narrow district around Immenstadt, Sonthofen, and Oberstdorf within the lordships' jurisdictional boundaries; they lived as far as sixty miles away from the seigneurial castle. About the same time the roll of the subjects of Ottobeuren described its most distant serfs as living in Nuremberg, Canstatt, Colmar, Salem, and St. Gallen (see Map 3). It was relatively easy to transform landlordship into territorial rule because distant possessions could be sold and the resulting capital could be used to buy up estates closer to home. This process generally moved forward quite smoothly because landlords were bound together by a common interest—consolidating estates and property in the immediate vicinity of the castle, the monastery, or the town. If at the same time one made the lease of lands contingent upon acceptance of serfdom, one achieved a compact domain in which one could later hope to control the rights to high justice as well.

It was more difficult to build territorial rule on serfdom than on landlordship. Serfs could not be sold.[44] So lords found a solution by trading serfs, at first one man for one man, a woman for a woman, but then in groups of ten to twenty persons, and finally in exchanges involving more than a thousand serfs. The peasant could still cultivate the same farm as before; only his lord had changed. Thus lords achieved the same thing they had with landlordship, except that the phases of this process occurred about fifty years later: territories arose in which there was only one master of serfs, a man who now claimed exclusive rights of justice, taxation, and military command over the peasants.

This process of territorial formation played itself out essentially in the fifteenth century although there had been modest beginnings in the fourteenth century and a rearguard action that stretched down to the mid-sixteenth century, especially where lords were building territories out of serfdom.[45] For the peasant the process spelled increased pressure from rulers in contrast to the older, looser relations of dependency. Landlordship, mastery over serfs, and to some degree also judicial lordship now flowed together, whereas previously the rivalry among claims had left the peasant in a governmental vacuum. The peasant now lived closer to his lord, and fell more easily under the grip of the administration; in short, he was now more effectively controlled. The bondsman of the soil, the tenant, the monastic peasant, and the leaseholder had all become subjects; lordship had become government.

ECONOMY, SOCIETY, LORDSHIP: THE COHERENCE OF THE PHENOMENA OF CRISIS

The agrarian crisis of the waning fourteenth century paved the way for the crisis of feudalism in the early sixteenth century. Emphasizing this causal connection need not imply that we must deny the independent weight of the political sphere or grant economic factors absolute priority for social and political development (especially since the agrarian crisis has not been shown to have started the process of forming territories). Still, it is true that the close dovetailing of economic, social, and political areas cannot be ignored. Each change in individual rights of lordship, whether over serfs or land (to name only the most important kinds), affected not only the structure of government but the entire economic and social framework as well.

To begin our analysis with the *economic* sphere, the development of personal dependency into serfdom had far-reaching secondary effects on the peasant economy. The limitation and prohibition of freedom of movement, even if prompted by the overriding goals of assuring a labor supply for cultivation of the lord's demesne and of strengthening the territorial state, also blocked the flow of rural population into the numerous imperial cities. Because of the visitations of plague during the fourteenth century and the economic recovery during the first half of the fifteenth, the cities could have taken in almost unlimited numbers of immigrants.[46] Admittedly some peasants did find ways of escaping to the towns, but they were the individual exceptions who eluded the tight mesh of the lords' administrative net. Just as the threat of confiscating all of a peasant's property hindered him from fleeing, so too his village neighbors had a definite interest in preventing such attempted escapes, for they were forced to reimburse out of their own property whatever loss the flight of their fellow serf might have caused their lord. By 1450 the harsh attack of masters on the inheritances of their serfs had in most cases eased off, but the regulations prohibiting freedom of movement remained in force; in fact, they were now employed more vigorously in order to support and supplement the movement to create territorial states.[47] The result was that more and more people had to gain their subsistence from a fixed amount of agricultural acreage.[48]

Indeed, the average acreage held by an individual family probably shrank because the confiscation of peasant-owned farms reduced peasant holdings to whatever they could lease, unless they could regain their own former allods as leaseholds. But these formerly private properties may also have been leased out to the growing class of day laborers. This would explain why the records reveal such a lively demand for peasant estates around 1500.[49] It is also possible that this demand was profit-motivated, since agricultural prices were rising from 1500 on; some landlords responded by introducing a tax on the transfer of property.

As we have seen, there was no rise in rents that caused peasants to complain of the heavy burdens on their farms, but it was a fact that more people had to earn their livelihood from each holding. From the late fifteenth century onwards, villages and lords both began proclaiming that moving into a village was now forbidden or burdened with an entry tax. It is extraordinarily difficult to obtain exact numbers for the growth of population because tax rolls, which usually provide the basis for such calculations, were not yet in use. As a substitute we may use the Ottobeuren serf and subject rolls from 1450–80 and 1548, rolls which have the special advantage of naming men, women, and children. In spite of various difficulties in interpretation[50] we can estimate a population rise of some 50 percent between 1450–80 and 1548 in the monastic territory of Ottobeuren. Although this is only a guess, the average family size can be determined much more accurately from a representative body of data of 400 to 500 families. In 1450–80 families had 5.04 persons on average, and in 1548 they had 5.6 persons.[51] That means that an average holding had to sustain 18.42 percent more people. Since the absolute rise in population of some 50 percent is not fully accounted for by the increased size of families, we can conclude that the number of families also increased; and if agricultural acreage did not expand, this implies a growth in the class of day laborers.[52] If the crowding in villages pushed at least some holdings to the brink of survival, any further burden might have seemed intolerable. Being forced to buy wood, as the Twelve Articles said, was perceived not only as a legal injury on the basis of older, almost unrestricted rights to wood supplies; but it was now economically oppressive too, especially since houses, built of wood in those days, often burned down. Thus the peasants needed large quantities of timber for construction, as well as for fencing in their fields and gardens. Restrictions on grazing rights stemmed partly from the lords' desire to limit access to woodland pasture, and partly from the villages' own custom of permitting day laborers to pasture their cattle on the meadow. Such limitations reduced the number of cattle on each holding and with them peasant incomes, for only cattle were not taxed by the lords.[53] In the seigneury of Messkirch the peasants in 1525 complained about one thing: "that they were overcrowded with cottagers or day laborers in the villages, so that they could no longer obtain their food and sustenance from their estates to the same extent as in the past." If one looked more closely at the case, or so at least the chronicle asserts, one discovered that "most of the same day laborers were the sons, sons-in-law, and nearest kin of the landed peasants." [54]

The already inflamed atmosphere produced by this kind of tension could only deteriorate further if the nobility persisted in keeping excessive stocks of wild game to satisfy its passion for the hunt, for game damaged the crops and thus reduced the land's yield. If lords also claimed exclusive fishing rights, that made things even worse. This is the sole explanation for the action of a peasant from Landolzweiler who sued the abbot of Rot through all courts up to the emperor in order to secure his right to collect acorns. Demands for services presumably hit the day laborers and cottagers harder because they had so little land that they depended on wages to supplement their incomes. By way of contrast, military taxes fell more heavily on the large and middling peasants, since taxes were assessed on property, of which the small peasants had very little.

Despite all the statistical difficulties one can probably say this much without completely distorting the situation: gradually, through the fifteenth century, the farmer's position worsened, and this process accelerated in the decades before 1525 because usage rights were restricted, services were increased, and tax burdens fell with full effect on farming enterprises. Even though the lively market for agricultural products around 1500 meant that market-oriented peasants could make higher profits than before, the resulting situation for most peasants must have been miserable. The fact that these extra burdens were experienced as innovations could only further antagonize the peasant and sharpen the conflict.

These economic difficulties had a *social* impact, especially because the landlord, as seen in the early sixteenth century, was not a party about whom one could legally complain. Rents had not been increased, old customs had not been injured, and consequently forceful demands could not be presented to the government since they could not be legally justified. Without a basis in law the peasant of the fifteenth and sixteenth centuries did not make demands; at most he made humble petitions.

Thus the village became a crucible of social conflicts between various village groups and also within families. Wealthy and middling peasants opposed the cottagers and small peasants because they invaded rights to common land and wood supplies and were more lightly taxed. In the families of the large and middle peasant stratum all the sons but the first-born, even if they could be given adequate portions, had to choose between hiring themselves out as field hands on their brother's farm and becoming mere cottagers in the village so long as the paternal holding remained undivided. Since Upper Swabia was and remained a region of single succession, and since rulers usually saw no reason to encourage the division of estates, such internal family conflicts were resolved only when younger sons decided to choose the uncertainties of mercenary military service rather than suffer a loss of social status within the village community. Some could certainly find work and earn their bread for several years in the city. By the early sixteenth century, however, cities had abundant economic problems of their own and were making it increasingly difficult to obtain citizenship, and so villages only postponed and did not solve their conflicts by exporting workers to the city. A division of land holdings, on the other hand, even if approved by the landlord, brought social decline as well, for a divided half-estate was a petty enterprise that verged on being a mere cottage holding. The uncertainties of inheritance often compounded these difficulties. Upper Swabia was a region of nonheritable leases, which meant that at the tenant's death the holding reverted to the landlord, at whose pleasure the land could be let once more. In some regions, such as Bavaria, the lords tried to keep the peasants on the land by improving their property rights, which led to the well-known development of heritable leases for peasants in the region of Bavarian law. In Upper Swabia, on the other hand, the lords reacted to economic troubles with force and renewed pressure on the peasants. Some parts of Swabia had better property rights, of course, such as the lease for three lifetimes in Weingarten, but this was unusual. Peasants had to fight for the right of inheritance. A chain of rebellions shook the monastic domains of Rot in the fifteenth century because the abbot and monks repeatedly tried to turn heritable leases back into lifetime leases. In the monastic lordship of Ochsenhausen inheritance rights were finally established in 1502, but only after a trial that had gone through seven courts and after rent strikes, renunciations of allegiance, and the threat of violent resistance and of military intervention by the Swabian League. Heritable leases were doubtless in the minority, and peasant existence remained insecure. To be sure, the landlord did lease reverted estates to the sons of previous tenants when he judged them capable of running the farm properly; but he could do otherwise, especially if the demand for farms was strong. Depending on the local inheritance customs therefore, the oldest or youngest son was unsure until the death of his father whether he could count on inheriting the farm.

Family and village tensions were further exacerbated by the fact that in a single village there were free peasants, rent-paying peasants, and the serfs of different lords. There was almost nothing so firmly engraved in the peasant mentality as the idea of original freedom, even though successful efforts to make everyone equal finally only turned all peasants into serfs. Yet even at the end of the fifteenth century the lords had not solved these problems, and therefore they survived for families and villages as well. Landlordship and mastery over serfs still did not exactly overlap. If a peasant on a lifetime lease married a serf from outside, he could be sure that his children, who as a rule took on the legal status of the mother, would not obtain a lease for the estate of their father. The children were in effect disinherited by the punishments for exogamous marriage.

There were even harsher burdens on rural society where serfdom had not yet become universal and where serfs and free tenants coexisted in the same village. In Allgäu during the second half of the fifteenth century the principle of the "baser hand" came to prevail, so that the children of a marriage between a serf and a free tenant automatically became serfs. It took no more than two generations for the peasants to feel the results of such a deterioration in their rights. Instead of the death taxes of best animal and best garment, which even the children of free tenants had to pay, the children of serfs now had to yield up half of the holding. Marrying could even result in exclusion from social fellowship if the outsider was punished by being kept from "receiving the worthy sacrament of the precious body of our Lord, Jesus Christ." [55]

The passage from tenancy to serfdom left scars on rural society, which could break open again even after the rebellion of 1525. Serfdom remained a problem right down to the liberation of the peasantry in the eighteenth and nineteenth centuries. There is no more devastating evidence of the humiliating manner in which a government could treat its subjects, in euphoric awareness of its newly won "petty-state sovereignty," than the toboggan ride to serfdom by which the free peasants of Kempten, the tenants of St. Nikolaus, St. Martin, and Allerheiligen, and the free ecclesiastical yeomen, free tenants all, were forced by jail sentences, monetary fines, and confiscation of estates "voluntarily" to accept the abbey's serfdom. Here and in similar cases, governmental action could provoke a cooperative solidarity that ignored all legal distinctions of status. If ancient custom as a legally formative principle could be so thoroughly perverted and disavowed, peasants did not have to seek further for justification of their resistance. Of course, such conditions did not prevail everywhere, and yet the memory of their legal status was still fresh among former free tenants, even when they had actually long since sunk to the level of serfdom; the copyholders of St. Cornelius at Buchau, for example, were still claiming in 1525 that "every Cornelius copyholder is as free as a bird on a branch and may move to and live in towns, markets, and villages unhindered by any lord. She [the abbess of Buchau] has forcibly squeezed our freedom from us and has monstrously burdened us with ruin,

MAP 4. SERFS AND FREEMEN IN THE MONASTIC LANDS OF OTTOBEUREN IN 1548

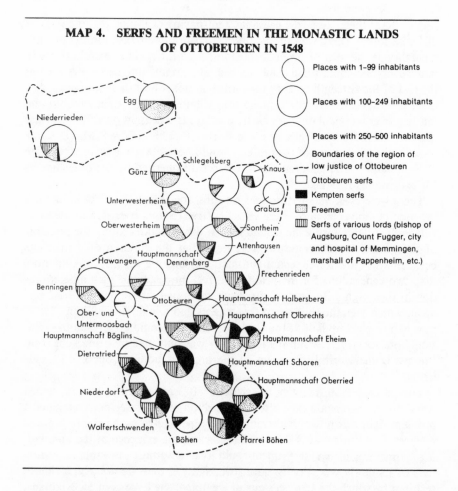

Places with 1–99 inhabitants

Places with 100–249 inhabitants

Places with 250–500 inhabitants

Boundaries of the region of
--- low justice of Ottobeuren

☐ Ottobeuren serfs

■ Kempten serfs

▨ Freemen

▥ Serfs of various lords (bishop of
Augsburg, Count Fugger, city
and hospital of Memmingen,
marshall of Pappenheim, etc.)

death taxes, marriage restrictions, and serfdom, defying God's decree and all reason and even her own edict of freedom."[56] We can imagine how the situation actually looked before this leveling process from the list of inhabitants in Ottobeuren in 1548, which reveals that only 20 percent of the total population of the monastic territory were still free (see Map 4).

Serfdom, or the "harsher servitude," as the peasants of Kempten called it, was socially humiliating. In Tannheim four brothers carried a case through all the ecclesiastical courts and even to Rome because they thought the abbot of Rot had illegally demanded the payment of clothing from their deceased mother. Another trial proceeded through all the secular appellate courts because the brothers Stefan refused to relinquish their free tenancy to the abbot of Kempten. The peasants of Staufen sent legations to the emperor and summoned up witnesses from all over Upper Germany simply to prove that they were not serfs. The peasants of Schussenried insisted on being labeled free tenants of the monastery and not serfs although their legal situation was no different from that of other peasants in neighboring territories. The awareness of a past freedom, surely justified in part only by the previously loose enforcement of dependence, was still alive among the peasants; but serfdom was also on its way to becoming a custom, an old tradition.

For rural society and the village community the still existing differences between tenants, monastic bondsmen, and serfs reflected a social stratification that was not congruent with the economic layers in the village. There were probably strong tensions among the peasants, but they could not lead to sharply opposed groups, especially since the rural structure of work forced peasants to depend on day laborers, and day laborers to depend on the peasants. The opposition between peasant and lordship was superimposed upon the tensions among peasants.

Both in economic and in social terms villagers still regarded the lord as its natural enemy, especially as changes in the *political* realm gradually affected the peasant. Serfdom and landlordship did not produce only economic problems and social tensions, for as these were introduced, the pressures of government grew as well. Lords had used serfdom and landlordship to develop an exclusive power to issue commands and prohibitions, and to establish their "laws" they had developed an exclusive judicial sovereignty. Having to swear "voluntarily" that one would not seek defense and protection elsewhere, that one would not flee, that one would not alienate wife and children, belongings and possessions, from the lord meant becoming "justiciable, taxable, serviceable, subordinate, and obedient" to the lord, as the documents on serfdom confirm. Even though such orders did not always explicitly prevent serfs from appealing their cases, either from the ecclesiastical court in Constance through Mainz to Rome, or from the village court through the Imperial High Court in Rottweil, or from the territorial high court up to the emperor, such an undertaking was not only financially ruinous but senseless besides, since papal bulls and imperial privileges both sanctioned the new forms of serfdom. The innumerable trials that were actually conducted, however, prove that peasants were not yet ready to accept such new forms of dependency without resistance. They could not believe that justice might be what they felt as injustice. In addition to these problems with serfdom, peasants had the same difficulties with the growth of landlordship. When he took over a holding, the peasant promised at first nothing more than that he would tend it "constructively and substantially" and that he would pay the stipulated rents on schedule. But from the second half of the fifteenth century on, the lease contracts extended the required duties, just as happened in the documents by which one accepted serfdom. The tenant promised for the length of his lease to be "justiciable, taxable, serviceable, and subordinate to his landlord." [57] Such provisions forced lords and peasants alike to permit landlordship and serfdom to merge. As a serf the peasant could no longer move to foreign soil; as a tenant he could not take on a different master. Claims like this could be effective only in a small region around the center of a domain.

Thus the territorial principle, fought for energetically and at high cost by the lords, was realized in the course of a few generations. For the history of government this meant an emancipation from the emperor or his representatives, the imperial vicegerents; and with respect to the subjects, a leveling of various dependent relationships and an increase of governmental pressure. For the kings and emperors the imperial vicegerencies were now valuable only as assets to be pawned. From the mid-fifteenth century onwards, as the imperial crown became attached to the archdukes of Austria, the competitive struggle between the rising territorial powers and the Habsburgs became more fierce. In the end the Upper Swabian nobles won out; they could no longer be denied the right of high justice or free imperial status.[58] For the peasants the emperor was no more; the office of vicegerent was now filled by Upper Swabian nobles, the Waldburgs and Königseggs, who were landlords and masters of many peasants. The emperors had withdrawn their defense and protection, and the former imperial territory of Swabia was now bereft of the symbols of emperor and empire. Instead, there were a host of "petty states" whose lords used the pattern of larger territories and the help of their own officials to achieve what they regarded as "a good polity." At an imperial diet the abbot of Weingarten was furious about the constant running to and fro of the estates so that business could not proceed. "That so annoyed the monk . . . that he spoke too loudly, 'You, my gracious and kind lords, you are running up and down, back and forth, just as my peasants do when they are choosing a swineherd.' With this speech, so free and so audacious, he brought them all to order." [59] Such cheerful irony barely masked the scorn he expressed toward the existing communal and associative institutions, whose elimination or disfranchisement was a basic goal of the territorial state. By 1525 nobles and prelates were still locked in this controversy with their stubborn communities and peasantry and still had to defend themselves against the complaints of their subjects before the magistrates of imperial cities, before imperial deputies, and before judicial commissioners of the Swabian League.

The cumulative effect of the growing economic difficulties, increasing social tensions, and the stronger dependence on lordly government was to create a critical, conflict-laden situation such as had probably never been seen in previous centuries. And yet not all of these tensions were equally strong. For the peasants their natural enemies formed a hierarchy. Complaints against towns were kept within limits. Rights to pasture, hunting, common land, and fishing were hardly mentioned; only with regard to wood supplies did subject peasants complain against their towns. Obviously their communal powers of government remained unrestricted, their tax burdens modest, and grievances against the administration of justice were confined to difficulties in sorting out jurisdictional claims among judicial lords. Complaints in the area of landlordship, formulated more as petitions than as demands, were more numerous than those against serfdom and as a whole were far less common than the demands of subjects in noble and monastic areas. Although the villages of the nobility had more to complain of concerning services (presumably the compulsory service at the hunt), land transfer taxes, and restrictions on use of the woods than monastic subjects, nonetheless their complaints as a whole weighed less heavily than the huge mass of complaints leveled at monasteries. Monastic villages attacked the high level of rents, restrictions on marriage, the demand for death taxes, and similar acts acknowledging servile status and did so much more vociferously than did other kinds of villages. They also polemicized against the administration of justice, the invasion of common fields and waters, and the military tax. The clergy became the main target of the revolutionary movement, not because peasants resented the mixture of spiritual claims and secular office, but because the burdens of monastic subjects were actually heavier. The first blow was also aimed at the nobility because relations between nobles and their peasants were only slightly less tense. Only the towns were largely spared the military attack of the peasants.

It remains to determine the effect of these causes on the program and announced goals of the Revolution of 1525; but first we must use our heightened awareness of the problems of peasant life, gained from the detailed analysis of Upper Swabian conditions, to survey the range of causes in all the areas of rebellion.

CHAPTER 3

The Spread and Influence of the Twelve Articles

If the feudalism of the High Middle Ages had preserved unchanged the pristine relationships between lord and peasant in Germany—which it did not—the wide dissemination of the Twelve Articles would come as no surprise. No other peasant platform attacked the questions of landlordship, serfdom, jurisdiction, and local dominion so comprehensively or kept them at the same time so free of obvious regional peculiarities, thereby lending them a cloak of general relevance.

In their native region the Twelve Articles fulfilled the twin functions of identifying the causes of the revolt and of setting forth its program. This is also generally true of those other lordships, territories, and regions where the Twelve Articles were adopted. The immediate task of a causal analysis of the revolution is to determine the extent to which the adoption of the articles can serve as an index to the similarity or interrelatedness of the economic, social, and political problems of different regions and territories.

The Twelve Articles were known in every region of the rebellion. Their author, Sebastian Lotzer, knew well the effectiveness of pamphlets because of his earlier work as a writer and propagandist. With over twenty printings in various places, the articles spread quickly during the months of April and May 1525. Peasants of Allgäu, who were recruiting in the alpine regions, brought them to Tyrol; itinerant merchants brought them to Fulda; the Alsatians asked their priests to interpret them; the imperial electors asked the Protestant reformers to evaluate them; the Bavarian dukes barred them from their lands; and Archduke Ferdinand tried in vain to keep them out of the Austrian lands.

To know the Twelve Articles, however, was not always to adopt them. They did become important as substitutes for local and regional demands, as supplements to earlier articles of grievance, or as a programatic statement in the following areas: the southwest—in the Black Forest, Breisgau, Markgräflerland, and Alsace; Franconia—in the villages around Rothenburg, the areas controlled by the peasant bands of the Neckar Valley and the Odenwald, the Hohenlohe lands, and the prince-bishopric of Bamberg; the Swabian-Franconian borderlands—in the Ries, the prince-priory of Ellwangen, among the Gaildorf and Limpurg peasants, the prince-bishopric of Eichstätt, the duchy of Württemberg, the Rhine Palatinate, and the prince-bishopric of Speyer, where the peasants based their debates on the articles; Thuringia, where they were adopted by the peasants of the Thuringian Forest, the prince-abbey of Fulda, and the county of Schwarzburg; and, finally, the Erzgebirge between Saxony and Bohemia, where the articles served as a program. They had no importance, however, in Switzerland, in the county of Tyrol, in the prince-archbishopric of Salzburg, or among the Franconian armies of the Tauber Valley and Bildhausen.

A reasonable but as yet unproved hypothesis is that even where the Twelve Articles attained merely programmatic status, they mirrored, at least roughly, the peasants' real tribulations. Wherever the articles did more than merely stimulate discussion, comparable structures of domination may be assumed to have existed; for it would have been fairly easy for the rulers to discredit them if they hadn't fitted local conditions. That the Twelve Articles circulated very widely, were known everywhere, and yet did not become the fundamental document in every revolutionary area of Germany, suggests that there were indeed limits to their relevance. It is conceivable that the economic, social, and legal problems of some territories were so different that the articles were irrelevant to them, as in the Tyrol, where relatively secure property rights and extensive personal liberties removed two central problems formulated by the articles. It is likely, too, that many places found the theoretical basis in the godly law unacceptable. This was so in the lands of the abbey of St. Gallen, for example, where the legitimizing principle remained strictly traditional. Moreover, identical content occasionally appears in independent local lists and in the Twelve Articles, though the former make no reference to the latter, an example of which is the grievance list of the Salzburg subjects at Gastein. To understand the causes of the revolution— and this is our only purpose in this section—we may set up reference points for framing the question precisely by establishing first where the Twelve Articles were adopted *in toto,* and then where they were changed to suit local and regional demands, in order to discover finally what grievances were voiced in the regions that did not adopt them at all.

THE TWELVE ARTICLES
AS BASIC REGIONAL DEMANDS

As the Upper Swabian material has shown, the local grievance lists reveal precisely which of the lords' prerogatives and practices triggered the crisis. Where local lists are lacking and the Twelve Articles take their place, the

MAP 5. THE REGIONAL DISTRIBUTION OF THE TWELVE ARTICLES

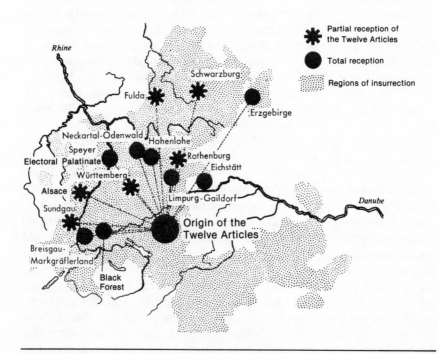

latter might be assumed to represent local and regional grievances if it could be shown that even outside Swabia local demands were absorbed into the articles.

In the Black Forest and Hegau, the preliminary risings of 1524 were followed by a second revolt in April 1525. At first the peasants resorted to the Twelve Articles, though a few days later they expressed even more advanced goals. They had earlier submitted their grievances to the Imperial Chamber Court, and this document permits us to test the congruence of the background of the Twelve Articles in Upper Swabia with the background of the articles of Hegau and the Black Forest.[1]

Careful comparison[2] of the latter with the articles of the Baltringen army shows that landlordship gave many fewer grounds for complaint in Hegau and the Black Forest: there were no complaints about entry fines and only a few about increased estate rents,[3] though there were many about seigneurial labor services.[4] This region, however, had many more complaints about serfdom. Radical demands for the total abolition of serfdom were indeed rarer here than in Upper Swabia,[5] but demands for the suppression of marriage restrictions, death taxes, and servile labor obligations were all the more vigorous.[6] The right to free movement and to inherit property, which did not appear specifically in the Baltringen articles, were treated extensively in those of Hegau and the Black Forest.[7] These pronounced differences concerning landlordship and serfdom were, however, balanced by extensive agreement about jurisdictional rights. The two regions placed about equal weight on denial of justice, abuses in the handing down of judgments, "alien" courts, the inflation of fines, and legislative practice. The lords' invasion of communal-corporate rights, however, was clearly more significant in Hegau and the Black Forest than in Upper Swabia.[8] The two regions gave equal emphasis to demands for adequate woodcutting rights and the right to use common pastures. In Hegau and the Black Forest, however, the peasants insisted much more vociferously on their fishing and hunting rights, the latter with special attention to crop damage by wild game.[9] Finally, forced services and taxes weighed much more heavily in the grievance catalogue of the Black Forest region than with the men of Baltringen.[10]

Two things emerge clearly from this comparison. First, adopting the Twelve Articles meant accepting their formulation of the revolt's causes, though the differences of emphasis within individual articles and groups of articles drafted by the Baltringen and Black Forest peasants prove that the Twelve Articles were flexible enough to allow considerable room for interpretation. We still have to discover the threshold beyond which the Twelve Articles became useless as a substitute for local demands, that is, the point at which their capacity for interpretation was overstrained. Second, where the Twelve Articles were adopted unchanged and *in toto,* they served to reinforce local demands (wherever such have survived). This is true for the Neckar Valley army and the peasants of Limpurg and Hohenlohe. Elsewhere, where the articles have swallowed up whatever local grievance lists there ever were (e.g., in Breisgau and Markgräflerland, in the Ries, around Ellwangen and Gaildorf, and in the prince-bishoprics of Eichstätt and Speyer, in the Werra Valley, and in the Erzgebirge), we can safely assume that the causes of revolt in Upper Swabia were the causes in those regions as well. Serfdom, landlordship, and judicial lordship, therefore, together with the secondary rights derived from these three sorts of authority, such as local government and territorial sovereignty, need to be examined over the entire area of rebellion. A closer examination of the territories in which the Twelve Articles underwent modification will show the extent to which other issues must be considered as well.

REGIONAL AND LOCAL MODIFICATIONS
OF THE TWELVE ARTICLES

The peasants west of the Rhine, like those of Breisgau and the Black Forest, based their case on the Twelve Articles. A comparison with the grievances submitted to an assembly at Basel in July 1525, however, reveals that the Twelve Articles covered only part of the spectrum of grievances in Alsace and Sundgau (southernmost Alsace). We may employ these Basel articles as a substitute for local grievances because they were clearly meant to supplement local demands formulated as far back as the era of the Bundschuh.* After the peasants' crushing defeat at the hands of the duke of Lorraine (May 17, 1525), however, the Basel articles could, of course, no longer proclaim a truly revolutionary program.

This Alsatian document, with its twenty-four articles, was much more detailed than the Twelve Articles, and its explications of individual items were as a rule both farther-reaching and more precisely phrased. They defined more exactly than did the Twelve Articles what was meant by "serfdom," [11] criticizing taxes, servile labor dues, death taxes, and restrictions on marriage and on freedom of movement. The demand for hunting rights was also more precisely grounded on the lords' refusal to reduce rents in money or in kind when wild game ruined the crops. Just one-half of these "Articles and Grievances of our United Peasantry of Sundgau and Upper Alsace" are identical in content with the Twelve Articles. [12] Two demands which appear here separately simply elaborate on themes from the Twelve Articles; these were demands for relief from the payment of the head tax (related to the Twelve Articles' passage on serfdom) and the elimination of the lords' grazing their livestock on the commons (related to the article on the commons).

The Upper Alsatian grievances, however, went on to demand a more careful, more just, and more practical judicial administration. Where, for example, a lord exercising high justice had formerly confiscated a convicted murderer's estate and had forced the court costs off on the peasants, from now on (the articles demand) such properties should be confiscated only as necessary to cover court costs, the rest being left to the widow and children. Whereas suits could move upward through four superior courts—from Ensisheim (seat of the Austrian regime in Upper Alsace), to Innsbruck, to the Imperial Chamber Court, to the High Court at Rottweil—in the future the judgments of local courts ought to be considered binding; and to lighten the peasants' financial load there should be but one appellate court, and this in the territory. Further, subjects were being jailed without a hearing, which should occur only in cases involving high justice. Finally, whereas the peasants were often excommunicated for debt, the ecclesiastical court should in the future be limited to its proper, ecclesiastical functions.

Alongside these detailed, high-priority grievances against the maladministration of justice stood others which were not in the Twelve Articles. These argued against territorial taxation, excise taxes, and customs duties; against the arbitrarily expanded powers of princely officials and the forced performance of certain services for them; and against the nobles' exemption

---

*The Bundschuh was a south German peasant conspiracy that nearly produced rebellions in 1493, 1502, 1513, and 1517. It took its name from the heavy peasant shoe, which served as an emblem on rebel banners.

from the territorial defense system. Moreover, in demanding that the monasteries be allowed to die out and that the Jews be driven from the land, the Upper Alsatian-Sundgau peasants went way beyond the limits of the Twelve Articles.

Regional characteristics and structures of domination peculiar to the Upper Rhine clearly emerge here, for complaints against the ecclesiastical courts and the High Court at Rottweil and the radically anticlerical and anti-Semitic demands were a hundred years old in this area. Complaints against territorial taxation, excises, customs, manipulations of the defense system, and machinations by officials all derived from a specific political development—the expanding territorial state, which strengthened its sovereign powers through its officials, which financed the state apparatus with taxes rather than traditional chancery receipts, and which in the case of Upper Alsace and Sundgau placed especially heavy defense burdens on its subjects (albeit with the consent of the territorial estates). The grievances' immediate targets were the nobility and the prelates, thereby providing evidence that lordship as a social structure affecting property, serfdom, and judicial rights was very widespread. But the grievances also reveal that the problems of the peasantry in a large territory, such as Nearer Austria,* were quite different from those in minuscule territories, where there was no prince to invade the lord's rule over the land, the serfs, and the local laws. This comparison of the Twelve Articles with the Upper Alsatian-Sundgau grievances shows that a statistical analysis of the various causes of the revolution must take two things into account: the homogeneous agrarian order from one region to the next (as outlined above), and the regionally varied structures of political domination. In Nearer Austria, for example, the prince was not attacked as territorial ruler but only as landlord and administrator of justice. Most grievances there were directed against noble and clerical landlords, serf-masters, and possessors of low justice (sometimes "local lord" is the best term), regardless of whether they had free imperial status or were subject to the Habsburg territorial ruler. Here we can recognize some priorities: landlordship, mastery over serfs, and judicial lordship aroused much more opposition than territorial government.

The duchy of Württemberg resembled Nearer Austria in some respects, though here the nobles and prelates had less control, and so the territorial sovereign as chief landlord (in 1525 the Austrian regime) became a main target of peasant aggression, along with the monasteries, which the rebels actually thought of dissolving. Matern Feuerbacher wanted "to introduce, encourage, and administer a Christian constitution based on the common articles, which, as you know, were issued in printed form." [13] But implement-

---

*Nearer Austria *(Vorderösterreich)* was a fragmented collection of small Habsburg territories in the German Southwest, including Breisgau, Sundgau, Ortenau, small areas of the Black Forest and sometimes also Swabian Austria (Burgau, Hohenberg, Nellenburg, and the province of Swabia) and Vorarlberg.

ing the Twelve Articles meant also realizing the articles' socioeconomic goals. Unfortunately, we have no grievance lists from villages or rural districts in Württemberg with which we might test the relevance or irrelevance of the Twelve Articles. In the absence of grievances from 1525, however, we can use the local lists prepared during the "Poor Conrad" uprising of 1514. These clearly show that forests and commons, hunting and fishing, had provided plenty of fuel for conflict, because the peasant economy had been gravely injured by the restrictions on rights of usage introduced by Württemberg's policy of forest conservation. The demand for complete or at least partial hunting rights (this demand is especially noteworthy) was justified almost solely by reference to the terrible damages to crops by wild game. Among the grievances of 1514 were complaints against services and compulsory labor, serfdom, and maladministration of justice. The allegation that "university men . . . have invaded the whole land with their practices, so that now a man can't get the same justice for 10 gulden that he got for 10 shillings about twelve years ago" [14] is similar to the ninth of the Twelve Articles. The decade after 1514 brought no structural improvements, so the same complaints were doubtless just as valid in 1525. At the start of the insurrections of 1525, Feuerbacher wrote that farm rents were unbearably high. The evidence as a whole indicates the conformity of conditions in Württemberg to those complained about in the Twelve Articles. We should not ignore the fact, however, that the grievances of 1514 were full of complaints unique to Württemberg, such as the numerous grievances of villages against the district towns for exploiting politically and economically their commanding positions, and a mass of charges against ducal officials.

Moving north to the territory of the prince-abbey of Fulda, we find that the townsmen's and peasants' grievances hardly went beyond the Twelve Articles, which they adopted as a whole, so that peculiarly local sources of the revolt remain obscure. This is only slightly less true of the county of Schwarzburg, whose local articles were generally congruent with the Twelve Articles, except that there was no article on serfdom. Regional peculiarities did crop up, however, in the numerous complaints against sheepherding and the even stronger ones against customs dues and taxes. To the southwest, in the prince-bishopric of Basel, the Twelve Articles dominated both quantitatively and qualitatively; the only regional peculiarities were fierce anticlerical and anti-Semitic prejudices and a strong opposition to moneylenders and foreigners.

Only in the larger territories was it obviously necessary to modify the Twelve Articles. Conflicts between local feudal lords and the peasantry, or between the territorial prince as landlord and his peasantry, could be well articulated by the Twelve Articles; but the articles, because of their origin, could not possibly give expression to problems created for the peasantry by the territorial principality. Among these were specifically the growing bureaucracy, which served to intensify the prince's domination, and the taxes and tolls which fed the state coffers. Taxes, much more than customs duties, burdened the peasant economy because they came on top of the prince's seigneurial dues, which were no longer sufficient for the needs of the early modern state. Officials were installed to realize the interests of their prince; and they necessarily invaded communal life, curbing, through their police power, the autonomy of the peasant community.

GRIEVANCE LISTS INDEPENDENT
OF THE TWELVE ARTICLES

Those rebellious regions whose grievances did not conform at all to the Twelve Articles were limited to parts of Franconia and Thuringia and, remarkably, Switzerland and the entire alpine region. An overview like this, which aims only at revealing the spectrum of potential for conflict, may focus on Salzburg, Tyrol, and Switzerland, because Franconia as a whole and Thuringia too can be assumed to have had comparable economic, social, and political structures, despite all of their local peculiarities.

Salzburg listed the causes of its revolt in the twenty-four articles of the whole territorial assembly of Salzburg, a forceful manifesto which painted a grim picture of clerical drunkenness and lechery, noble oppression, and princely despotism. Here, the noble and clerical landlords, the lords of petty estates, and the holders of judicial lordships were charged with having taken over the allodial possessions and inheritance rights of farms, raised dues and services, and introduced new transfer fines. Serfdom was attacked as being untraditional in Salzburg; the common form of tenancy was copyhold, which barred the lords from subjecting their peasants to political control and from robbing them of their property through the imposition of death taxes—in short, from "treating the poor folk as if they were cattle." [15] Compared with such grievances against the lords as landlords and serfmasters, complaints about complete or partial access to the forests and fishing and hunting rights (justified by the damages caused by wild game) seem to have taken second place, if we can judge the weight of the articles by their breadth and polemical vigor. Thus far the Salzburg articles corresponded very well to the Twelve Articles; but the catalogue of grievances went on. There were also complaints, although less vehement ones, against the territorial prince and his officials as "tyrants and bloodsuckers." [16] Such men denied the poor their rights; they either neglected or financially exploited the administration of justice; they misused the ecclesiastical courts by excommunicating for secular offenses; they oppressed the land with taxes [17] which should have been levied only for territorial defense.

Despite the fact that the Twelve Articles did not become a platform for the Salzburg territory, the local grievances show that the difficulties in the agrarian economy that unleashed the crisis were the same there as elsewhere, and that political structures shaped the grievances in the same direction we have already seen in Nearer Austria and Württemberg. Our rough distinction between small and large territories within the area of revolt, a distinction that is now becoming clearer, is further confirmed by the Tyrolean grievances.

In the Tyrolean local grievances, and also in the comprehensive articles from Merano and Innsbruck,[18] complaints against landlords are extremely numerous,[19] despite the widespread existence of heritable tenures in Tyrol; on the other hand, the local lists lack demands for the abolition or restriction of serfdom. The districts of Matrei and Schlanders did complain of a head tax, but that was really a form of protection and not a mark of serfdom. Comparable in weight to the complaints against landlordship were those against restrictions on pasture and forest usage and the demand for extending fishing and hunting rights. The latter was motivated by the extensive damages by wild game in Tyrol, which by the time of Maximilian's death (1519) had already driven peasants to a relentless campaign against deer and boar. Finally, the articles questioned the meaning and justice of forced labor services, both to the landlord and to the territorial prince. The grievances addressed to the prince were much more reserved than those of the Salzburg peasants, for, with regard to taxes, the Tyroleans questioned less their justice than their inequitable distribution. Frequently, however, they attacked customs duties, excises, and exactions of all kinds. In criticizing the maladministration of justice, they blamed not the prince but his judges and overseers, mostly nobles to whom many of the Tyrolean courts were pawned.

A wide variety of political structures determined the Swiss grievance lists, making them very difficult to reduce to a common denominator. Only those of the assemblies of St. Gallen and the Thurgau betray a strong kinship to lists from southwest Germany.

The St. Gallen and Thurgau lists complained about rising charges by the landlords and the putting of new legal disabilities on peasant properties by subjecting allodial lands to seigneurial dues and rents and by charging for property transfers. Both lists demanded the abolition or at least the easing of serfdom, and they demanded that illegitimate children be given inheritance rights. They demanded free hunting and the right to fish in Lake Constance; they insisted that lords contribute to general taxes and military taxes; and they wanted unrestricted rights of manufacturing in the countryside. Both lists further complained about maladministration of justice, particularly the needless jailing of defendants of good reputation in nonfelony cases who were ready to cooperate with the court. And both lists complained against the invasion of the autonomy of the village commons and courts. The Thurgauers objected to the lords' appointing all the district officers; and the men of St. Gallen complained that they were not consulted about new regulations.[20]

Other agreements in content among the various Swiss grievance lists are very few, hardly going beyond the demand for the abolition or curbing of serfdom. The districts of the city of Basel preferred to complain about taxes and customs duties (the salt duty, the "bad Penny," the duty on grain), the jurisdictional aggrandizements of the ecclesiastical courts, compulsory labor services, and the restriction of fishing and hunting rights; and they demanded the restriction of military duties to real emergencies. The demands from the villages of the town of Schaffhausen were restricted, except for a complaint about the tithe (which we have excluded as an "exogenous" factor here and elsewhere), to the abolition of serfdom and the reduction of compulsory labor dues and rents. The Solothurn peasants emphasized in three articles their demand for the abolition of serfdom—although after treaties signed in 1514 this demand was largely unnecessary—but they were otherwise content with the most general demands, such as some access to the forests, hunting and fishing rights, abrogation of the tax on foodstuffs, and improvement in the administration of justice. Finally, the grievance lists from the territories of Bern and Zurich are so different that they cannot be used to discover similarities among the causes for revolt.

These independently developed grievance lists were clearly uninfluenced by the Twelve Articles. Despite regional peculiarities, especially in Switzerland, where feudal structures had weakened, they allow us to differentiate a variety of causes of the rebellion. The manorial nexus between tenants and lords, the most enduring determinant of everyday peasant life, was overloaded with the most severe tensions and burdens. None of lordship's privileges escaped peasant criticism: neither landlordship, nor serfdom, nor rights of low justice, nor the police power, nor the power to execute punishments. And on top of the agrarian-feudal system, partly exacerbating but partly relieving its tensions, lay the nascent territorial state, whose administrative and fiscal practices the peasants also attacked.

Because we have found a high degree of objectivity and uniformity in the peasant's grievances, we are now ready to use them for a close analysis of the causes of the Revolution of 1525.

CHAPTER 4

The Crisis of the Agrarian Order and the Critique of the Early Modern State

THE CRISIS OF THE FEUDAL AGRARIAN ORDER

Between Freedom and Bondage

The "Reformation of Emperor Sigismund," an anonymous reform proposal from about 1438, had pilloried few things so savagely as the enserfment of peasants by the noble and clerical lords. The purpose of this treatise was not so much to brand as oppressive an unchanging legal situation as to halt an ongoing trend in its tracks. From the laconic complaints expressed by the rebels of the Bundschuh, to the violent charges of the Upper Rhenish Revolutionary,* to the discussions at the Diet of Speyer (1526), serfdom remained a topic of vehement political and literary debate. The grievance lists from all the regions of the insurrection make it clear that these debates reached their climax in 1525. The use of the godly law nearly everywhere as the justification for the anti-serfdom article might lead one to suppose that the peasants wanted to abolish serfdom only in order to realize the gospel, as they understood it. Historians in the West have thus argued that the explicit desire for personal freedom was not really triggered by economic oppression or by familial or village tensions. The urgency, determined spirit, and passionate language leave no doubt that, at least during the early phase of the revolt, the abolition of serfdom was the peasants' main desire. The Twelve Articles confirm this impression in the preamble, where the peasants are compared to the people of Israel, whom God guided through the Red Sea. In so doing God was freeing his enslaved people from the steadily increasing labors that the tyrannical overloads imposed. But if such grievance articles truly reveal the rebels' motives and reliably present peasant problems—and we have conclusively demonstrated that they do for Upper Swabia—then the demands

---

*The anonymous author of an apocalyptic reform pamphlet dating from ca. 1500. The work is properly referred to as the *Book of One Hundred Chapters and Forty Statutes.*

for an abolition of serfdom should not be isolated from the other articles. Instead of being a merely theoretical objection, the attack on serfdom must be seen in the context of other articles demanding an end to the death tax and to restrictions on freedom of movement and freedom to marry—all of which flowed from serfdom. Yet it is very difficult to prove in any general way that grievances against serfdom mirrored actual historical conditions. All that can be offered at this time are generalizations, deliberately formulated as theses, which can only occasionally be supplied with empirical supports.

The zone of serfdom was roughly coterminous with the area of insurrection in 1525, stretching from Salzburg to Alsace along the east-west axis (with the exception of Tyrol, which had only remnants of serfdom by 1525) and from Franconia to Switzerland along the north-south axis.

Territorial rulers in 1525 had not yet generally succeeded in reducing their subjects to a uniform body of legally equal serfs.[1] The greater the differences created by more or less oppressive forms of personal dependence within a given region, the more repulsive must have seemed the legal consequences of serfdom, such as prohibitions on free movement and limits on the right to marry. The serfs of the lords of Thun, for example, reported to the territorial diet at Innsbruck in 1525 that they had "no other complaint about serfdom except that they find it shameful and are not able to marry respectably."[2] Such witnesses can be multiplied, and together they reveal the complexities serfdom could produce: around 1500 the circle of those in a given area who could marry one another was often so restricted that the degrees of consanguinity made it impossible for the peasants to marry at all.

The economic burdens stemming from serfdom were usually limited to a symbolic fine in the form of a "bond-shilling" or "bond-chicken," an annual servile head tax, and a death tax of the best cow and best garment. If he had to pay all these charges, then a serf doubtless felt their weight, especially since the servile head tax could be very high. Of these three dues, however, only death taxes were common to most regions, so that the fewer cattle a peasant had, the heavier was the burden. Along with his tools, livestock were the only form of property fully controlled by the peasant himself, and the seizure of livestock as taxes must have hit the peasants very hard. We rarely have reliable figures for estimating the average number of animals per farm; and the variations were certainly great. Even so, we can say that a substantial peasant normally had four horses and several times that many cattle, and he could fairly easily bear the death tax; but the same charge could become a crushing burden for small peasants and day laborers. It is estimated that in Switzerland the average farming unit had three or four cows, and the comparable figures for Inner Austria (Styria, Carinthia, and Carniola) ranged from 2.1 to 4.6 animals per inhabitant (i.e., per person liable to heriot), figures which certainly meant that the economic consequences of serfdom were oppressive.

The obligations deriving from personal dependence in the sixteenth century suggest a blurring of the lines between late medieval serfs and other tenants. Death taxes of the best cow to the lord had originally been a mark of free tenancy, while from the serf the master normally collected either the entire estate or part of it (although this rule was usually enforced only when the serf left behind only married children or no children at all). This practice survived in some places down to 1500. We cannot tell how often rulers confiscated the personal property of a family, accumulated sometimes for generations, by excluding all relatives except for children from the inheritance. When this was combined with the complete or partial appropriation of the real and personal property of serfs who married outside the circle of their lord's dependents (an ever more lucrative source, because the peasants were forced by diminishing marriage possibilities to resort more frequently to these outside marriages), we can scarcely doubt that the larger picture was one of gradual, if perhaps modest, enrichment for the lords and impoverishment for their peasants.[3]

Complaints against serfdom would have been debunked as empty revolutionary rhetoric had the process of blending the status of tenants and serfs brought a uniformly improved legal condition for the peasantry as well as economic relief. It is, to be sure, incontestable that the forms of bondage loosened in the wake of economic development during the twelfth and thirteenth centuries. Mobility increased, as did economic independence, and the differences between freedom and servility as criteria of social distinction simultaneously faded. In the Alemannic-Swabian region this development was reflected in the often successful claim by subjects that they were *"free* men of the monastery" or *"free* men of the lordship." The legal institution of serfdom did not disappear, however, and could be reactivated when needed. The conditions for such a reactivation occurred during the late medieval agrarian crisis. Mobility had to be curbed to assure the cultivation of the land; marriage to outsiders had to be severely punished in order to avoid difficulties with inheritances and legal complications with other lords in the process of territorial state-building; and rents and dues had to be pushed to the limit in order to make up the for landlords' losses of income because of falling grain prices. Because of the leveling of legal differences down to the fourteenth century, the new intensification of personal dependence meant that free clients, tenants, and serfs could without distinction be subjected to the new serfdom. The right to enserf squatters was another means of increasing the number of serfs. The fifteenth century was dominated by complaints against rising burdens and restrictions on mobility, neither of which had been at all common before. Could this impression be merely the result of accidents in the survival of records?

When these doubtless fragmentary data are combined with the empirically better-grounded findings for Swabia, two points can be established: first, an intensification of personal dependence between the late fourteenth and the mid-fifteenth century; and secondly, a gradual mitigation of serfdom during the last decades of the fifteenth century. Thus, we may truly speak of a "second serfdom" not only for Germany east of the Elbe but for southern Germany as well. Still, it is true that the climax of this second serfdom in about 1450 could produce nothing more than scattered revolts and obviously provoked nothing like the reaction of 1525—which was inspired (as Erasmus of Rotterdam put it) by the argument that "by nature all men are born free, and serfdom has been set up against nature." [4] Therefore, we are still left wondering what the true weight of serfdom was in the context of all the other rights of lordship.

The Costs of Landlordship on Agriculture

The improvement of peasant property rights was characteristic of late medieval tendencies in the agrarian order. Tenure expanded from a limited tenancy for a definite number of years, or for life, to the heritable tenancy. From the lords' point of view, this process may have had several advantages: it reduced the attractiveness of emigration, it encouraged investments, and it converted legal privileges into cash. There is no doubt, however, that pressure from the peasants themselves also contributed greatly to the improvement of their legal position.

All this has little to do with the question of peasant's burdens. [5] Charges on heritable farms could not be increased, to be sure, but the records from nonheritable leaseholds, on which rents could be renegotiated each time the land changed hands, also show that rents and dues rose little, if at all, before the sixteenth century. Even if here and there hereditary tenures were less heavily burdened than annual or life tenures, still in Central Europe the differences were not marked. During the second half of the fifteenth century the average burden on a peasant holding, including the tithe, came to something like 30 percent of the gross product. The real incomes of peasants varied markedly according to the size of the farm, the degree of specialization, and access to markets, but there can be no doubt that in general the total costs were high. In the broad stratum of middling peasants, the net product was just barely sufficient to live on. In contrast to the caricatures of chronicler and litterateur, who delighted in caustic but lively images of luxuriously clothed peasants wallowing in gluttony and drunkenness, true prosperity among peasants was exceptional and limited to the thin upper class of villagers. [6]

The increasing differentiation of rural society into separate upper, middle, and lower classes was only strengthened by the growing involvement of peasants with the markets to be found in the numerous towns throughout the area of insurrection. Moreover, extraordinary fluctuations in harvest yields meant that peasants were sometimes unable to pay their fixed rents. Especially for market-oriented peasants, who had specialized in garden crops, cattle, or wine growing, a harvest failure produced no surplus for the market (at least for small and middle-sized farms), and therefore no cash with which to pay for the necessities no longer produced at home, let alone cash for the landlord's rent. In Alsace, which has been very well studied in this respect, we know of harvest failures for 1480-83, 1490-92, 1500-1503, and 1516-19. These were precisely the years when many farms were abandoned. The causal link seems obvious.

If I may hazard a generalization, it seems clear that before 1525 the costs of landlordship on agriculture were high but that they were not rising. If one insists on seeing the regional differences, then it must be added that during the decades before 1525 in some places lords tried to raise their incomes by imposing land transfer fees. This was true mainly of the lesser noble landlords, whose feudal rents no longer came anywhere near supporting a noble lifestyle.

Landlords did have alternatives, however: they could accept their situation as given and sell out to the free cities, or they could invent new sources of income, thereby inviting suits from their subjects. Land transfer fees remained the only direct way to raise feudal rents.[7] Moreover, the smaller the landholding was, the more oppressive were the fixed dues to the landlord. There can be no doubt that there were more and more persons on the land from the late fifteenth through the sixteenth centuries; and so peasant holdings rarely attained the size of a normal hide (15-40 acres). By the end of the fifteenth century the numbers of day laborers, cotters, and gardeners were climbing steadily, taking land from fragmented farms or, less often, from the commons. Thorough studies of several districts in Thuringia have brought a number of details in this process to light. Between 1496 and 1542 the number of taxpayers rose from 763 to 1,231, and the number of peasant farms rose from 670 to 784 (through the division of estates). But the servant population rose from 58 to 249. In other words, only one quarter of the additional population could be outfitted with a farm of some sort. By far the greater number obviously sank to the lowest level in the village or moved away. Wherever we can glimpse the rural class structure, the lowest classes make up half the village population.

If one analyzes rural society according to property holdings rather than according to the size of farms, the figures on village poverty are only slightly lower. In Thuringia, Saxony, Franconia, and Württemberg the propertyless (worth up to 25 gulden) make up 40 to 50 percent of the population (for parts of Saxony the figure is smaller; in parts of Thuringia, larger). Compared with the relative wealth of German cities, especially in Hesse and along the middle Rhine, the widespread conditions of poverty in the countryside are incontestable.

This finding helps to firm up our data about rural indebtedness. In parts of Styria the number of debtors was appallingly high, but the actual debts surprisingly low, corresponding on the average to the market price of one or two oxen. Yet such debts often encumbered the farms for up to ten years, which means that even small debts could not be paid off. And the average indebtedness in parts of Tyrol reached half the worth of the farm. Throughout

Alsace, too, a wide variety of sources testify to the over-indebtedness of the peasants.

It is hard to estimate just how socially explosive these developments were, especially since the available sources naturally do not speak of conflicts within the village.[8] We must assume an extremely complex web of antagonistic village interests, shaped by at least three major groups: full peasants, small peasants (cottagers), and rural day laborers. It seems possible that these internal conflicts actually neutralized one another; that would then explain why these tensions never became visible among the rebels themselves, at least not in 1525.

Collective Usage Rights and Fiscally Motivated Usage Restrictions

Late medieval agriculture normally had a safety valve in that, alongside the relatively independent farm or leasehold, there were extensive usage rights in the forests and common pastures, which permitted the keeping of many more animals than would have been possible with the resources of the farm alone. These rights also produced timber for building and fencing, without forcing the peasant to draw on his own financial resources. At the beginning of the fifteenth century there were still extensive forests, so there were few conflicts between peasants and forest overlords; and even where lumbering and pasturage were precisely regulated, usage was rarely restricted in any serious way.

By 1525 the situation was entirely changed. Hardly a peasant grievance list neglected to demand emphatically logging rights, hunting rights (with the usual argument about damages by wild game), pasturage rights, and the right to graze the forests. Where such grievances are lacking, as in Kempten or the Black Forest, a glance at historical forestation maps shows that in such areas the balance between forest and arable had changed decisively in favor of forests. Reaching far back into the fifteenth century there were conflicts between peasants and rulers about overexploitation of the forests, which had caused swiftly rising timber prices that drove the lords to define their vaguely phrased forest rights with greater precision. By 1525 things had not yet deteriorated to the point that one could succeed legally with the argument used by the imperial city of Memmingen against the imperial vicegerency of Swabia, that "he who owns the stags may also hang the thieves," [9] a lively analogy concocted by a Memmingen senator seeking to base sovereignty over the city's urban hinterland on its rights over wild game. Yet this unsuccessful argument shows the real threat to which peasants were subject: rights over game (plus other rights, too, of course) might be developed into territorial sovereignty. This had already succeeded in Württemberg, where "the Counts of Württemberg built their territory not on their rights as counts but on hunting rights." [10] Not until the seventeenth century had things gone so far that forest rights actually became regalian rights. By then forest lordship was seen as an integral part of territorial sovereignty, and princes could enforce their own interests with special laws and special courts.

Princely forest conservation policies began cautiously in the fifteenth century but expanded rapidly during the sixteenth. Before 1525 Saxony, Württemberg, Salzburg, and Tyrol—to name only the most important—promulgated forest regulations. Of course these edicts drew on older customaries and local regulations, but there can be no doubt that governmental interference in the woods became more energetic. Indeed, the flood of forest laws proves the point, especially since the new legislation on forests was not limited to princely forests but was applied to village and private woods as well.

Princely forest policies were shaped by a mixture of several competing interests: the growing scarcity of timber, caused by clearing at the hands of both peasants and nobles plus the enormous timber consumption of the cities; the increasing profitability of the forests; and the lords' passion for hunting. Forest laws and their enforcement varied in severity, of course, according to the severity of the timber shortage; but sometimes the forest laws only masked the lords' passion for the hunt. Peasant complaints in Tyrol were doubtless based on the region's huge need for wood in the mining and smelting of copper and silver, but just as vehement were those from Vorarlberg, where the forests served mainly as Habsburg hunting preserves. The complaints of Württemberg's rebellious peasants during the "Poor Conrad" against restrictions on their forest rights were surely due to real timber shortages in that densely settled territory, but in the margraviate of Baden the forest ordinances simply protected the game, large and small, from the peasants. The end result was everywhere the same: the peasants were barred from the forests as completely as possible unless they had clear legal title to their woodland. Wherever we get a close look into the forest economy around 1500, the same picture emerges: prohibitions on clearing; clear-cutting in place of the earlier selective harvest practices, plus the fencing off of young trees for long periods; and restrictions on mastage and forest grazing rights. The peasants could not simply be deprived of their forest rights through edicts, but the lords did try to shift over to them the burden of proving their rights. Only rarely, of course, could the peasants produce a sealed charter to prove their rights; and the lords, who could not produce analogous proof of their exclusive claims any more frequently, emphasized with all the more verbiage their "princely sovereignty." This dilemma of legal insecurity became obvious in the Twelve Articles, which turned the princes' argument upside down and demanded that lords prove with sealed charters that they had not stolen the forests from the villages.

The details of forest laws aimed at limiting mastage for hogs, forest grazing, and lumbering. Whether fifteenth-century forest rights always limited the amounts to be cut, or whether they always required that the peasants pay the lord in cash for the timber, may well be doubted.[11] By the sixteenth century, however, such regulations had become common. Wherever they did not limit the mastage of hogs in favor of game parks, the lords of the forest leased or rented mastage rights for large sums of cash. Forest grazing harmed the forests, of course, because the cattle and sheep hindered the growth of young trees. And the danger of deforestation grew with the increase in numbers of farmsteads and cottages in the woods, though just as harmful to good forest management was overpopulation by wild game. Young trees were fenced off for at least three to ten years, thereby eliminating the possibility of forest grazing for the peasants; for the young trees were off limits while the tall, mature stands provided no grazing. As for lumbering, the peasants were barred from marketing timber, though earlier (so far as we can tell from the forest laws) the practice had been quite usual. In place of the old practice of unregulated lumbering according to need, now the different species of trees were marked for particular purposes. Oak and beech went exclusively for building timber, windfallen trees for firewood. The allotment of timber occurred under the supervision of the foresters, sometimes even with consultation by carpenters. We cannot determine accurately how much of a peasant's needs could still be completely supplied under these restrictions; but we know that sometimes and in some places the peasants did have to buy wood. Peasants near Nuremberg allowed their fields to grow up in trees because of the timber shortage, which is surely an extreme but instructive example of how desperate peasants could be. The policy of conserving the woods did not always have to mean greater restrictions for the peasants, but their harsh complaints form a bitter counterpoint to the lyrical rhetoric of the chanceries and confirm that the "father of his country" did not always have the interests of his "children" at heart.

Although forest conservation emphasized preserving and increasing game stocks, its unintended consequence was severe crop damage by deer, boar, and the hunters themselves. Peasants could not solve this problem satisfactorily until long after 1525—that is, until they could administer the forest themselves, cut back on game populations and kill those that damaged their crops. In all the grievance lists, or at least in all those that went beyond mere theory, the freedom to hunt was demanded because of crop damage by wild game. We get no concrete impression of the damages, but the truth of the claims may be judged by the fact that peasants continued to complain emphatically about this issue right down to the early nineteenth century. So long as peasants could not hunt in their own fields and so long as they were forbidden even to keep dogs and to fence in their fields, they could not regard forest conservation as being really in the common interest. They knew only too well that, in vast areas of the Holy Roman Empire, prohibitions against clearing and forest grazing served only to multiply game populations, so that the noble passion for the hunt ultimately dictated forest policy. Peasant opposition to "conservation" is even more understandable when we note that the penalty for poaching (this example should at least be mentioned) could be so severe that a peasant who killed a stag in his own fields was sewn into the stag's skin and torn to pieces by the hounds. That they should nonetheless be forced to serve as beaters and to tend the lord's dogs went well beyond what they could view as the tolerable limits of arbitrary power.

Fishing was akin to hunting. Just as the peasant got his timber from the woods, so he fished in the streams, the rivers, and the lakes. In the later fifteenth century the lords began to put fishing waters off limits, depriving the peasant of his fishing rights. We don't know whether fish played a significant role in the peasant family's caloric intake,[12] and the grievance lists give us no help here. To the extent that fishing rights could be justified by the traditional law, the grievance lists only demanded access to fish for the sick and for pregnant women. Free use of the waters meant more, of course, than just fishing rights, for watering livestock and irrigating meadows were often restricted in the interest of conserving fish stocks.

In general, legal rights concerning the commons were probably clearer than those connected with the forests, though both property and lordship rights could atrophy when pasture was plentiful, as it was during the decades after the initial siege of Black Death in the fourteenth century. Exploiting their lordship over the commons, landlords and rulers could easily issue restrictions on the use of commons, settle day laborers on the commons, or stock the commons exclusively with their own livestock, thereby forcing the peasants to reduce their own livestock holdings. Along with urban growth and the rise of urban incomes, such restrictions on the commons may have been partly responsible for the shortages in the meat supply of Central Europe, shortages which were met only by huge imports. The few estimates we have of livestock holdings,[13] plus indirect evidence from import figures, prices, and peasant diet, suggest the same conclusion: a very low livestock population.

External Factors: Population Movements

The tensions within rural society grew more and more acute, both because incomes were falling and because it proved difficult to blame the lords. The fact that objections to landlordship were rarely grounded in the old law (and the Bible was certainly not very helpful in providing arguments for rent reductions) and usually limited themselves to demanding a reduction in rents and other burdens, surely suggests that other factors than the relationship between lord and peasant had depressed the profits of agriculture.

We are told where to find these other factors by sixteenth-century chroniclers, who complained constantly of a rising population. Sebastian Franck believed that even after the 100,000 peasant deaths in the military defeats of 1525, another 100,000 (plus women and children) could be spared for emigration to Hungary. Franck, like Ulrich von Hutten, thought that only war and plague could blunt the edge of overpopulation.

The reliability of such chroniclers may be questioned in principle, because their data rested on personal observations limited by the naturally narrow horizons of their experience. Demographic studies have now determined that around 1500 there was a density of thirty to forty inhabitants per square kilometer, but it goes without saying that there were great differences in population density, depending on the quality of the soil, the proportion of forest to arable, and the urban density—to name only the most important variables. Such absolute numbers thus tell us little. We may doubt that the population had reached the actual limits of its ability to feed itself, because it continued growing until the Thirty Years' War without any corresponding change either in the amount of arable or in the intensity of cultivation. We must still discover whether the population was increasing during the decades just before 1525—that is, whether more persons had to be fed from unchanging harvests.

Visitations of the plague during the fourteenth century had drastically reduced the European population, including that of Central Europe; and a demographic downturn—or at least stagnation—continued through the middle of the next century. Demographic growth during the sixteenth century is well attested, though its point of onset and its strength are debatable and not at all clear. Precise calculations which may be typical for Germany as a whole are first available only from 1520 onwards; and they indicate an annual growth rate of around 0.7 percent, which eased off towards the end of the century. There were naturally some regional differences, and the general impression is one of an earlier and faster upswing in western than in eastern Germany. Apparently growth also began earlier in the south than in the north.[14] Although Saxony began rising in population in the decades just before 1550, reliable figures for upper Germany show an annual growth of 1.4 percent ever since the end of the fifteenth century. In the parts of Thuringia bordering on Franconia the number of taxpayers increased between 1496 and 1542 by about 62 percent. In the archbishopric of Salzburg between 1497 and 1531 the population rose by at least 14.3 percent, but perhaps by as much as 69 percent, depending on how one evaluates the data. This is a good example of just how hard it is to go beyond general trends to a detailed demographic history. We have figures of this kind only for particular regions, of course, and they offer no firm basis for broad generalizations. Indirect sources tell us, however, that the growth of population was in many places rapid enough to cause concern. After 1500, for example, the "law and order" sought by territorial princes was increasingly concerned with beggars;[15] landless laborers and gardeners multiplied in the countryside; landlords tried to put an end to partible inheritance; villages now set entry fees to discourage newcomers; clearings were made in the woods wherever possible; and even in 1525 cities and the Swabian League had no trouble recruiting mercenary soldiers.[16] These are all signs of a growing population.

We can get a real sense of what demographic expansion meant in the countryside only by looking at the possibilities for and limits on horizontal mobility between town and countryside. During the epidemics of the fourteenth and fifteenth centuries, the cities had experienced an economic upswing and a strong demand for labor. Urban growth was due only in part to natural increase, for about half the new citizens were immigrants from the immediate hinterland. This immigration lasted until well into the fifteenth century, when incipient economic difficulties in the cities began to cut down on the peasant influx, so that rural population growth now had to be absorbed by the agricultural economy.[17] The differences in these processes between east and west and between north and south in the Holy Roman Empire may well help to account for the fact that in 1525 there was no insurrection either in northern Germany or in Germany east of the Elbe.

THE DYNAMICS OF THE EARLY MODERN STATE

The concept of the "early modern state"[18] is best applied to those territories in the empire, such as Brandenburg and Austria, which were characterized by an "uncommon rise in the tempo of politics and the self-consciousness of the state."[19] This means that such states dissolved the feudal ties of vassalage across the territory, claimed for themselves a legislative monopoly, and simultaneously opened up new sources of income outside the feudal economy. Such criteria for the early modern state exclude those territories whose political structures continued to rest principally on the agrarian order, as was the case in Swabia and Franconia, on the Upper Rhine, and in Switzerland—precisely those small states whose problems were summed up in the Twelve Articles. It is very difficult to distinguish sharply between the "small state" and the "large state" around 1500 because of the fluidity of the categories; but some classification is possible if it is done with care. Territories of the type of the prince-abbey of Kempten are small states, while those like Tyrol are large states. In analyzing the causes of the Revolution of 1525, the only important question is the extent to which, regardless of the generally uniform agrarian order, the early modern state invaded peasants' lives, an invasion which came in two prongs, taxation and princely officials.

The tremendous financial needs of the German territorial states can be documented from the fourteenth century onward, a growth whose causes we need not examine here.[20] Although state finance during the fourteenth century developed nothing more than primitive financial forms, chiefly using mortgages to commercialize the ruler's rights, during the next century conditions changed appreciably. The change came when the state hit upon taxation as a means of finance alongside the fiscal exploitation of regalian rights. Taxes, though undeveloped in the small states, were the rule in all the large states. Before princes could levy taxes on their people, however, the people had to become their direct subjects. As for the peasantry and their role in this process, it is impossible now to determine if the leveling of the forms of personal dependence and the erosion of serfdom (as can be clearly documented for Tyrol) brought them economic relief; or whether the price of freedom from serfdom was actually higher taxes to the prince.

One thing at least is certain: tax burdens grew during the decades before 1525. Where the territorial diet's approval was required, the estates naturally tried to keep the territorial burden as light as possible. Faced with the constant danger of state bankruptcy, however, the estates regularly had to make enormous sums available to their princes, in the illusory hope of finally freeing the prince's own mortgaged incomes, paying off his debts, and thus securing some long-term relief from taxes. In addition to the property tax, princes added the excise, which sometimes even took the place of property taxes. Then there were the consecration taxes in ecclesiastical states, and throughout southern Germany the contributions to the Swabian League. Last, but by no means least, there was the imperial tax for the Turkish wars, the importance of which for the late fifteenth and early sixteenth centuries can only be roughly inferred from its vast consequences for the development of the state in the late sixteenth century.

Wherever we get glimpses or better views of the financial history of the large states—for example, in Salzburg and the Palatinate, in Tyrol and Württemberg, and in Vorarlberg and the prince-bishopric of Speyer—the importance of taxes stands out. Franconia affords highly detailed pictures of the peasants' tax burdens. Here, the territorial tax was assessed on personal property at 5 to 10 percent during the years before 1525. The episcopal consecration tax assessed at the enthronement of a bishop—and thus not a regular tax, though in Bamberg it was paid in 1501, 1503, 1505, and 1522—was set at 10 percent of all property in episcopal fiefs and up to 10 gulden each for properties outside the episcopal domain. There were also indirect taxes on wine and beer, and sometimes on meat and flour as well, which raised prices 10 to 20 percent. Together with the military levy, which was raised in 1519, 1523, and 1524, this was an enormous tax burden; all told, the peasants paid about half their annual incomes in taxes and dues.

Although one should not overgeneralize from these data, they do help us to penetrate to the real background of the peasants' grievances against taxation in the large state. Even some small city-states, such as Basel, adopted this state-building method and thereby provoked complaints from their peasants. Princely financial demands necessarily affected the territorial administration and bureaucracy, whose constant expansion over the centuries reached a first plateau around 1500 in the creation of privy councils and prerogative courts in Upper and Lower Austria, Bavaria, Baden, Hesse, Saxony, and other territories. The native nobility and the bourgeoisie (a class which was closely bound together by marriage and already had some legal education) filled the key positions in the chief departments of government; from these posts they pursued their prince's interests. An increasingly centralized judicial administration tended to force legal customs to become more uniform, thereby favoring a more widely applicable set of territorial laws. Social policy tended towards a stricter regulation of the social and private life through enforcing "law and order," whose purpose was to nip every difficulty and every crime in the bud. Finally, economic policy issued forest and mining laws and strove for stricter control of the princely domain, in order to swell princely revenues.

To ascribe these measures entirely to the naked self-interest of the princes would be simplistic. Any growth in the chancery or cameral revenues of the prince also served peasant interests, as did the codification of law on the territorial level; for the former was an indispensable prerequisite to lowering the territorial tax burden, while the latter was unavoidable in the face of increasing mobility. It can be demonstrated for south Germany that the peasants at the very least supported these developments. The reconstruction of the state did nonetheless produce conflicts. To increase chancery revenues it was not enough to collect feudal dues more efficiently; other sources of income also had to be tapped. One source was the forests, now protected by forest laws issued by regalian authority and necessarily bringing restrictions on peasant usage in their wake. Protecting the village from strangers, beggars, and vagabonds required new controls, which violated the immunity of the individual home. If law were to be made more uniform, princely courts had to nullify many judgments from lower courts. Unquestionably, arrogant bureaucrats went too far. Including the commons among his regalian rights, for example, did not justify the prince's appropriation of those parts of the district which had been allowed to lie fallow and grow up in grass. Law and order overshot the mark when it closed the taverns at nine o'clock instead of the usual ten. And the courts made too much of a good thing when they transferred cases from lower courts in order to enforce the Roman law of inheritance in the territory.[21]

Beyond these areas in which the interests of prince and peasant might collide, there were more frequent and more basic conflicts at the communal level. Princes, to be sure, implemented the new idea of the territorial state with a framework of privy councils, prerogative courts, supreme courts, chancelleries, central administrative bodies, and chambers of accounts; but these organs could not yet penetrate down to the people. This required a local administrative apparatus, which developed in the form of district government. The district, sometimes coterminous with the older village commune and sometimes not, was the province of the district governor, usually a noble, who, as the prince's official, had to try to realize the regime's goals on the local level. Although appointed for a set term and responsible to the central government, the district officer enjoyed broad judicial, police, and administrative powers; his judicial authority might well collide with that of the communal court, his police power might well limit the functions of analogous communal officials, and his administrative competence might well make old village institutions superfluous.

For the town and rural districts of South Tyrol, the peasants demanded officials, "who will annually collect, administer, and disburse Your Serene Highness's rents, dues, and revenues, but who will have no judicial power either to punish us or to hear our cases; for they should only be called Your Serene Highness's district governors." This grievance concerned officials' arbitrary expansion of their authority, and the plaintiffs wanted it stopped. They did not thereby deny the prince any judicial authority at all, demanding only that "the judges in all criminal and civil cases, major or minor, should have no interest or stake in the cases, but they should refer everything to Your Serene Highness alone." [22] Thereby unjust punishments and self-seeking judges would be avoided. This demand was provoked by the fact that more than 60 percent of the Tyrolean courts were mortgaged; and the judicial authorities installed badly paid judges and administrators, who supplemented their meager incomes from fines they levied.

In Württemberg we find a similar problem with the duke's regalian rights. With a relatively dense settlement and an acute timber shortage, and with its dukes' passion for the chase, Württemberg saw an early and vigorous development of forest conservation laws. Numerous foresters were appointed to enforce the laws; and they were especially tempted to misuse their powers because the chancery was ordered to accept no complaints against them. Using their police powers, they barred peasants not only from the forests but also from the commons and the streams. They used their criminal jurisdiction to slap heavy cash fines on peasants who "could not find" the hunting dogs entrusted to their care. The forest wardens and their servants lived at the peasants' expense, while at the same time they forbade the peasants to let the dogs run free to chase wild game from the crops.

Thus, the enforcement of law and order may have prevented some judicial and administrative errors, but it also created a host of new ones. In addition to their tax burdens, the villages now had also to support this network of local officials, who were often poorly paid and often venal.

THE PEASANT POLITICAL CONSCIOUSNESS

The deterioration of their economic condition, the heightening of social tensions, the increasing pressure from their lords—all served to sharpen the peasants' political consciousness. A remarkable constitutional shift had occurred during the fifteenth century, and a fateful one for southern Germany: political responsibility for peasant affairs had been transferred from the rural commune to the territorial assembly.

Whatever the origin of the rural commune, the fourteenth and fifteenth centuries were the crucial time of its maturation. The continued spread of nucleated villages in the wake of late medieval depopulation had brought political problems to rural society. Through the dissolution of manorial structures and the growing alienability and commercialization of the rights of lordship, competing claims to lordship over the village developed which forced the peasant to form corporate administrative and judicial institutions to fill the resulting governmental vacuum. These changes strengthened the sense of local corporate and communal autonomy, which had already developed because the landlords, local rulers, and judicial authorities lacked strong administrative organs of their own. Such fragmentation and competition forced them to delegate governmental functions to these smallest political units. The village community, the judicial commune, the valley community, the mountain commune—all had comparable structures owing to their similar tasks.[23] Peasants of the community—sometimes elected, sometimes appointed, and sometimes selected jointly by community and lord—provided as harmonious an economic regime as was possible where individual and communal interests often stood in conflict with one another, as they did over the three-field system, pasturage rights, and the use of the commons and the woods. These village officials fulfilled the tasks of supervising construction, preventing fires, and regulating the market. They issued edicts and injunctions to guard the local economy, protect property relationships, and preserve internal peace. They exercised criminal jurisdiction to enforce their regulations. They appointed jurors to the village courts, which were empowered to handle all sorts of administrative, petty, and even criminal cases with the exception of the three or four capital felonies reserved for high justice. In brief, the most elementary state functions, such as guarding the peace and protecting civic rights, were handled by the peasants themselves; and in this they were supervised sometimes by the ruler but more often by the commune itself, which could assemble whenever it needed to.

We must emphasize these fundamental facts if we are to secure a precise conception of the late medieval political order—that is, of the political order that involved the peasants as well as the emperor and the imperial estates. Problems of political order in the countryside no doubt grew during the fourteenth century because of the increasingly concentrated settlement patterns, and in the fifteenth because of rural population growth. The most elementary needs of human society could at that time certainly be better supplied by the village commune itself, which experienced the needs, than by the lords. The villages thus harmonized with a second voice in the roundsong the cities had begun centuries before.

The early modern state was the first to succeed in putting its officials into the village, district, valley, and mountain communities. Clothed in the ruler's authority, these officials tried to enforce whatever the prince and his councillors regarded as promoting the common weal, law and order, and, of course, their own interests.

In emphasizing the broad range and common characteristics of communal powers in the fifteenth century, we must not overlook differences of time and place. There are plenty of good examples of such differences. During the early modern era the communal districts of Vorarlberg developed into nearly autonomous political entities, because of the increasing complexity of social and economic conditions and because of the Habsburgs' declining interest in these distant territories. Finally, these communes were issuing their own territorial laws. On the other hand, the landlords of fifteenth-century Saxony had already stripped village communities of their powers. In Franconia, villagers may have used the old associations of king's freemen to create politically active and responsible communes much earlier than in the Black Forest, for example, where settlement came relatively late. Local and regional variations in the intensity of communal political development are also to be found in the fifteenth century. In a village lying at the foot of the lord's castle, corporate or communal self-government could hardly develop vigorously, whereas a remote valley, reachable by the lord's officer only after several days' ride (and in winter not at all), was naturally thrown upon its own resources. Regional differences also occurred both within the counties, baronies, duchies, and electorates, and from one territory to the next. In the prince-abbey of St. Gallen, for example, the scope of communal self-administration was narrower in the "Old Land" than in the dependent area of Toggenburg. And in the old county of Württemberg,* village autonomy was subject to the presidency of the district town and the influence of the district administrator and had much narrower limits than in Upper Swabia. In the Rheingau peasants had political rights, but in the rest of the electorate of Mainz they probably had none. The conclusion that geography as well as the obvious political factors could also be responsible for the varying strength of the commune is perhaps nowhere clearer than among the Tyrolean communes, which had generally won greater rights than even those of Salzburg, just as communal autonomy in the Alpine area was greater than in Upper or Central Germany. Such differences form a spectrum, of course, and not polar opposites.

From the early fifteenth century onwards at least, a new dimension is visible in the lord-peasant relationship, something which from the ruler's point of view may be crudely called "territorialization." Complementing the process of externally consolidating a land through the exchange and purchase of estates, people, and political rights, there was an internal intensification of government through the elimination of noble and clerical lords as intermediate powers between prince and peasant. The varying degrees of personal dependence were also smoothed out to make a uniform body of subjects of the territorial ruler, and sovereign rights were invented or reactivated. This process led noble and ecclesiastical lords to react to the pressure placed on them by the prince by increasing the pressure on their own peasants; at the same time they discovered in the territorial diet a suitable instrument with which to offer corporate resistance to the prince. Conflicts between peasants and lords, on the other hand, had to be resolved on the village level. The more

*Württemberg was a county until 1495, when it was raised to a duchy.

the villagers became subjects of a lord in the wake of territorialization, the narrower became the area that was free of lordship. The more a local ruler made use of his power to command, the more limited became the creative legal powers of village courts. The more intensively a lord took over local administration, the more village officials shifted allegiance from their community to their lord. The more energetically sovereign rights were exercised, the more restrictions there were on all sorts of common usage rights for the village. In short, a theoretical polarity between lord and community became an actual antagonism. The simplest proof of this development is supplied by the village court decisions and ordinances, which are more numerous for the fifteenth century than for any other time in their thousand-year span.[24]

There is no doubt that the lord's regulations for the village encroached on local customary law and that the ruler's justice replaced the old corporate standards of justice[25]—not just to serve princely self-interest more completely, but also to make the law uniform for the entire territory. The longer this process went on, the less able were village and village court to defend themselves against the ruler's invasion. But the peasants were not inclined to suffer these losses passively, and in the ensuing hard struggles (accompanied by rent strikes and refusals to pay homage) the territorial assemblies (*Landschaften*) were born. These bodies were the theoretical correlate of lordships (*Herrschaften*); as such, they were associative institutions, corporations of the entire territory, partly allied with the old territorial estates in opposition to the territorial prince. The Tyrolean peasants (that is, the subjects of the counts of Tyrol) had already obtained the right to be part of the territorial diet around 1400, an achievement repeated somewhat later in the Habsburg lands further west. The Habsburg subjects in Nearer Austria gained the right of representation at diets for parts of the Austrian lands and at diets for all the Habsburg lands, and finally in their own Nearer Austrian diets around the mid-fifteenth century. Similar developments occurred in Swabian Austria and in Vorarlberg around 1500. In Salzburg the subjects of the archbishop had striven since the 1460s for inclusion in the corporation of territorial estates. In the smaller territories of southern Germany—such as the county of Toggenburg; the abbeys of Schussenried, Ochsenhausen, and Kempten; the Baden lordships of Rötteln-Sausenberg, Hochberg, and Badenweiler; and the prince-priory of Berchtesgaden—subjects forced their princes, despite vehement resistance, to recognize legally the body of all subjects as a corporate association. Peasants made their political conceptions known decisively in such acts of political emancipation, even where they achieved only the weakest rudiments of territorial assemblies, as in the Palatinate in the first half of the fifteenth century and in the prince-bishopric of Speyer shortly after 1500.

With our eye on the Revolution of 1525, it is worth emphasizing the violent aspects of this earlier process of political emancipation.[26] The archbishop of

Salzburg suppressed the rebellion of his peasants only with the aid of the Bavarian dukes, and even so, the revolt cleared the way for peasant participation in the territorial diets. The prince-prior of Berchtesgaden needed Emperor Maximilian's intervention to win even a modest victory over his assembly. The abbots of Ochsenhausen and Kempten had to call on the Swabian League to intervene with troops against their rebellious subjects. The story of the formation of the territorial assembly was thus often a story of imprisonment, flight, and banishment. Even though assemblies did not always result from such acts of violence, stubborn peasants risked their economic survival, their freedom, and their very lives to keep from becoming mere pawns of the territorial state. The "common man" had become politicized. Emissaries of the peasantries of Swabia, for example, moved through upper Germany collecting witnesses for suits against their lords. Communes refused to do homage to newly elected prelates until their own grievances were met. Village elders threatened the prince's officials with force if dues were not lowered. Representatives of the peasants even went to the universities to secure jurists' opinions against their rulers. And peasant delegations appeared at imperial diets, at the imperial court, at the assemblies of the Swiss Confederation, and in the Swiss towns to plead for military or legal aid against their lords.

Successes won by the peasants on every front necessarily heightened their political expectations. In 1462, for example, the Salzburg peasants forced their archbishop to repeal tax increases and other innovations. In 1474 the Tyrolean peasants combined with the urban assembly delegates to force through a territorial constitution. The Berchtesgaden peasants in 1506 forced the prince-prior to revoke invasions of the existing agrarian system; and in 1502 the Ochsenhausen peasants secured, against their abbot's will, a transformation of nonheritable tenures into heritable ones. In 1500 the third estate of Nearer Austria, peasants and townsmen, were able to extract a set of regulations framed to their own liking. And the territorial assembly of Rötteln-Sausenberg basically constructed its own territorial constitution in 1518. These examples may suffice.

What the peasants achieved was codified in the edicts of territorial diets, in official territorial constitutions, or in charters of which the subjects got one of the two copies. Comparing and contrasting these documents with one another, we find once more some problems that the small state and the large state shared and others that they did not. In the minor territories of Swabia, the Upper Rhine, and Switzerland, the chief problem was a clarification or definition of the agrarian order that would work throughout the entire territory, including clear statements regarding servile obligations, property rights, and usage rights. This was true for the larger territories only to a limited degree. Where the territorial prince was also the greatest landlord, as in Salzburg or in Tyrol, the assemblies made an effort to regulate the agrarian order and agrarian economy more to the peasants' liking by changing the territorial laws. Where the territorial prince was much less important as landlord than were the nobles and clergy, as in Nearer Austria, the agrarian order could hardly become the object of territorial laws, and here only direct negotiations between peasant and landlord would serve the purpose. But everywhere the peasants' aim was the same: participation in framing the constitution of the territorial state. And if in the small states such efforts were largely confined to the agrarian order, this was because here, that order was nearly the same as the constitution of the small territorial state. Just as the territorial state had progressed beyond the purely agrarian state, so too, the large states' territorial laws went well beyond purely agrarian matters. One other characteristic distinguished the large states from the small ones. From Salzburg to Nearer Austria, wherever peasants went unrepresented, the diets of large states voted for taxes that were thoughtlessly extracted only from townsmen and villagers and not from the wealthier estates.

Peasant successes did have their limits. A remarkable feature of the edicts of the territorial diets, the territorial laws, and the treaties is the emphasis on the old law. The old law set limits on the peasants' ability to get their will. They might achieve much, little, or nothing at all: much, if the customary law could be shown to have been violated by innovations; little, when it was so overlaid by decades of innovations that nothing could be proved; and nothing at all, where new social and political problems clearly demanded solutions never dreamed of in the old law. Wherever the territorial state made use of Roman law, or uniform common law, or statute law, even if only as a supplement to tradition, and wherever the state's jurisprudence abandoned the German tradition of finding or discovering the law, it left the helpless peasant behind. And yet both sides felt the need for legitimacy. Lords fought with the weapon of the "common imperial [i.e., Roman] and ecclesiastical [i.e., canon] law," while the peasant defended himself with the now blunted weapon of ancient tradition. Reason stood opposed to morality. Fettered by his own concept of law as whatever was customary and reasonable, the peasant could only demand what he could legally justify. What he needed was the equivalent of the "common imperial and ecclesiastical law," and he finally found it in 1525 in the divine law.

CHAPTER 5

Biblicism versus Feudalism

The crisis of feudalism was not to be solved in the traditional way of cooperative law-finding by lords and peasants. Why not? If we are to answer this question, the contacts, overlaps, and interdependence among the issues under dispute must be laid bare, and the weights of the critical elements must be evaluated in such a way as to explain both general relationships and regional peculiarities.

Although the situation of Central European agriculture around 1500 is difficult to understand, it is clear that during the last fifty years before 1525 the peasant's position worsened as agricultural land became scarcer, as usage rights were vigorously pruned back for the first time, and as taxes increased substantially. Whether this process played itself out against a backdrop of recession or one of agricultural upswing cannot now be determined. Although not necessarily primary, this sharp deterioration of conditions was at least one cause of the revolution, for it was felt by only two generations and was therefore perceived as an actual deterioration.

One might object here that it is wrong to emphasize the economic condition of agriculture as a cause of the rebellion, because neither before nor after 1500 was change in the agrarian sector very rapid. This is correct, but it overlooks the fact that added economic burdens had been, in fact, sufficient to unleash revolts before 1525. The rising of the Salzburg peasants had been their answer to a doubling of the consecration tax; the disturbances in the monastic lands of Weissenau, Schussenried, and St. Blasien were reactions to increases in servile dues; and the "Poor Conrad" revolt in Württemberg was a response to a new ducal forest policy. No doubt the deeper causes of such revolts can be sought in the deeper levels of peasant consciousness, such as an offended sense of justice, but it is highly relevant that in each individual case the conflict was provoked by a ruler's actions which directly affected the peasant economy. The fact that from the mid-fifteenth century onward revolts erupted ever more frequently speaks for a sharpening of the crisis before 1525. Further, the increase in the number of revolts can be synchro-nized with rising economic exactions. The elector of Mainz advanced this view as early as the imperial election of 1519, and he explicitly backed Charles V because of the Habsburgs' economic power, "so that the poor common man will not be overloaded and burdened by obligations and levies without cause or need, for from this will follow nothing if not a Bundschuh." [1]

Two things about these revolts are noteworthy. First, they were accom-panied by the rationalization that in the time of "our parents and grand-parents," such-and-such an obligation was not customary; and secondly, they were conducted with the goal of abolishing concrete abuses. Motives and goals flowed together. Each demand had its legitimation, and the legitimation was the old law—the key concept in the entire medieval legal mentality. It is nearly self-evident, after all, that nothing was demanded during the late medieval revolts and insurrections in the empire that could not be justified. In other words, revolts could aim only at the abolition of specific innovations. This explains why the revolts remained territorially localized and why no revolution occurred in the fifteenth century comparable to that of 1525.

The added economic burdens struck a world of village and family that was already charged with tension. Since the flight from land to city had halted, a growing population struggled for the parcelling out of an inelastic supply of arable land. In regions with partible inheritance, society was levelled downward; while in regions where only one heir was permitted, the growth of a rural lower class sharpened the contrast between rich and poor. At first glance it seems absurd, in view of such troubles within the villages, that the lords hindered peasant mobility; but lords were concerned not with cottagers and small peasants but with tapping the wealth of the big farms. The same motive, reinforced by the interests of the territorial state, also prompted noble prohibitions of marriage outside the lord's jurisdiction, which prevented the satisfaction of the most elementary needs.

These social and economic developments stand in sharp contrast to political trends which could be simply described as the political emancipation of the peasants. If widespread village self-government fostered the ability to make political decisions, the peasants' successes in confrontation with their lords must have also raised their political expectations.

Greater attention to regional variation is necessary at this point. It cannot be denied that there existed a wide variety of economic burdens, social ten-sions, and political expectations among the peasants, and it is just this variety that prevents us from establishing any definitive hierarchy of causes of revolution; on the contrary, these factors must be considered as regionally specific variables. In Tyrol high political expectations counterbalanced lesser economic burdens, and the subjects moved step-by-step towards their goal of a territorial constitution. In Franconia the economic burden weighed more heavily than did the political expectations, for here the dues owed to landlord and prince ate up half the peasant's income and went well beyond tolerable

limits. Such examples, which could easily be multiplied, show that the con-
junction of variables always had the same effect in the end: the relationship
between lord and peasant had reached the limits of what it could bear. Where
the limit had not yet been reached, as may have been the case in Thuringia
(where south German forms of serfdom and communal autonomy were
unknown), the fire of a revolutionary leader such as Thomas Müntzer could
easily burn the remaining bridges.

But the revolutionary breakthrough did not come quite yet, and this
lethargy among the peasantry is incomprehensible if one excludes from the
lord-subject complex the bond of loyalty, the ethical component that bound a
peasant to his lord. Loyalty, that pervasive yeast of the medieval social and
political order, had in fact been devalued—and peasants obviously knew
it—by the overwhelming weight of economic dependence; but the peasant
was not yet in a position to break out of these older ethical bonds. These
bonds dominated his legal thinking, which fell prey to its own highly moral
nature and could not master the problems of a rapidly changing social and
political order, being bound to "ancient tradition." Ancient tradition did not
offer any solution to the demographic problem, for example. Further,
wherever the lord could cite "old law," ancient tradition was powerless. The
Sybilline judgment proclaimed that written law—even forgeries—was
superior to ancient tradition. Ancient tradition could prevent innovations, in
fact, only if it could appear as "documented" ancient tradition; and in
doubtful cases the stronger party prevailed. Yet, because this situation was
still novel, and because customary law did indeed sometimes win, the peasant
placed all his hopes in the power of the old law. It naturally took some time
before he realized that this hope was illusory,* and when it finally did become
clear to him that conflicts could no longer be resolved through the traditional
means of arbitration, his only alternatives were either to renounce the attempt
to justify his demands or to seek refuge in a "new" law. Ethically or legally
justified demands were naturally superior to unjustified ones. If the new law
were congenial to the peasants' legal mentality—if it could transform the
distresses, tensions, hopes, and expectations into legitimate, ethical
demands—then that law would obviously appear as a redeeming force.
Peasants found this new law in the "godly law."

The Peasants' War proper began in the months of January and February
1525, in Upper Swabia.[2] In Allgäu, around Lake Constance, and all about
Baltringen the peasants rose and organized themselves into the Allgäu, Lake
Constance, and Baltringen armies. We know of no mutual interaction among

---

*These relationships may be expressed by the following equation:

$$\text{readiness to revolt} = \frac{\text{economic burden} + \text{social tension} + \text{political expectations}}{\text{strength of legitimation}}$$

The weaker the force of legitimation, the greater the readiness to revolt.

the armies during this initial phase, but the increase of economic burdens, social tensions, and political expectations had clearly reached comparable levels. One sign of the homogeneity of agrarian and political conditions is the fact that noble and clerical lords had been consulting one another about ways to strengthen their territorial rule and to intensify their own power. The frequent law suits during the fifteenth century must have fostered this sort of communication among lords because they had staffed the various legal arbitration commissions and had thus become familiar with Upper Swabian conditions far beyond the bounds of their own petty lordships. An institution such as the Swabian League, whose assemblies brought together nobles, prelates and urban magistrates, also promoted the exchange of opinions and the adoption of uniform practices towards peasants. The remarkable frequency with which lords justified their own restrictive measures by reference to the customs of neighboring territories proves that these exchanges went on.

The hallmark of the revolts in the first two months of 1525 was their supraterritorial character. Peasants from widely different lordships came together, and whole villages rose, not just the subjects of a single lord. The real novelty lay in the fact that never before had peasant revolts broken through the narrow political boundaries.[3] Before such supraterritorial development could occur, however, the old forms of legitimacy had to be overcome. This was so because only individual lords and no one else could break the ancient tradition, and therefore demands couched in terms of ancient tradition could be addressed only to specific lords. This traditional sense of legitimacy and localism could be overcome in two ways, either through a new law, which would dissolve the legal community of peasant and lord, or through a renunciation of law altogether. The first path was taken by the Allgäuers, the second by the Baltringers.

The serfs and tenants of the abbey of Kempten in Allgäu had pressed with ever-increasing vigor since the mid-fifteenth century for loosening the forms of personal dependence. A revolt in 1491–92 formed the first peak in this dramatic campaign, while the second came with the sharply limited obeisance to the abbot sworn by peasants in 1523, both actions which the peasants undertook solely with the weapon of the ancient tradition. In January of 1525 an attempt to arbitrate among the abbot, the monks, and the territorial assembly failed. On January 23 at Leubas, seat of the Imperial Territorial Court of Kempten, the assembly then debated the alternatives—whether to resort to arms or the law—and the majority voted for the law. At this time the assembly still was composed exclusively of Kempten's ecclesiastical subjects. When the abbot charged that peasants of other lords had joined the sworn association, the assembly vigorously rejected the accusation and claimed to have excluded all foreigners. These events reveal with utmost clarity the combination of the old law and political action limited to a specific region and its people.

The envoy of the Kempten territorial assembly, Jörg Schmid (also known as Knopf) of Leubas, went to Tübingen to consult a university jurist. The assembly waited until February 20 before recalling him, by which time all of Allgäu was in an uproar and the peasants had found a new legitimation for their demands in "the holy gospel and the godly law." [4] Territorial limits were not breached, and dependence on different lords no longer posed an impassable obstacle to cooperation. By the end of the month the peasants of the count of Montfort, together with the nonresident citizens of Wangen, the serfs of the abbot of Kempten, and the subjects of the bishop of Augsburg, found a common institutional vehicle for their cause in "the Christian Association of the Land of Allgäu." [5] The Kempten peasants had never renounced legitimacy, but they had exchanged old, worn-out legal conceptions for new and handier ones—the old law for the divine law.

The second alternative to the old law emerged in the rebellion around Baltringen. In the month before mid-February, 7,000 to 10,000 peasants from the most diverse territories south of the Danube, from Messkirch to the Lech, streamed into the encampment at Baltringen. Although the peasants did not send many of their complaints directly to their individual lords, on February 16 they did submit their articles of grievance to the Swabian League when requested to do so. If we examine the kinds of legitimacy claimed in these lists, only 5 percent of the articles called on the godly law, and 11 percent on the old law; 84 percent appealed to no law at all. [6] Now and then arguments that were based on older usages crept into individual articles, understandably enough. But a very careful classification of the articles appears to confirm the conclusion that some demands simply could not be justified because there had been no demonstrable violation of the old law. Arguments based on ancient tradition were rarely presented in articles dealing with serfdom (1.5 percent) and landlordship (8 percent), but more frequently in those on judicial administration (14.81 percent) and usage rights (20.73 percent).

This acute lack of legitimacy was overcome within ten days. On February 27 the Baltringen army, now calling itself a "Christian Assembly," made the enforcement of God's word into a program: "Whatever this same word of God grants us or takes from us we will gladly accept and suffer whatever good or pain comes from it." [7] It was now superfluous to search out legal justifications for demands, to submit complaints, or to strive for a compromise with each individual lord. The revolt had acquired its legitimation; the revolution now had its goal. There remained only to express this goal more precisely, to harmonize the economic, social, and political demands with the word of God. The revolution now needed a manifesto—which it found in the Twelve Articles.

The enforcement of the godly law—whatever the peasants might have understood in detail by this phrase—became the goal of the revolution. The Twelve Articles acquired their explosive force from the formulation of God's law as a new legal principle, a law which could provide the legal basis for overcoming the structural problems of feudalism or even for destroying feudalism altogether. Even where the Twelve Articles themselves could not serve as the basic peasant demands, either because feudalism was still too stable or because the early modern state had already leached out the inner strength of feudalism, the superstructure of the godly law could be stripped off and made independent of the original demands, and thus be used to support demands with quite a different content.

The Twelve Articles, mirror of the peasant's aims in the first phase of the revolution, at first simply had to give biblical proof of the justice of peasant demands, logically branding as unchristian the lords' measures that had provoked their demands. For the peasants, using the word of God as a legal principle had a truly redemptive effect: the lords were now blamed for the rebellion, while the Bible justified it.[8] It remained unsettled what means could and should be used to establish the word of God.

Godly law was potentially dynamic in three senses. First, demands of any kind could be submitted, so long as they could be supported from the Bible. Secondly, corporate barriers, which had formerly divided peasants from townsmen, could be dissolved. And thirdly, the social and political order of the future now became an open question.

Wherever we can understand the lords' reaction to peasant demands in some detail, we see once more how useless ancient tradition was as a defense against innovations. In responding to the grievances their subjects had submitted to the Swabian League, the nobles all denied that any novelites had been introduced at all. From the lords' perspective, their policies were perfectly in accord with ancient tradition and territorial custom. This blocked any sort of compromise and left the peasant in a defensive position from which only the divine law could free him. To be sure, the legitimizing force of ancient tradition crippled the peasant only in those regions where purely feudal structures of domination still existed. The cities, on the other hand, replied to their peasants' demands more pragmatically, sometimes even defusing them with a shot of irony. Thus Memmingen, in answering the demand that entry fines be abolished, said by way of parody that in the future farms would be let out "on just the same terms that the subjects demand for their pastors."[9] This acceptance of the fact that there would continue to be conflicts of interest, as demonstrated by the free city of Memmingen here, naturally made it easier to reach an understanding. The lay and clerical lords, on the other hand, fled to the old law as a trusted refuge from the godly law. At a meeting in Basel, for example, the attorneys of the free knights and prelates of Alsace and Sundgau argued consistently against the peasants on the basis of ancient tradition: labor obligations were "of ancient origin"; death taxes were also "not newly invented but have been in force for many years"; the Shrovetide hen, that mark of servility, ought to be paid "because they and their ancestors have paid it for such a long time"; and the estates of murderers were confiscated because "this has been the custom for as long as anyone can remember."[10] In Tyrol, Salzburg, and Franconia, everywhere the

lords increasingly insisted on the ancient tradition. It was a surprising exception when Elector Frederick the Wise of Saxony admitted to his brother,
Duke John, that "the poor are burdened in many ways by us lay and ecclesiastical lords," and that "perhaps . . . the poor folk have been given sufficient cause for their revolt." [11]

Without the principle of God's law (and the above examples are only to
document this point) the revolution would have been impossible. The explosive power of God's law was also evident in the towns. Regardless of the fact
that it was a city that gave peasants the argument from Godly law—and this
is unquestionably the case with the Twelve Articles—we must insist that it
was through the peasants that the principle of God's law returned to the cities
as a possible principle for reshaping the social and political order. In general,
cities took up the slogan of God's law only well after the peasants had
thoroughly adopted it. And already in the Twelve Articles one finds the claim
that the reformation of the political order was basically an open question,
with the qualification that if these articles were found to "be unjust, they
shall be dead, null, and void from that moment on. Likewise, if Scripture
truly reveals further grievances as offensive to God and a burden to our
neighbor, we will reserve a place for them and declare them included in our
list" (article 12). Peasants wanted not only to hear the gospel but "to live
accordingly"; and the specific grievances listed were not their final word,
since their belief in the power of God's word to discover the truth and to per-
suade men of it was still unshaken. This was not only a liberation, however,
but a new bondage as well, for the application of biblical truth to the life of
this world was a private realm reserved to theologians, and the lords were
simply expected to submit themselves to the theologians' judgments. But
where would the revolution go when the theologians refused to guide and the
lords would not obey?

THE GOALS
OF THE REVOLUTION:
CHRISTIAN WELFARE
OF THE COMMUNITY
AND BROTHERLY LOVE

Although the commoners of a land may tolerate for a long time the despotism
and corruption of their lord, hoping that he will improve, if he does not, then
the commoners of a land should boldly take up the sword.
— *An die versamlung gemeyner Pawerschafft* (1525)

CHAPTER 6

The Christian Association and Assemblies: Models of a New Social and Political Order?

Between the months of January and May of 1525 a large number of groups with military, social, and political objectives banded together throughout the whole region of insurrection in central and southern Germany, taking names like "crowd," "vast multitude," "Christian federation," "Christian union," "evangelical brotherly league," "assembly," and "brotherhood." Most commonly they used the labels "Christian Association" and "Assembly." Taking only two examples, but two highly representative ones, let us examine how their social and political concepts were able to produce more than a mere catalogue of grievances, and how their formation and organization actually pointed the way to new forms of the state. These two are the Christian Association and Assembly of Allgäu, Lake Constance, and Baltringen and the Assembly and Honorable Christian Community of Salzburg.

At the beginning of March the troops from Baltringen urged a union with the troops from Allgäu and Lake Constance. On March 6 about fifty representatives of these armies came together in the merchant guild's chamber in Memmingen; on March 7, in writing to the Swabian League, they gave themselves an institutional framework with the Federal Ordinance and called themselves the Assembly of Troops from Allgäu, Lake Constance, and Baltringen and also the Christian Association. By using the term "Assembly," they expressed the corporative character and political claims of this supraregional association; with the name "Christian Association," they made it clear that the new norm of political order was the gospel and godly law. The Federal Ordinance, which was most likely based on a draft written by Sebastian Lotzer,[1] was discussed for a day and then accepted by the representatives of the individual troops on March 7, printed, and broadcast from the pulpits. Its immediate task was to fill the existing political vacuum, but at the same time it represents a first vague attempt to frame a new constitution.

The preamble is similar to that of the Twelve Articles in describing the intent of the Christian Association to establish the "gospel" and the "divine word," "justice and godly law." Proclamation of God's word was assured by requiring pastors to preach the pure gospel under pain of dismissal. Godly law was established by the remaining provisions of this Federal Ordinance. The program of the Twelve Articles was partially implemented by reducing seigneurial incomes to a contractually established level, but the lords' judicial authority was not explicitly abolished.

The vague and general restrictions on landlords' rights stand out more clearly if we examine the authority assumed by the association and the security precautions that it took. Any new treaty with the lords needed the association's approval and was valid only if it did not require anyone to withdraw from the assembly. A committee of three commanders and twelve councillors, elected from the three armies, took over leadership of the Christian Association; their authority was, however, clearly limited to military matters. In agreeing to keep the peace among themselves, the members used precisely the same formula that rural laws of the fifteenth and sixteenth centuries employed to keep the peace within the village. Several police regulations forbidding robbery, blasphemy, and other things completed the legislation. Artisans and mercenary soldiers, who could not earn their living from the land, had to swear before the parish captain that they would not join any army hostile to the association, and they would give notice of any preparations they made for war, and that they would stand ready in emergencies to defend the association. Servants of feudal lords were to join the assembly after renouncing their oath of service or they would be banished from the land. Finally, an article on castles strengthened the peasants' security by forbidding nobles and prelates to stockpile guns and troops except for members of the assembly.

The Federal Ordinance was doubtless provisional in many respects. Its contours were indistinct, and problems of political order remained unsolved,[2] all of which is understandable in view of its hasty composition: the peasants spent no more than one day on it. Godly law, as the peasants at that point understood it, provided no basis for aggressive, implacable, militarily disciplined actions against the nobles and prelates. Although one cannot deny the military character of the assembly, this Federal Ordinance was fundamentally defensive, and the "Territorial Constitution" framed slightly later remained basically faithful to this idea. Nobles still occupied their castles and prelates their abbeys, unless they had already fled to the refuge of the imperial cities. Feudal lordship was clearly locked in a struggle to the death, but what the peasants initially set up to replace it could only be temporary even though the Christian Association itself had been organized as a permanent body. It was conceivable, of course, that the commanders and councillors might be granted more than just the military powers they had. After the inescapable collapse of all governmental functions, one could imagine that the assembly itself would finally take over the administration of justice; the detailed provisions in the "Territorial Constitution" for keeping the peace at least point in this direction. Moreover, a remarkable optimism had not yet died—the hope expressed in the Federal Ordinance that the nobility would join the Christian Association. For the moment, however, there was an organizational vacuum that urgently needed to be filled. The Christian Association was on its way to becoming a new Switzerland in Upper Swabia. The members of the association had, after all, bound themselves together by an oath, and it was not for nothing that they called themselves an assembly (*Landschaft*). Yet just as obviously the peasants and their leaders were still too bound up in feudal relations even to imagine a radical alternative to the existing order, let alone to establish one. Both of the surviving formal oaths of the Christian Association illustrate this kind of uncertainty. In the first version we find an oath aimed at establishing the gospel and godly law and at protecting existing governmental and seigneurial rights within this framework; in the second version, the peasants aimed at the replacement of governmental powers with the statement that they wanted no other lord than the emperor.

This inability to conceive political alternatives was reinforced by the Upper Swabian interpretation of the Bible, which was adequate for the task of digging up biblical proof-texts for concrete economic, social, and political complaints against the lords, but which turned to the expertise of theologians for any advance of the peasants' program and any political interpretation of "divine truth." One week after the promulgation of the Federal Ordinance, at a second league assembly in Memmingen, the theological referees were named: Luther and Zwingli, Philip Melanchthon and Andreas Osiander, Conrad Billican and Matthew Zell, together with a series of others whom the peasants knew not by name but only by office and place of residence. To the extent that these theologians responded to the peasant inquiries at all, their reaction was a brusque rejection of peasant attempts to use God's word to change, improve, or even Christianize the political order. In an advisory document for the elector of the Palatinate, Melanchthon held that "since the Gospel requires obedience to the government and forbids rebellion even if the princes behave wickedly, and since it also requires that one suffer injustice, the peasants are acting against the Gospel in that they have mutinied against their government, intending violence and crime against it. . . . Obviously they are opposing God in this, so one can see that it is the devil that pushes them on." [3] Martin Luther sounded the same note, and even Zwingli, whose *Sixty-seven Conclusions* had unmistakably urged the bringing of positive law into accord with the norms of godly law, refused to support peasant efforts to actualize God's law. Instead, Zwingli abandoned the peasants, as we can see clearly in the case of St. Gallen, where he had stridently called for the secularization of the abbey of St. Gallen. Thus, the godly law remained silent because no one spelled it out. It lost its authority because it did not solve the crisis, and it lost its explosive power because the military and political leaders, including Lotzer and Schappeler, did not know how to exploit it to produce a new political order. Their political thinking simply oscillated between a Swiss-style sworn fellowship and free imperial status; their tactical operations were exhausted in either passivity or defensive postures.[4]

This Christian Association steadily grew in numbers, and by the second half of March, excepting only the imperial cities and a very few territorial cities, almost all rural and urban communities in Upper Swabia had joined the association. Even so, its representatives and strategists proved unable to develop their program any further. As the assembly swelled and it became more and more crucial to solve the problem of the nobles and prelates and establish a viable political order, the leaders of the Christian Association seemed less and less able to push beyond negotiation for settlement of their demands. Twenty days had passed since the framing of the Federal Ordinance. The godly law, which sustained the Christian Association, had had a liberating but not a revolutionary effect. It had not sufficed to set castles to the torch or to drive the nobility into exile.

Radical elements within the Christian Association, who had a different concept of the law of God, pushed on beyond these restraints. On March 26 the first castle went up in flames; on April 4 the first unit of the army of the Swabian League was defeated near Leipheim, east of Ulm. Countless monasteries, castles, and fortresses were now stormed before the army of the Swabian League could push into the area of Lake Constance and finally disperse the peasant masses by means of the Treaty of Weingarten, which forced them into a peaceful, arbitrated settlement. With those castles went the symbols of feudal lordship; with the destruction of altar hangings, relics, libraries, and archives peasants renounced (consciously or unconsciously) their whole cultural tradition, the past altogether; they replaced it with a better future which, their unseeing eye presumed, lay ahead at some uncertain distance. For a military clash with trained soldiers, however, these peasants lacked both concrete goals and fanatical convictions. Political alternatives became blurred, and the magical force of ideology collapsed when the leaders of the Christian Association refused to preach the harmony of force and the godly law.

This Upper Swabian development brings to light one fact whose general applicability must be tested for the whole area of rebellion. It is the observation that once the peasants acknowledged the godly law, they no longer aimed only at the abolition of concrete grievances but pushed more for a new political order, even if it was still only a vague idea. This new order would remove all differences of status and build on such local and regional corporations as village and urban communities, local courts, and territorial assemblies. Instead of eliminating these older corporations, the new order would use their experience with elections to work toward a broader political union based on the same electoral principle.

The Common Assembly (*Landschaft*) of Salzburg, or, as they also called themselves, the Honorable Christian Community of this Province in the Mountains of the Bishopric of Salzburg,[5] came together in the second half of May 1525. An uprising had spread out of Gastein a few days before; and under the leadership of peasants from Pinzgau and Pongau and of miners from Gastein, it had swept over the countryside, making contact with the city of Salzburg and forcing the archbishop to retreat to his stronghold, Hohensalzburg. These Salzburgers put godly law at the very center of their written program, demanding the authentic proclamation of God's word and grounding their economic demands on the gospel. Even the concrete demands of this platform pointed beyond economic grievances, since they would, if realized, have required changes in the social structure and the political order of the Salzburg territory. The communal authority of the Salzburg villages and districts was to be strengthened by giving them the right to choose pastors and to participate in the selection of judges. Seigneurs were to be reduced to the status of mere rentiers as their sovereign powers were transferred to the territorial prince, the archbishop. Property relations were not attacked in principle, but the political order certainly was, for the program foresaw the ultimate abolition of all intermediate authorities, especially the clergy, who were to be subject to the regular jurisdiction of the rural communes.

The Twenty-Four Articles of the Common Assembly of Salzburg described only negatively what the peasants and miners of the archbishopric of Salzburg intended to do to reshape the political order, but the city of Salzburg brought forward much more concrete proposals. A governing council of the Salzburg assembly with members from the three estates (probably meaning nobility, burghers, and peasants)[6] was to take over the official functions of the archbishop, cathedral chapter, and council. This new government was to be responsible for administering the monasteries, filling vacant offices, and managing the finances. The archbishop was to retain his ecclesiastical rights (although even they were reduced), and receive a set income to be established by the assembly. The structural effects of this reform are shown in Figure 1.

This program obviously presumed a functioning constitution of estates. It grew out of corporate political traditions and simply shifted the authority of the territorial sovereign to the estates (the assembly). Replacing the former government with representatives of the assembly appeared to be the easiest way of changing power relations without fundamentally attacking the structure of the state and the bureaucratic machinery.

Even though the idea was first propagated by the city, a government by the territorial assembly became a goal for all factions, and especially for the peasants, who for decades had been proclaiming their desire to be included in

FIGURE 1. THE TERRITORIAL CONSTITUTION OF SALZBURG

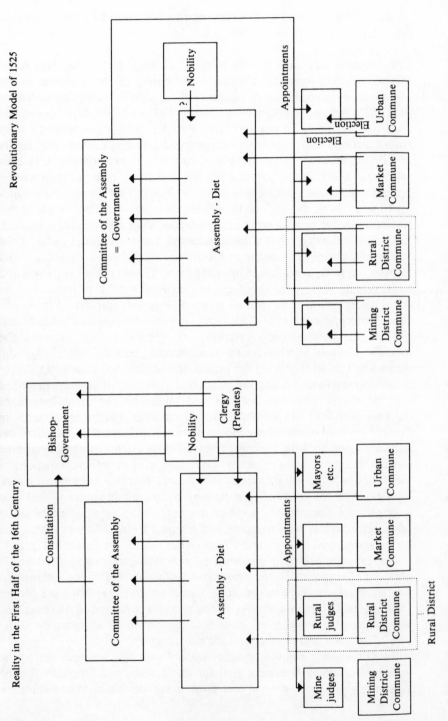

Reality in the First Half of the 16th Century

Revolutionary Model of 1525

the assembly. Of course everything depended upon what groups of people were specifically included in a territorial assembly. There had to be a decision as to which of two competing groups could rightly claim the title of "Assembly": the territorial estates in the traditional sense (on whom the archbishop had relied extensively in his desperate situation) or the rebellious peasants and miners.

In June 1525, after receiving homage as the "Assembly" from the archiepiscopal district officials, fiscal officers, and customs officials, the rebels took these men under their territorial assembly's protection and began issuing commands and injunctions. Relations became embittered only after a truce on August 31, when some of the rebels proved ready to accept conditional cooperation with the archbishop, while others uncompromisingly insisted on an assembly government composed of peasants, miners, marketplaces, and towns. This radical faction had earlier demanded the transformation of the archbishopric into a secular principality, perhaps a Bavarian suggestion. Although a regular territorial diet was to discuss reform of the territorial constitution in March 1526, the radicals, who had not attended the diet, insisted on framing the territorial constitution without the participation of the archbishop. They deliberately rejected any cooperation with the archbishop by explicitly claiming the title of "Assembly" for themselves and by holding a counterdiet. Our only source for this whole episode is the one-sided view from the March diet called by Archbishop Matthew Lang. Writing to Archduke Ferdinand, the emperor's brother, the diet claimed that the rebels had "forcibly subverted civil authority and had arrogated to themselves the title of Salzburg Assembly, although they have neither the authority nor the power to a common, proper territorial diet or of the proper constituent estates. Such rabble masses cannot be a true assembly." [7] The estates found it monstrous, too, that the rebels "during the current proper common diet" had "called together a diet of their own." [8] Only the military intervention of the Swabian League put a stop to these struggles for legitimacy and prevented the formation of "a new Switzerland," as the paymaster of the Swabian League, Leonhard Strauss, called it. [9]

Salzburg and Upper Swabia obviously had things in common, but there were also large differences. Differing territorial constitutions strongly influenced the social and political ideas of both regions. The Salzburg program clearly and unambiguously aimed at a seizure of sovereignty by the common assembly of the rebels. The peasants of Baltringen, Allgäu, and Lake Constance, lacking the models and traditions of the state, had a much harder time making their still vague social and political visions more precise; they could not discriminate between the blurred, entangled notions of a Swiss-style confederation and free imperial status. Such differences were also reflected in their terminology. Although the Salzburgers also called their association "Christian," this label remained much less meaningful than the stronger constitutional concept of "assembly." In contrast, the masses from Baltringen, Allgäu, and Lake Constance gave heavy emphasis to the adjective "Christian," while the concept of assembly had none of the primacy it enjoyed in Salzburg. Gospel and godly law were necessary in both places as the basis of a revolutionary program, but in Salzburg this biblicism could fade into the background during the second phase of the revolt because the political program was moving confidently within the framework of the established territorial constitution. But in Upper Swabia, where there was no established large territorial state or constitution, the political program had to justify a new, supraterritorial political association. Later we shall see whether such programmatic differences appeared throughout the whole area of the rebellion.

Salzburg and Upper Swabia were similar, however, in that both quickly extended participation in the rebellion beyond the peasants. In Upper Swabia the towns joined in, while in Salzburg the miners took part. Therefore we may doubt whether the concept of the "Peasants' War" correctly represents the social structure of the Revolution of 1525.[10]

CHAPTER 7

The Peasants' War
as the Rebellion
of the Common Man

In order to understand the Revolution of 1525 it is important to determine just how strong the connections were among peasants, burghers, and miners in the various areas of the rebellion, whether common miseries or similar goals lay at the basis of their coalitions, and whether cooperation, when it occurred, was forced or voluntary. It is generally true that the sharp differences in urban wealth in central and southern Germany made possible a cooperation between town and country dissidents, but cooperation with miners was naturally restricted to specific mining regions, like Salzburg, Tyrol, and Thuringia. A survey of Upper Swabian conditions shows, however, that distinguishing imperial from territorial cities also helps to sharpen our understanding of this problem. Not one imperial city from Upper Swabia joined the Christian Association, while a majority of the territorial towns did. A kind of parallelism in the development of the archbishopric of Salzburg is unmistakable, for the rebels there met no great obstacles to coordinating political goals and military operations between town and country.

IMPERIAL CITIES AND THE PEASANTS' WAR

A primary clue to the significance of the imperial cities (to take them up first) may be found in the suggestive fact that the Twelve Articles were formulated with the help of "the city," and the same city, Memmingen, opened its gates to the Christian Association of Upper Swabia for their meetings. We must assume the active participation in the peasant movement of at least some townsmen, and at least the benevolent neutrality of the burgomaster and senate. Following these clues in Memmingen more closely, let us examine the attitudes of the urban regime and of specific groups and individual townsmen, in order to discover what was truly important and so gain a clearer

105

conceptual structure for analyzing the relations between town and country generally in 1525. Then we can proceed to a quick survey of the areas of rebellion that had the highest density of imperial cities: Upper Swabia, the Upper Rhine, and Franconia.

Memmingen was one of those imperial cities of southern Germany which had destroyed the former political monopoly of its patricians. Strong tensions were already visible within the city during the fifteenth century, tensions created in part by the great poverty of the weavers. Numbering 256, they had doubled in the hundred years before 1530, but even so, the taxable wealth of all guild members had sunk by 50 percent between 1450 and 1521. In opposition to the town senate, the guilds succeeded between 1482 and 1512 in closing the urban market to the linen weavers from the Memmingen villages. The lifting of this prohibition in 1518 led to an uprising supported by all the guilds. The city secretary described the growing difficulties of the senate in maintaining internal stability with this laconic sentence in the senate's records: "The populus want to seize the upper hand; it appears that nothing good will come of it." [1]

Because civic officials' salaries were mere honoraria, the magistracy necessarily remained de facto the province of the rich. Just prior to 1525 they had to deal not only with social tensions but also with religious and ecclesiastical tensions, which often intersected the socioeconomic ones and finally led to factions within the city that were composed of all the social classes. The key figure in these religious and social disputes was the preacher at St. Martin's, Christoph Schappeler, a theologically educated man with academic degrees (as required by the endowment of the preachership by the family and trading house of Vöhlin) and a man also engaged in social questions, as became clear in the first years of his activity. The senate, fearing an "uprising" in 1516, found it necessary to regulate Schappeler's sermons, because he sided with the poor against the rich, but in 1521 they listened in silence to his charge that the poor had been more harshly punished than the rich. "It was found," remarked the senate's records, "that he told us the truth." [2]

Such events reflected tensions which became ever more serious as they gradually moved out into the streets. In 1521 Schappeler had "preached his felonious sermons . . . in the streets," pressing the community to look after its interests better. The worry "that it might lead to a rebellion" [3] caused the magistrates again to send a delegation from the senate to Schappeler. As time passed, the pulpit became more Schappeler's rostrum, from which he sharply criticized the conduct of priests, the position of the pope, and the canon law. The situation became acute, and Schappeler decided to go to Switzerland; [4] the bishop of Augsburg demanded that the senate take more severe measures against the dissidents. A "conventicle" made up of middling and upper-class burghers accosted the priest of the Church of Our Lady on a public street and forced upon him a document which contained not only a clear confession of the new gospel but also a sharp attack on the priest's conduct. Again the senate intervened, not out of worry about rebellion this time, but out of fear of the emperor's reaction. A few months later Schappeler returned from the Second Religious Disputation of Zurich (October 1523), at which he had presided. Partly reflecting the theological results of this disputation, he now preached against the mass, against the invocation of saints, and against the biblical basis of tithes. He was excommunicated by the bishop of Augsburg in February of 1524. The senate was now forced to a decision, since banishment from the city was supposed to follow excommunication, and they moved to support their preachers, partly from true conviction and partly from helplessness. Schappeler's following had become so large "not only in our city but also in the countryside," [5] that a revolt seemed unavoidable if they did not support him.

The clergy and the city senate came to feel all too sharply the political bite of Schappeler's sermons during the summer of 1524. Almost simultaneously the Memmingen peasants and some of the citizenry refused to pay tithes. Since refusal of tithes struck at the existence not only of the parishes but also of the civic hospital, one of the most important social institutions of the city, the senate reacted vigorously. [6] The announcement of heavy penalties and negotiations with the senate sufficed to change the minds of those who had refused to pay. Only a master baker, Hans Hölzlin, still adamantly refused and was thrown in jail. That was enough to mobilize several hundred burghers. An *ad hoc* committee organized by guilds formed at the marketplace, demanded his immediate release, and presented four more articles of complaints: (1) jail arrest only in felony cases; (2) preaching "without human additions" in all the churches of the city; (3) no intervention by the senate in tithe controversies between the "common man" and the priests; (4) punishment of priests who insulted Schappeler and others; and possibly (5) a religious disputation between those of the old faith and the new faith. The senate approved all these demands, and the "commune" duly dissolved.

It is worth noting that even the senate admitted that there were close ties between town and country in the matter of tithes and that inside the city a firm core of opposition to the senate had obviously formed. The spokesman for the Memmingen "commune" of 1524, Ambrosius Baesch, a relatively well-to-do weaver, belonged to the conventicle. Hans Hölzlin, who had so stubbornly refused to pay tithes, fled to Switzerland after the military defeat of the peasants and tried from there to instigate a second uprising in Allgäu. Of the other members of the conventicle, Paul Höpp, a teacher in the Latin school who played a key role in the internal urban disturbances of April and May 1525, and Georg Lamprecht were both executed in July of 1525, while Sebastian Lotzer, the field secretary for the Baltringen troops, escaped to Switzerland in April of 1525.

The citizen opposition group, together with the hesitant approach of the senate toward the new doctrine and the persuasive power of Schappeler himself, combined to push the Reformation rapidly forward in Memmingen.

Riots at Christmas 1524 forced the priests of the old faith into a religious disputation with Schappeler, and the laity claimed the right to judge it. This made Schappeler's victory certain. There was now no stopping reform. The clergy were made equal to the burghers in rights and duties; the mass was abolished; communion was offered under both species; ecclesiastical tithes became voluntary, while secularized tithes were still compulsory. These reforms testify to Schappeler's influence and to the weight of his following, which had long since expanded beyond the confines of the city community. Long before peasants began to mass in the countryside, the senate strengthened the guard at the city gates with two guildmasters at each one and ordered the field guards to keep order in the churches. Schappeler preached in the countryside and in neighboring imperial cities even though only the Memmingen senate stood between him and the attack of the bishop of Augsburg.

The senate's hot-and-cold attitude towards the new doctrine appeared truly progressive to the countryside. Memmingen was recognized as the vanguard of the Reformation in Upper Swabia. This explains the choice of Memmingen as the meeting place for the Christian Association; it explains the many attempts by subjects of nearby abbeys and nobles to have the senate arbitrate their complaints; and it explains the restraint of the Memmingen villages vis-à-vis the regime of their imperial city. While the peasants of northern Upper Swabia and Allgäu had long since banded together, complaints from Memmingen's hinterland first appeared only after mid-February 1525.[7] The senate and guilds adroitly intercepted the separate disorders by sending a delegation to the villages just a week after the first village deputation appeared in the city. The regime's envoys called for the election of a committee and the listing of grievances and admonished the villagers to be peaceful. Two days later all of the Memmingen villages submitted a document which renounced the listing of separate complaints and requested instead that the senate simply "treat us according to the interpretation and content of God's word. . . . Whatever God's word gives or takes from us, we will always gladly accept and maintain."[8] The emphasis on "God's word" was characteristic of Sebastian Lotzer, a vigorous partisan of Schappeler. The urban reformers were providing the Memmingen peasants with the argument from godly law.[9] Only a few days later the peasants turned in the Memmingen articles, which were largely identical with the Twelve Articles in both content and wording. The senate responded fairly generously by abolishing serfdom and entry fines, by giving villagers hunting and fishing rights, and by agreeing to find suitable preachers for the villages. Possibly for these reasons the Memmingen villages never joined one of the larger peasant armies. Given the attitude of the Memmingen senate, this is not hard to understand. For the peasants Memmingen was an open city; weapons were sold to them there; and Schappeler and his assistant preachers were brought in as advisers or sent to the villages for negotiations with the peasants. Memmingen permitted loans to the Swabian

League only with the explicit condition that the moneys not be used for armaments against the peasants.

Toward the end of March the Christian Association held its third meeting in Memmingen, and the peasant army expanded rapidly around the city. We can only guess how close the relations were between the burghers and the peasants, but we do know that, with the approval of the senate, the city fed the army. And it was only with difficulty and against the will of the community that the senate was able to turn down the peasant requests for heavy artillery. One indicator of how threatening the situation was may be that on March 20 the senate demanded, for the first time, that the peasants leave their weapons at the gates. The captain of the Memmingen contingent in the army of the Swabian League reported to the city that his men refused to move against the peasants. The League general, Georg Truchess von Waldburg, held the city's radical "commune" responsible for desertions.

In the second half of April there occurred new, sharp conflicts within the city. The peasants had intercepted a letter from the senate which obviously requested military support against the peasants and protection for the city. The senate could now recover its position only by making concessions to the guilds regarding the election of the privy Council of the Eleven, but then in the thick of events it still had to call for the help of the soldiers of the Swabian League. Memmingen was occupied in June. Those who failed to follow Schappeler and many others fleeing to escape the grasp of the Swabian League had to reckon with execution or jail. Those who thought that they could save the reforms of January found that they had deceived themselves. All of the old ecclesiastical conditions were restored.

It is difficult to render a final judgment concerning the political groupings within the city because parties oriented to internal or external politics shifted rapidly, and it would be simple-minded to look in only one social stratum for the forces favoring the Reformation and the peasant program while opposing the senate. We can, however, sketch the bare outlines of the radical minority, which constantly agitated for the Reformation, for the peasants, and against the senate. It was largely identical with the conventicle, comprising a handful of rich or at least well-to-do men and a larger number of propertyless. Using tax registers and a city map to locate them, one finds the centers of radical activity in the poorest quarters. Between 1450 and 1525 the city's rich had declined in numbers while the poor had grown. Meanwhile the middle layer, owing to these shifts in the distribution of wealth, had achieved some prosperity; and despite their sympathies with the revolutionary elements in the city and countryside, they remained in the end supporters of the senate. Ever since the military successes of the Swabian League during April, the Memmingen senate, divided against itself, grappled with the alternatives of either living up to its obligations to the League and empire or else risking its autonomy and free imperial status. Beginning in 1524 the pressure from the bishop of

Augsburg, the Swabian League, and the empire had been considerable. The Memmingen tithe dispute of 1524 had not remained a local affair. When Memmingen became the meeting place for the Christian Association, the Swabian League concluded that the city belonged to the peasants' party. To counteract such conclusions the senate, in its reply to the Memmingen articles, made a conciliatory gesture toward the Swabian League by reserving to the League the regulations of the tithe question (which certainly ought to have been managed internally), a move that had not been intended in the draft of their reply. Such gestures were superfluous. For the League Memmingen was "thoroughly dangerous," [10] and the firmness with which it urged the removal of Schappeler and Lotzer left no doubt as to what Memmingen could expect if the radical commune should gain the upper hand and conclude an alliance with the peasant army.

Three forces determined the general constellation in Memmingen during 1524 and 1525; the senate, the guilds or the commons, and the villages of the urban hinterland. The city-state's extremely complicated institutional architecture had a certain elasticity, but it could not be tampered with at will. If the tensions between two quantities in this three-way structure were to grow or shrink, the third was bound to be affected as well. In concrete language, the senate was the ruler of both the burghers and peasants. In 1524–25 this relationship between regime and subject was doubtless polarized. Common opposition to the senate made it much easier for urban and rural populations to come together, an alliance which was strengthened all the more by the common desire for religious reformation. In order to maintain stability, the senate could have relieved the tensions in three ways: by accommodation in ecclesiastical questions, and by concessions either to the urban community or to the villages in its territory. The imperial city with its territory was, of course, no island, especially not in the war years 1524 and 1525. In the larger picture of strained relations between the authorities and the peasantry in 1525, any concessions by the senate would be viewed by both sides as joining the camp of the peasants. And that, in turn, would threaten the city-state from without. Firmly asserting the position of the magistracy, and thereby following the line of the imperial estates, however, could blow up the city-state from within. Thus, the conciliatory attitude toward both sides seemed to be the epitome of political wisdom for the councillors of this imperial city.

It remains to be seen whether these conclusions about Memmingen can be applied to all the imperial cities. (1) Which groups inside the city worked together with the peasants? (2) What attitude did the imperial city's authorities take? (3) To what extent did the intelligentsia of the city supply the peasant revolution with an ideology by offering them God's word, the Bible, and godly law? This third question can already be regarded as answered conclusively, because of the wide distribution of the Twelve Articles.

To begin an answer, it appears that the Upper Swabian towns did orient themselves to Memmingen. At urban diets they sought to find a common political position; their mayors and councillors struggled to find a compromise between the peasants, the seigneurs, and the Swabian League.[11]

The officials of the imperial cities sought a policy of compromise which became ever more necessary as the massing of peasant armies everywhere sharpened the tensions between communities and their rulers. The Swabian League could hardly raise troops in the cities, for the common folk generally (but not always) stood on the peasants' side. Kempten explicitly counseled the Swabian League at the end of March to avoid military actions, for in case of attack "all of the Upper Swabian cities would go over to the peasants." [12] The glimpses we get of conditions inside these cities confirm that it was difficult to prevent an alliance between peasants and burghers. The senate of Augsburg, which finally did manage to hold the citizenry on its side, had trouble at first preventing a union of peasants and burghers, especially the weavers. In Kempten in March the senate just barely prevented a guild rebellion. The burghers of Biberach promised the peasant troops from Baltringen that within three days they would throw their own lords over the walls. One of the Swabian League commanders, Ulrich Artzt, wrote anxiously to Conrad Peutinger: "We from the cities are making a reputation for ourselves in this war that will be long with us"; [13] his judgment was surely based on more detailed knowledge that we can reconstruct today from surviving materials.

The Lower Alsatian peasants, who had been massing since mid-April, sought from the beginning an alliance with the city of Strasbourg and its preachers.[14] They hoped that their common interests in religious Reformation would result in common political aims. With the approval of the senate and doubtless intending to represent the senate's interests, the Strasbourg reformers—Wolfgang Capito, Matthew Zell, and Martin Bucer—negotiated with the peasants, though without success, for they had nothing more to offer them than the advice that they should break up their association. All pragmatic considerations aside, their reasoning flowed from the conviction that "we have found no Scripture which, to the honor of God and the common good, would justify the murder of unjust magistrates by the people." [15] This was not the view that peasants now held of godly law and divine justice.

With that the opposing positions were defined. The peasants could not count on the active support of either the preachers or the senate of Strasbourg. In fact, the best they could hope for was benevolent neutrality. Strasbourg did try, hesitantly but with eventual success, to arbitrate between peasants and lords on both banks of the Rhine, far beyond its immediate sphere of interest. The Treaty of Renchen, remarkable for its favorable treatment of the peasants, was essentially the result of Strasbourg's efforts at arbitration.

In deciding only to arbitrate but not to intervene actively, the senate was far from having the support of Strasbourg's burghers. We know that the master of the guilds (*Ammeister*) and members of the Council of the XIII went from guild to guild, "warning" and "requesting" the burghers "to stay at home in these troublesome, difficult times, and not to unite with" the peasants, and so one can hardly doubt—in fact, the council conceded—that the burghers, to say nothing of the lower classes, were indeed going out to join the peasants.[16] There must have been close connections between the peasants and specific guilds—the butchers and gardeners were especially mentioned—because the peasants bypassed the city government altogether and sent the guilds their invitation to help them establish the Twelve Articles and to supply them with cannon and other weapons. We cannot tell how many Strasbourgeois joined the peasant armies, but judging from the city's diplomatic correspondence there must have been many. The senate even had to arrest sixteen burghers for allegedly conspiring to guide the peasant armies into the city.

Especially instructive are the negotiations which the senate carried on with the individual guilds between May 11 and 14. Rumors had led the senate to fear that the peasants would march on the city and forcibly take over ecclesiastical and monastic lands.[17] The senate's attitude was unambiguous. It wanted to protect the clergy, especially since they enjoyed Strasbourg citizenship, and to oppose peasant demands; "they should feel and see that we do not approve their project, which is neither honorable, Christian, nor evangelical, but is rather completely opposed to our desire." Yet the senate was not sure of its own citizens, and it questioned each guildsman personally as to whether he would support the senate. Probably to help bring the burghers over to the senate's policy, cheap flour was now dispensed from the city's supplies, and the indirect taxes on food were lifted. These measures sufficed to bring the guilds into line behind the senate's policy. And yet the cloth guild made it clear that they did not think the peasants' actions were unjustified in all respects. Their oath of loyalty to the regime was to be binding only if the requests of the city were "not against God and brotherly love." After such an answer one could hardly depend on the cloth guild. The gardeners went so far in opposing the senate's wishes as to vote to sacrifice those clergy and clerical possessions which had come under city law only as a result of the rebellion. More than 20 percent of the members of the butchers' guild could not even be questioned, which makes one suspect that they were active partisans of the peasants.

One day after this general inquiry was held, Erasmus Gerber, the highest captain of the Lower Alsatian peasant armies, sent his devastating warning to the city. By referring to the many Strasbourgeois serving in the peasant army, he hoped to move the senate to aid him against Duke Antoine of Lorraine: "Look at your poor citizens and vassals, and the fruit of our land, that you may do right and not abandon us completely. . . . Do it for God's sake; come, help us. . . . Given in fear at Saverne." [18] Three hours later, just a few hours before the most gruesome butchery of 1525: "Oh, you Christian lords, we pray to you as your citizens and children, do not abandon us in our distress and misery. If you will not come to our aid, we will not hold out longer against the enemy, and we and the whole country will be ruined. We want to defend ourselves with your help as long as we can, and request your graces' protection, hoping that you will not abandon us, etc. Given at Saverne in haste and distress." [19] The bloodbath of Saverne relieved Strasbourg of the task of preventing burghers and peasants from uniting.

Strasbourg's key role for the attitude of the other Alsatian cities resembled that of Memmingen for Upper Swabia. Yet in Alsace the cooperation between peasants and burghers from imperial cities went much farther than in Upper Swabia. Wissembourg provided the peasants with cannon and barely prevented an alliance with the peasants, which vineyard workers especially wanted, only when the town secularized the monasteries. Kaisersberg was forced to yield to the peasants, presumably because of strong sympathies within the town. If a defensive alliance among the towns could not be organized, as Kaisersberg complained to Strasbourg, it was probably because the ties between peasants and townsmen were too strong. Such ties were possibly strengthened too by the patriotic tunes played by the Alsatian humanists, emphasizing the unity of the nation. Such efforts bore a kind of fruit, as is proved by the unrest at Sélestat, when the duke of Lorraine had to use "foreign troops" against the peasants at Saverne. Moreover, most of the Alsatian imperial cities contained large numbers of burghers who were actually farmers, and so common economic interests must have strengthened the ties between town and country. Towns such as Colmar formulated grievances that were not very different from the Twelve Articles.

The only town on the Upper Rhine equal in importance to Strasbourg was Basel. They were similar in their cautious policy of favoring an arbitrated settlement of the conflict. In both cities the Reformation movement had won considerable ground by 1525, and both Strasbourg and Basel had trouble mastering the internal dissension of their burghers and the external threats of their peasants.

Long before 1525 there had been social tensions in Basel, struggles between artisans and the merchant guilds that led finally in January of 1526 to a new guild constitution in favor of the artisans. In 1525 it seems to have been mainly the weavers who were causing trouble for the senate. It was a weaver, for example, who drafted a plan for revolution. Some senators, obviously fearing a sudden attack, negotiated at the weavers' guildhall, and one weaver was arrested. Finally, at the beginning of May, under pressure from the guilds as in other imperial cities, the canons and monks were forced to become citizens, bound by the oath of citizenship, and burdened with the usual taxes. Clearly the high point of the crisis came at the beginning of May. The senate bound all guild members and burghers to obedience while the Basel peasants at the same time were establishing contacts with the guilds and finally marched in arms against the city. It is not certain whether these events were connected with the arrest of thirty weavers.

When the Carmelites from near Heilbronn fled from the peasants to their house in the imperial city of Heilbronn in mid-April, it was evident that the senate there could no longer curb the commoners. The monks ran a gauntlet of burghers from the city gate to their house, "and as we walked along in our habits, they yelled so against us that I cannot describe it adequately; for if we had been Jews, it would not have been worse. They yanked one out here and another there; here they wanted to stab us to death; next they wanted to hang us. And everyone mocked us." [20] This event occurred only a few days before the city surrendered to peasant armies.

At the beginning of April the senate of Heilbronn had still been able to keep most of the guilds on its side, although individual groups of burghers had already moved out to join the peasants. In vain the senate reminded them of their oath of citizenship and demanded that they return to the city. At the same time commoners vigorously voiced their complaints against the free city's regime. They were ready, of course, to protect the city from attack, but the citizens saw no reason why the peasants should be prevented from taking over ecclesiastical lands, whose owners did not share in the burdens and duties common to all. The community ought to be responsible for the hiring of mercenaries and for taking clerics in as citizens. Letters "of interest to the whole commune" ought to be made public.[21] With these measures the commune would have decisively strengthened its control. As might be expected, the senate replied cautiously but negatively. It had sent couriers to the emperor, to the Imperial Governing Council (*Reichsregiment*), and to the Swabian League asking for embassies which would be able to restore the senate's now fragile authority. Yet the pressure from the burghers' ranks only grew stronger. Although the senate had still refused on April 4 to tax the Teutonic Knights, the monasteries, and the clergy as they did the burghers, on April 12 they announced to the guilds that they would accede to this demand. The reformer of Heilbronn, Johann Lachmann, whose pacific warnings to the peasants echoed away unheard, now thought it possible that the twenty men of the sorry city guard would be overpowered by the burghers, especially since "many citizens favor the peasants more than the city." [22] Just two days later he thought it fitting that the senate accept unconditionally all of the demands of the commoners, since it was "better to give in some than to lose everything." [23] Everything was lost anyway. On April 18 the peasant leaders entered Heilbronn, and on the following day the city entered into a pact of brotherhood with the peasants and made a contingent of troops available to the peasant army.

Looking more closely at the leaders of the revolt in Heilbronn confirms and enlarges our conclusions from Memmingen and Strasbourg. The fifty-six Heilbronn townsmen whom we know to have been leaders of the rebellion were mostly wine growers and artisans. They belonged, not to the poorest section of the lower class, but rather, to a stratum that was financially better off but still politically insignificant. The real urban lower class, which lived in Heilbronn's "New Street," hardly ever pushed forward with demands and programs of their own for the city; they did, however, join the peasants. It is noteworthy that the leaders came forward with a demand for change in the urban constitution. The same thing seems to have happened in Memmingen. Urban rebels used the revolt of 1525 to achieve their own internal changes.

We may take Heilbronn as paradigmatic for the attitude of imperial cities in Franconia and Lower Swabia if, in making comparisons, we emphasize only the main lines of development and don't lose track of generalizations in the maze of local differences. Except for Nuremberg and Schwäbisch Hall, which prevented an alliance between town and countryside by making concessions to their inhabitants and rural subjects, townsmen did enter into pacts with the peasants in the imperial cities of Rothenburg, Dinkelsbühl, and Nördlingen.

There was in these urban rebellions a typical course of development, one that has been worked out in detail for Frankfurt, on the periphery of the main region of the Peasants' War. This pattern confirms once again the close but indirect connection between these urban and peasant movements. Once a town knew of the Peasants' War, the "social movement" within the town went through three phases. In the first phase of protest the leaders were "the poor and the day laborers, those who lived off agriculture, apprentices and servants, but also the artisans who had no guild." In the second phase the social basis broadened to include guild artisans, who then moved on with even broader burgher support to the third phase of actually taking control of the city government. In Frankfurt the burghers were said to have become "emperor, pope, bishop, council, and burgomaster," all in one.[24]

Wherever the sources allow a glimpse of conditions inside a city, the council and the community opposed each other as enemies in 1525. The factors that allowed the community to win an upper hand, as in Rothenburg, or the senate to maintain its authority undiminished, as in Schwäbisch Hall, were mainly regional and local variables, such as the persuasive force of specific peasant programs, or the status of the Reformation, or the tensions within a particular city, or the pressures of external politics. It would be forced and artificial to try to establish a uniform sequence of causes.

One conclusion we may draw, however, is that the revolution in the countryside was definitely imported into the city in the sense that there had to be an initial massing of the peasants before city populations could be mobilized. Only when peasants reached the point where they were no longer concerned with the removal of individual economic burdens and converted their original grounds for rebellion into a much more open and revolutionary program capable of further development, only then did the barriers between town and country fall, barriers created by the different economic structures of urban and rural life. Clearly, what united the common project of peasants and townsmen was the gospel, or more precisely, the transformation of Reformation theology into a political theology.

The latent tensions within the imperial cities of the fifteenth and sixteenth centuries seem to have increased because of the growing feudalization of the urban upper classes, who, aided by their control of urban territories, were able to climb into the lesser nobility. Such tensions could be unleashed either internally when the lower orders struggled with the city council for economic relief and for the communal right to a voice in government or externally when they ignored the senate and joined the peasant armies.

The relative scarcity of sources prevents any further general conclusions. Urban senate records for 1525 are remarkably tight-lipped, so that one cannot really understand the internal urban troubles from official city records, and even the usually verbose city chronicles, with their penchant for displaying conflicts on an epic scale, are silent and try to divert our attention to the deeds of the peasants. After the victories of the Swabian League the cities obviously had no interest in emphasizing their own roles in the revolution.

Nowhere did the regimes of the imperial cities themselves initiate alliances with the peasants. Where such alliances did occur, they came from the pressure of burghers, guilds, and the lower classes of the town or as a result of military threats by the peasants, who used force against the town more for strategic purposes than out of principle. It was obviously impossible for the regimes of the imperial cities to escape the traditional political categories of emperor, empire, and Swabian League. In any event they probably saw no alternative to the existing political system. Thus, they had to direct their policies toward preserving the established structures while restricting as far as possible the areas of tension. In this way the imperial cities became the true mediators between peasants and lords while the Imperial Governing Council rode helplessly back and forth between Esslingen and Ulm.

PEASANTS AND TERRITORIAL TOWNS

When the peasants revolted in Hegau, a mob marched up to the town of Messkirch: "In the town it was then discussed whether they should remain loyal to their lords, or let the peasants in, or actually join the peasants. The majority favored opening the gates and letting the rebellious peasants in, and that is what happened." [25] Only two peasants in the seigneury of Messkirch failed to join the rebels. In the Thuringian town of Fulda the mayor and council reported to the coadjutor of the abbey that they had been ordered by the rebels to take over the monasteries around Fulda "or they would do it; and they wanted to know from us if we wanted to do it or not, and whether we wanted to support and uphold the gospel and the word of God and the laws or not; to which we, along with your princely grace's councillors, answered that we intended with all our heart and will to support and uphold the gospel, the word of God, and the laws as if our whole salvation depended on it; and so the above-mentioned monastery . . . was taken over." [26]

These two examples may stand for many, because they show that from

Salzburg to Alsace, from Trent to Saxony, cooperation between peasants and territorial towns was achieved without difficulty. We shall select just three regions—Tyrol, Württemberg, and Thuringia—to show how and why town and country worked so well together in the revolution. In Tyrol nearly all the towns joined the rebels, and where they didn't, as in North Tyrol, they did finally support the common program in the territorial diets. In Württemberg nearly all the districts rose in rebellion; only six district towns failed to participate. In Thuringia the towns that refused to join the general uprising, such as Goslar, were clearly exceptional.

The lists of grievances make it clear why territorial towns could cooperate with the peasants so much more easily than the imperial cities could. Local grievances from Tyrol confirm that in addition to the unifying cause of the gospel and the godly law rural and urban interests were identical. Country districts and towns were equally affected by the rising early modern state, which they encountered in the form of new taxes and in kinds of authority given to district officials and judges, as we can see in the complaints from Merano, Bolzano, Lienz, and Kitzbühl. Town and country, especially when far from the great trade route through the Brenner Pass and the Inn Valley, were so similar in their economic structure that they could generate exactly the same complaints, as in the towns Mals and Glurns in Vinschgau, which complained of restrictions on their agrarian usage rights.

With the exception of Stuttgart and Tübingen, the district centers of Württemberg were farming towns, so that the Twelve Articles could easily provide the basis of demands for district villages and towns. Without discounting the differences between the urban "notables" and the peasants, who had assailed the district towns during the "Poor Conrad" revolt (1514), the political ideas they held in common were strong enough in 1525 to bridge the gaps between townsmen and peasants. The goal of their common efforts was a major change in the territorial constitution, by which a committee composed equally of burghers, peasants, and nobles would have set aside the territorial prince in most respects while entirely replacing his government.

The cooperation of peasants and townsmen in Thuringia and Saxony is well-known, and recent research had deepened our insights into the leadership groups and their specific interests in rebellion. It is remarkable, for example, that in these regions the Reformation established a very firm foothold in the suburbs, and that the connection between the rural and urban social movements was mainly a cooperation between the countryside and the suburbs. This is worth noting because towns in this region were distant from the main centers of insurrection and hence provide us with a way of testing which social groups were most enthusiastically caught up in the revolutionary movement. At the center of the zone of insurrection this is often hard or even impossible to determine because the tumultuous course of events swept up cities as a whole, complicating the task of localizing the basis of revolt either topographically or sociologically.

From 1522 onwards the followers of the Reformation in Leipzig found places to preach, not in the city churches, which long remained closed to them despite countless petitions from burghers and the residents of the suburbs, but instead, in the small churches and chapels of the suburbs. In 1525, with the approach of rebellious peasant armies and with Duke George of Saxony mobilizing for war in the city, the broad coalition in favor of the Reformation came apart at the seams. The urban upper class now defended the interests of the duke and the magistrates, while a radical lower-class movement, firmly anchored in the suburbs, pressed for the abolition of territorial, urban, and ecclesiastical government.

In Magdeburg a radical variant of the Reformation developed in the suburban quarter, set off by Luther's sermons of 1524, despite his intention of having a moderating influence. In addition to violent scenes in the churches of St. Agnes and St. Lawrence and in the Franciscan cloister, 1524 saw a series of rent strikes against the archbishop's bailiff and demands by rebels that "a new senate more to their liking be chosen," that the archbishop give up control of the city, and that "they would be their own lords and not obey the government any longer." [27] Similar disruptions occurred in Erfurt in April 1525, with suburban rebels again at the forefront.

The suburbs were brought to revolutionary action more easily than the city centers for a number of reasons. By the beginning of the sixteenth century the population of the suburbs had often reached or even surpassed that of the inner city. Suburban dwellers were therefore no longer a negligible factor in the life of the city. Occupationally the suburbs were made up of farmers and artisans—in addition to the beggars, vagabonds, and unemployed poor, who were usually exiled to the suburbs. The soil was tilled either by peasants who owned their own plots or by tenants, both free and servile, for whom the seigneur might be the city, a monastery or church, or an individual burgher. Manufacturing was usually concentrated on the production of linen, as in the suburbs of Chemnitz. These factors created a relatively unified structure of wealth, in contrast to the inner city. The total wealth of the suburbs lagged well behind that of the inner city, as we can see clearly from the example of Weimar (Table 1).

Suburbs also had a legal and constitutional position significantly different from that of the inner city. Although the suburbs of Leipzig, for example, had a few streets and sections that enjoyed the protection of city law, most of the suburbs were legally disadvantaged or simply identified with the countryside. These unequal relations are also exemplified in the laws of the imperial city of Mühlhausen, which warned burghers that if they wounded a resident of the suburbs, they would receive a fine of six gulden and four weeks' house arrest. If a suburbanite wounded a burgher, however, the penalty was death.

The following provisional balance can probably be drawn, and it is very likely true of regions far distant from Thuringia and Saxony too. Suburban occupations, and especially the agricultural pursuits, made for natural ties

TABLE 1
WEALTH AND POPULATION IN WEIMAR

Wealth in 1542 (in gulden)	Number of Taxable Households	
	Inner City	Suburbs
1–100	*125*	*80*
1–25	41	49
26–50	41	20
51–75	21	5
76–100	22	6
101–200	*35*	*3*
101–150	18	2
151–200	17	1
201–800	*40*	*0*
All categories	*200*	*83*
Total Houses in 1557	338	230

SOURCE: K. Czok, "Zur sozialökonomischen Struktur," p. 58.

between town and country. Moreover, a relatively unified wealth structure created a unity of interests in the suburbs and reduced social tensions within this narrow geographical sector, thus producing a greater sense of solidarity than was easily achieved in the inner city. The constitutional position of the suburbs, ruled by either the territorial sovereign or by the town senate, also allowed peasants and suburban residents to join their political goals easily.

In cases where the suburbs were not clearly distinct from the rest of the city, or in other words, where the city had a thoroughly agricultural character, as in the Saxon towns of Sangershausen, Frankenhausen, and Apolda, the peasant and urban movements blended together in a common protest against the territorial government.

The gospel and the godly law had been able to forge some bridges between peasants and the commoners from imperial cities. But the much closer cooperation between peasants and territorial towns was possible because their agreement on the Reformation was fortified by similar forms of dependence and similar economic interests. Such generalizations are rough, of course, but we can see their usefulness if we turn our attention more closely to one territorial town which could not be voluntarily integrated into the revolutionary movement—Freiburg im Breisgau. Freiburg's exceptional position among the towns of Nearer Austria found expression in the town's presidency over the third estate in the territorial diet. Because of the disinterest of the Habsburgs, the Upper Rhine felt much less pressure from the expanding early modern state than, say, Tyrol; and Freiburg could thus assume a position somewhat like that of the imperial cities and accordingly came to behave like an imperial city. From the records of legal oaths taken by convicted criminals we can conclude that Freiburg obviously experienced tensions similar to those found between council and community in the imperial cities. And indeed one faction inside the city pushed for alliance with the peasant armies. The example of Freiburg shows that the schematic categories of imperial city and territorial city are indeed helpful in organizing the variety of urban reactions to the peasant movement. But we should readily concede that some cities may not fit these ideal types.

In light of the active participation by territorial towns and by the common people of the imperial cities, we may question whether we should continue to speak of a *peasants'* war. This is even more true when we note that in addition to townsmen the miners were deeply involved in the Revolution of 1525.

PEASANTS AND MINERS

In the course of the year 1525, all the mining areas within the region of rebellion broke out in disturbances. Though the miners remained somewhat isolated and did not always seek an alliance with the peasants, this was because the peasant masses in many places, as in North Tyrol, often lacked the necessary radicalism and forcefulness.

In January and February of 1525 the Tyrolean miners of Schwaz rebelled, well before one could really speak of peasant disturbances in the valley of the Inn River. Even so, the miners' rebellion presented Archduke Ferdinand with a real danger, because the miners publicly demonstrated their power and insisted relentlessly on their demands. On January 21 some 3,000 miners at Hall forced their list of grievances on Ferdinand. When the archduke's first reply, on February 15, turned out to be evasive, the miners undertook a second march on Innsbruck, to which Ferdinand finally responded by dismissing all of his mining judges, country judges, and overseers on February 18. Ferdinand and his government also sought to avert the potential danger of an alliance of peasants, burghers, and miners in the Inn Valley by summoning the country districts, towns, and mining communes to a territorial diet at Innsbruck in May. This policy succeeded in channeling the unrest into the framing of grievances. Although this was a real victory for Ferdinand, a mining judge from Schwaz warned that "if the miners here rebel again, the peasants from the bishopric of Salzburg and others from Bavaria will join them." [28] South of the Brenner, by contrast, in the center of the Tyrolean rebellion, the miners of Sterzing were full participants in the movement of peasants and townsmen.

In the archbishopric of Salzburg the so-called Peasants' War was led from the very beginning by both peasants and miners, with men from the largest mining operations taking major roles as leaders. In the Gastein Valley the smelters and miners, who also created the Twenty-Four Articles of the Common Assembly of Salzburg, sent out shock waves of rebellion not only through the archbishopric but also to the miners of Austria and Styria. Their military prowess showed its temper in the Battle of Schladming, the most convincing military victory of the Revolution of 1525 and essentially their achievement; and it helps explain the rebels' rapid successes in Salzburg. Alongside envoys from the towns, markets, and country districts, the companies and miners from Gastein and Rauris represented their own interests at the territorial diets. Perhaps this explains why the smelters from Gastein could not be roused again to take part in a second rebellion, in 1526, but the sources are too scanty for us to be sure. On the other hand, Tyrolean miners from Schwaz seem to have joined the then hard-pressed Salzburgers; but they failed to arrive in the hoped-for numbers, as is shown by the heart-rending open letter to the miners of Schwaz from the "common countryside and mines of the mountain territory of Salzburg, your brothers in Christ Jesus" [29]: "We pray to you all, as one Christian to another, that you will defend us against this tyrannical, unchristian, and bloodthirsty villian [the Swabian League], lest we wretchedly lose our wives and children and miserably spill our blood. . . . and we pray that you will come forcefully to our aid and hurry, hurry, hurry." [30]

Some have doubted that the participation of miners in the revolt in Salzburg should be taken as proof that these different classes recognized common goals that transcended their occupations; for it was said that the miners of Salzburg "fought from the first day on at full pay." [31] It would be shortsighted, however, to conclude that these miners were simply acting as mercenary soldiers. There was an important and simple difference between miners and peasants in the fact that the miner and his family had no income apart from his wages and therefore could not survive without a replacement for his mining wages. Unlike peasants, miners had to be paid for their military service. And the conclusion that miners had no common cause with the peasants also overlooks the fact that some miners were actually "peasant-miners" who lived in the village and for at least some of the time worked at agricultural tasks.

In Thuringia, Thomas Müntzer was successful in bringing some of the Mansfeld miners into the "faithful union of the godly will" that he had organized with the rebels from Allstedt,[32] but in the Erzgebirge along the Bohemian border there were apparently only isolated instances of cooperation between peasants and miners. In any case, the mountain towns of Schneeberg and Freiberg remained relatively calm, while Annaberg experienced only ephemeral disturbances. Only in Joachimstal did the miners assemble by the thousands in an armed camp. They did have connections with the peasants, but compared to the radicalism of the peasants from Franconia, Swabia, or the Upper Rhine, their enthusiasm was pale.

The miners' complaints mirrored local and regional peculiarities. The Schwazers, for example, demanded that the territorial prince cancel mortgages on the mines; the Annabergers requested a quarterly accounting for the tin pennies produced by the miners; and the Joachimstalers asked that the authorities not interfere in relations between miners and mine inspectors. And yet behind these special grievances one can still see clearly the common objective of peasants, burghers, and miners: the establishment of the gospel and the suppression of arbitrary interference by government officials in favor of a more extensive autonomy. Since as a rule miners were exempt from the ordinary jurisdiction of the district and territorial courts and were subject both legally and administratively to their own often quite despotic mining judges, and since these separate mining courts lacked the sort of developed traditions found in the seigneurial courts, the miners' desire for greater autonomy was the same as the peasants' goal of restoring unlimited rights of self-government. In Tyrol the miners demanded the recall of local officials, and at the territorial diet they joined townsmen and peasants in demanding the pure proclamation of the gospel and the suppression of secular power in clerical hands. In Salzburg the protests of miners and peasants against the arbitrary administration of justice and the despotism of seigneurial officials, along with their demand for the establishment of godly law, were included in the Twenty-Four Articles of the Salzburg Assembly. In Joachimstal the main articles complained of defects in the administration of justice, demanded more participation of miners in filling offices, and requested miners' rights to choose their own pastors. It seems fair to call these the common goals of the "common man."

THE "COMMON MAN": INVESTIGATIONS INTO THE HISTORY OF A CONCEPT

At least from the time when Peter Harer composed his "True and Thorough Description of the Peasants' War" (before 1531), the use of the term "Peasants' War" for the Revolution of 1525 has been pervasive.[33] Contempories too, from urban and monastic chroniclers to noble and ecclesiastical lords, labeled the events of 1525 a peasants' war. In doing so they presented an outsider's view of the revolution, determined, in fact, by the peasant armies. And yet it must be doubted whether this term is adequate to the phenomenon, for it occurs in sources that were generated exclusively by the seigneurial side and mostly from the years after 1525. From the perspective of the nobility and prelates the rebellion was a violation of the public peace by the peasants; retrospectively the cities strengthened this conclusion in order to ward off the suspicion that they had benevolently tolerated or even actively supported the rebellion. In actuality, it was only the first phase of the rebellion, represented by the Twelve Articles, that had a strong identity as a peasant movement. The rebels themselves did not see their uprising as one of just peasants. The Letters of Articles from the Black Forest described the leaders of the revolt as "the poor common man in town and countryside."

Wendel Hipler's intended advice for the Heilbronn peasants' diet attempted, among other things, to compare the "common man"—the "subject"—with the "princes, lords and nobles." It was a "meeting of burghers and peasants" in Württemberg that formulated the grievances sent to the Swabian League.[34] These examples suffice. Even the Habsburg government in Innsbruck referred to the uprising, which was then still confined to Hegau and the Black Forest, as a rebellion of the common man, while Margrave Philipp of Baden, who did not merely represent the interests of the seigneurial party, spoke simply of a "union of the common man."[35] The Treaty of Renchen spoke not of a peasants' war or of a peasant rebellion but of "bands of subjects" and described the assembly of "considerable numbers of the common man."[36]

Given the involvement of the territorial cities, of the commoners from the imperial cities, and of the miners, it may be asked how broadly applicable the concept of the common man was and whether it might not be really more appropriate to call this war the Revolution of the Common Man.

"Common man" was current as a term for the peasants in the sources of the sixteenth century, and it can be found quite often with this meaning in 1525 as well. In the cities the term obviously could mean that social group which was ineligible for the senate, although here there was no generally sharp distinction. The term certainly included, however, the underprivileged groups without citizenship, such as journeymen, servants, and those with dishonorable occupations. At the imperial diet the imperial cities demanded more rights, threatening that otherwise "rebellion and resistance would grow between magistrates and the common man in the towns."[37] Following a proposal of Conrad Peutinger of Augsburg, the Swabian League was to publish its stance toward the uprising and distribute it in the towns to prevent the "common man" from making common cause with the peasants.[38] In addition to being used for peasants and for parts of the urban population, the term "common man" could also be used as a general concept for a specific stratum. From Salzburg, through Tyrol, Upper Swabia, Württemberg, and on to Franconia, in 1525 the common man was widely regarded as the leader of the revolution. Even politically experienced observers, such as the elector of Saxony, viewed the events of 1525 in these terms: "If it be God's will, it will end with the common man governing."[39]

On the basis of these references, the concept can be considerably sharpened. In sources from Salzburg, Tyrol, and Franconia, the common man was understood as a subject, as one incapable of ruling. In Tyrol in 1525 the complaint appeared that "the common man could not bring ecclesiastics and noblemen to justice without difficulty and heavy expenses."[40] The Franconian peasants demanded that "from now on all spiritual and secular persons, noble and nonnoble, should obey the laws of common burghers and peasants and not claim to be above what other common men have to do."[41] The pamphlet *To the Association of the Common Peasantry* complained of the "arbitrary power of nobles and other authorities . . . who daily push and compel the common man ruthlessly and against all reason, using unchristian and tyrannical force." [42] In these examples the concept of common man is the polar opposite of that of government, whether represented by the territorial sovereign or his urban analogue, the senate. This explains why such diverse groups as peasants, miners, the residents of territorial cities, and the politically powerless members of imperial cities could all call themselves common men. This also explains its relative usefulness as well as its vagueness. In 1525 the social contours of this concept were broadened by the equation of "rebel" and "common man," for generally in the sixteenth century the term "common man" meant more narrowly the "head of household" (*Hausvater*). It was heads of families who had political rights in the old estates system of houselordships, and it was only they who were fully integrated into the lowest organs of the state. [43] It was they who fought to preserve or expand their inherited political rights when the complex relationship of lord and his man (*Holder*) was transformed into the complex relationship of government and subject. That helps explain why the concept of common man cannot be found before the late Middle Ages. And with this conclusion we confirm once again the basic correlation between the "common man" and the "government."

This conceptual analysis thus converges with our empirical findings. The common man was the peasant, the miner, the resident of a territorial town; in the imperial cities he was the townsman ineligible for public office. Insofar as the common man constituted the counterpart of the lord, we should really speak of a rising of the common man. And in view of the social structure of the revolution it is high time to bid farewell to the *Peasants'* War, or at least to use that word with such discretion that it helps rather than hinders our understanding of the phenomenon of 1525. It remains to be seen just how revolutionary the war actually was.

CHAPTER 8

The Rebellion of the Common Man as a Revolution

Both the alternative offered by the Christian Association to the existing structures of authority in Upper Swabia and the Salzburg Assembly's plan for the early modern state were revolutionary. The Christian Association wanted a federal league on a corporate basis. Village communes, urban communes, and assemblies, on the model of the Kempten Assembly, formed the lowest political units on which a governmental superstructure was to be built. Communal associations were to be brought together regionally into political units (the groups from Allgäu, Lake Constance, Baltringen); and these units, in turn, would form legally equal parts of a federal union constituting an Upper Swabian state. Lordship, wherever it was necessary, would be legitimized through the principle of election. Logically, there was room for the nobility and clergy in this political order only if they made themselves part of the communal associations, and this would mean the loss of their previous privileged political position and the restriction if not the complete abolition of their economic power. The peasants knew very well that they would sooner or later have to figure out what to do with the larger political association of the Holy Roman Empire, but they left the question open. The emperor was by no means a necessary complement to the Christian Association, but he was also not disruptive, providing he accepted the existence of the league. This Upper Swabian plan was revolutionary from several points of view. Small states based on patriarchal and authoritarian structures were to be replaced by a constitution based on corporative alliance. The welter of small feudal seigneuries was to be dissolved in favor of a large political alliance, comparable to the Swiss Confederation, in which the cooperative traditions of the village communes, town communes, and assemblies would be preserved in the refined form of elections. The gospel and godly law provided the state with its norm; its ethical goals were the common welfare and brotherly love.

The Salzburg rebels, on the other hand, accepted the existing territorial constitution as the framework for their political and social ideas. The terri-

125

tory in their sense was the totality of Salzburg mining communes, rural communes, markets, and towns, which were to choose a territorial committee as the government of their territory, perhaps through territorial diets. Otherwise, there were parallels to the model of Upper Swabia. Communal associations formed the cells of the state; the political organism grew out from them and received its legitimacy at every level from the elections.[1] Ecclesiastical lords could hang on to the doubtful hope of at least preserving monastic life under territorial administration. The position of secular nobles appears uncertain and was in any event not logically thought through, although this could be the result of gaps in our sources. Here too the gospel, godly law, and brotherly love gave the state its ethos and goal. In Salzburg as in Upper Swabia the common man—the peasant, the miner, the townsman—resolutely demanded political rights which until then had been reserved for nobles and clergy, insisting that selfish needs yield to the common weal, in order that the world might thus be made more peaceful and more just.[2] How this goal was to be realized depended on the regional structure of lordship.

ALTERNATIVES TO FEUDALISM:
THE CORPORATIVE-ASSOCIATIVE CONSTITUTION

Although the godly law was used at first only to justify complaints as legitimate demands, in a second phase of the uprising it was used as the formative (although not yet clearly formulated) principle of a new society. The law of God offered a means of overcoming feudalism if it could weld together a political order which could absorb the state functions previously exercised by feudal lords, thereby making them dispensable. The Christian Association of the troops from Allgäu, Lake Constance, and Baltringen seized and developed this possiblity, though in contrary directions. One faction of the rebels emphasized the peaceful character of godly law and struggled for compromise on a supraterritorial level, while a second faction (which prevailed in the end) reconciled the law of God with the use of force. Both factions developed in a matrix of society and lordship that can be called "feudal" in a rough but still meaningful sense, because the feudal elements in the system of landlordship and serfdom were much stronger here than in larger territories, where the bureaucracy and new methods of state finance had already left this kind of feudalism behind.

Feudal lords obviously survived as territorial nobles and prelates in the large territories, and these lords were the first to feel the violent thrust of rural revolution. Yet these large territories were significantly different from the politically splintered regions of Swabia, Franconia, and the Upper Rhine, since in the early modern state the large territory already presented an important alternative to feudalism.

At the beginning of April, as the Swabian League moved toward its first decisive military blow against the Christian Association in Upper Swabia, other peasants were gathering in the Black Forest and Hegau. Their "Christian Association," as the rebels called it without being more precise, brought together the villages and towns of the Black Forest, the Upper Neckar, and the Upper Danube, taking control of monasteries and castles without meeting any notable resistance. Although Commander Georg Truchsess von Waldburg had wanted to open his campaign as leader of the army of the Swabian League by attacking the peasants from Hegau and the Black Forest, the League forced his army to depart, allowing the Christian Association to expand its federation easily. The rebels seized the Black Forest monasteries of St. George, St. Peter, and St. Margaret; and during the first days of May the regions of Markgräflerland, Breisgau, Kaiserstuhl, and Ortenau joined this group of rebels. The revolutionaries' strategy was the same wherever they went: admission of peasants and burghers, villages and towns, under oath into the Christian Association, and the takeover or destruction of convents and castles, in some instances neutralizing military strongholds and paralyzing corrupt old customs (as the wrecking of archives shows), but elsewhere simply spreading the league without any gaps across the land. After a siege of eight days, on May 23, Freiburg surrendered, too, and three days later Breisach, the last town on the right bank of the Rhine, was taken.

The last days of May were both the high point and the fatal turning point in the German southwest. They were the high point because now the whole region from Lake Constance westward was under the rebels' control. But they were also a disastrous turning point because the separate peasant armies now returned to their homes without having filled the political vacuum, and also because the threat from outside was growing after May 16, when thousands of Lower Alsatians were butchered at Saverne by the brutal forces of the duke of Lorraine, and finally, because the rebels from Ortenau now reached negotiated settlements with their lords. After the victories of the duke of Lorraine in Alsace and of the Swabian League in Württemberg and Franconia, the rebels could look for salvation only to negotiated settlements; and if negotiations were undertaken by separate groups, they would destroy the league of the Christian Association. The men of Breisgau wobbled toward negotiations in June, while the first days of July saw the men from Hegau and the Black Forest retreat before the makeshift army of Archduke Ferdinand, which then reduced twenty-four villages to cinders and ashes and extorted an unconditional surrender. In November the peasants of Klettgau were conquered, and those of Hauenstein laid down their arms.

The program of the Christian Association, which had been conceived and developed in April and May, was too weak to give the German southwest enough stability to resist the "seduction" of negotiated settlements once the lords began to achieve military success. Yet we would be wrong to estimate the goals of the 1525 revolution from its results. For the peasants of Hegau and the Black Forest, who had founded the Christian Association, the major goal was to use the Twelve Articles as a basis for "freeing" [3] the "poor common man in towns and in the countryside" from economic burdens, or as the so-called Article-Letter of the Black Forest peasants more positively put it, to foster the "common Christian welfare and brotherly love." [4] To achieve this end the Black Forest rebels threatened to banish anyone who refused to join the Christian Association, a threat aimed especially at monasteries and castles. To be sure, nobles, monks, and clergy were not required to enter the Christian Association if they were willing to surrender their fortresses and castles. Godly law and love of neighbor were explicitly proclaimed as legal norms. Nobles and clergy could still survive in this legal and social framework, which remained vague and lacking in close definition. The correspondence of the peasant armies with Freiburg, Schaffhausen, and Switzerland, carried on in the next couple of months after the Article-Letter, does not suggest that the Christian Association ever developed its program any further. The goals of the association were always set forth in the same formulas. In place of the lords' "exploitation," the "common welfare" and "brotherly love" must come to prevail as the gospel and the law of God demanded.

Only the peasants of Hegau made their goal clearer, when they resolutely objected to any compromise not based on godly law and aimed at restoring the old conditions of political and social domination.[5] Faced with the militant opposition of the rulers, the people of Hegau seem to have hoped to flee to Switzerland, as they revealed in a letter of June 20 to three cities in the Swiss Confederation: "Gracious and favorable lords, take note that our purpose is godly and Christian, and that our persecution is unprecedented and worse than that of the Turks, so that it might even move a hard stone to sympathy. Therefore we implore your severity, firmness, and wisdom . . . that you might . . . graciously receive us into your protection." [6] If we consider this one letter as representative at least of the peasants of Hegau—they had not yet been beaten by the Habsburg army—then we may conclude that at least one part of the southwest German contingent wanted to incorporate their imperfect alliance in the Swiss confederation. For the Christian Association in Upper Swabia such incorporation would also have been attractive, in view of the associations' constitution, but it was out of the question because of the geographic separation.* Concerning the inner structure of this Christian Association in southwest Germany and of its separate armies, no more than its corporative basis is known, if we use "corporative" in the sense that rural and urban communes made up the lowest political units. Thus we do not yet know how compatible these peasant armies and their association would have been with the Swiss Confederation. But we do have a fairly straightforward witness to the events in the Upper Rhineland—the council and city secretary

---

*Hegau had a common border with Schaffhausen, while Upper Swabia was a one or two days' journey from St. Gallen.

of Basel, Heinrich Ryhiner, who set down verbatim the program of the Breisgau and Sundgau peasants in the chronicle that he wrote in 1525. This program was nothing less than the Federal Ordinance of the Christian Association in Upper Swabia. Assuming that Ryhiner was correct in thus connecting Upper Swabia and the Upper Rhine,[7] the common program of the Christian Association in Upper Swabia and of the Christian Association in southwestern Germany was not only the Twelve Articles but also the actual Federal Ordinance. Since the program of the Christian Association in Upper Swabia was very close to a federation along Swiss lines, a petition of the peasants of Hegau to be taken under the protection of the cities of Basel, Zurich, and Schaffhausen (possibly with the further goal of integration into the Swiss confederation) is a bit easier to understand.

As we noted earlier, the basis of demands in Alsace was the Twelve Articles, with the gospel and godly law as the legal framework for a new social and political order. Here it was easier than elsewhere to pull the separate bands of troops tightly together and to ready them for organized action under their leader, Erasmus Gerber. At the end of April, before the rebellion in Alsace was even a month old, Gerber issued a sort of army ordinance, which aimed at long-term military measures to fend off possible attacks, but which also emphasized that the Alsatian troops intended to give their momentary alliance some lasting and practical coherence. Every seven days the troops in the field were replaced, since each village and city had to draft one quarter of its able-bodied men for each week. Through this rotation the army both attained a longer-term security and overcame the disorganized conditions of the first weeks of the rebellion. Political order at the communal level was thus maintained, and orderly economic life could continue. Erasmus Gerber stressed again and again in his proclamation, "that we should and will remain united among ourselves in the name of Jesus Christ, our Lord, to the praise and honor of God the Lord, in order to confirm his word and to comfort and help the poor, common man."[8]

Gerber's ordinance took the existence of functioning leagues of communes for granted, and they did actually exist in the sense that during the late Middle Ages the villages of Alsace had been required to cooperate in choosing delegates. Alsace was thus prepared to meet emergencies, like the present one, rather easily. The village institutions lay ready to hand, but they were now accountable to the communities themselves and no longer to the lords. Villages, even when their inhabitants belonged to different lords, came together in armed bands, which operated as autonomous units. These bands, for their part, named representatives to a common committee which coordinated the whole enterprise and, together with Erasmus Gerber, made up a kind of high command, empowered to proclaim binding orders and injunctions on everyone. At Molsheim in the beginning of May this common committee was composed of forty-two peasants. It proclaimed the "articles to which towns and villages must swear when they are captured," [9] articles which gave powers of command to captains, colonels, and governors[10] but obviously subordinated such officers to the control of all the troops, or to a committee elected for the purpose. Article 10 made this point by decreeing that "the captains shall not do anything secretly or without the knowledge of the troops or the appropriate governors." A report that these articles were passed "by the high captains and the common brethren" confirms our conclusion that these wide-ranging ordinances depended on the will of all of the rebels.

Even assuming that the organization of the Alsatian troops was intended only for military security, it is nonetheless clear that such an idea also provided a workable political model.[11] Autonomous rural and urban communes, bound "to God's word and holy gospel and to justice," [12] were grouped together in regional bands which had captains (possibly with only military powers) and governors (presumably with general governmental authority). The bands delegated representatives to a general committee which was military government, war council, and highest territorial authority all in one. At the head of the government was an elected supreme captain, who represented the association in its contacts with the outside world. There was hardly room in this association for governing authorities of the traditional sort, unless they unconditionally subjected themselves to the gospel, a general principle whose concrete economic, social, and political implications, beyond the Twelve Articles, had not yet been formulated.

It is very hard to know how seriously we should take the scattered reports that the Alsatians wanted to recognize only the emperor as their superior. Two of the four crucial passages come from the correspondence of Nikolaus Ziegler, lord of Barr, while the other two witnesses were peasants who confessed after the defeat, probably under torture. The symbolism of the army banners weighs against the idea that the Alsatians aimed at a specific relation to the emperor, since only one out of more than twenty banners featured the imperial eagle.

The army of the Tauber Valley included the subjects of the imperial city of Rothenburg, and the peasants of several Franconian nobles, the Teutonic Knights, and the Cathedral of Würzburg. Like all the other armies, it regarded godly law, or more specifically, the gospel and the word of God, as the foundation of all its demands and goals. The earliest normative program of the Tauber Valley men forbade their lords to collect any income or service dues until a settlement could be reached, and it set forth measures, closely related to the efforts of the Christian Association in Upper Swabia, to fill the new political vacuum by taking over some of the most pressing governmental functions. They supported "brotherly love" as a rule for living together by proclaiming a peace ordinance along the lines of village peace-keeping, with the provisions for local order (forbidding drunkenness and blasphemy) and with an elected provost who should hold judicial and punitive powers.

This earliest ordinance was later sharpened by the Ochsenfurt Field Ordinance of April 27, but its range of application was obviously limited, since it referred repeatedly to military field conditions. The earlier model was clearly a more appropriate framework for settling general problems of political order. The Ochsenfurt Field Ordinance did, however, express much more clearly the Tauber Valley troops' vision of the future. The old rulers would now have to give up more than just their income. Nobles (there was no mention of prelates), once they had abandoned and destroyed their castles, could, if they wished, join the "Christian Brotherhood" of the Tauber Valley men. Here then, not only did the nobles (and logically the clergy, too) lose their rights of lordship (as in a supplementary article which held that nobles were subject to the same jurisdiction as peasants and burghers), but the existing property relations were also radically rejected. Nobles were to be left with nothing more than their personal property.[13]

The "reformation" intended by this Field Ordinance left room for the reformers to create a new social and political order on the basis of an interpretation of the word of God and the gospel. Yet a major part of the interpretive work was anticipated by the way in which the Tauber Valley men politicized the Bible. The subordination and integration of the nobility necessarily meant their loss of both lordship rights and real property. Other mandates pressed in a similar direction, edicts that obviously were sent from Ochsenfurt. One of them ordered toll collectors to stop collecting tolls from carters and teamsters and to take over the administration of all noble granaries and wine cellars.

So long as men waited for religious reformation and for the biblical scholars to speak, the political order remained in suspense. Like the Upper Swabians, the men of the Tauber Valley had not thought the revolution through to its end but had delivered it up to the theologians. This explains the fragmentary nature of their extant ordinances. In Franconia, unlike Alsace, military organization could not be simply translated into political order, for the organizing principle of the army was not the villages and towns, and Franconia also lacked the smoothly functioning communes which might have supported a state structure from below.

The armies from the Neckar Valley and the Odenwald confined themselves to a program more moderate than that of the men of the Tauber Valley. These subjects of the archbishop of Mainz, of the imperial city Heilbronn, of the counts of Hohenlohe, and of many other lords fell together; and after seizing Weinsberg and killing its noble defenders, they had little difficulty forcing towns and nobles to join their ranks. The oath of the elector of Mainz to the "whole Christian meeting of the bright army"[14] was only the most spectacular of these forced admissions. Lords promised to uphold the provisions of the Twelve Articles until a reformation was introduced. To be sure, the armies of the Neckar Valley and Odenwald demanded the unconditional subjection of lords to this intended reformation, but they did not propose to abolish all aristocratic rights. This more moderate attitude of the rebels toward the lords can also be seen in the fact that, although they demanded preaching of the pure word of God, and accordingly, the communal election of ministers (which the Twelve Articles had already adequately justified), still their insistence on godly law remained very much a minor issue, at least in demands above the local level. This explains why the men from the Neckar Valley and Odenwald were unwilling to relegate the reformation to theologians alone. Even if we see this as a conciliatory gesture toward the lords, it is obvious that settlements between individual lords and their subjects were now inconceivable. Any compromise had to be binding on the whole peasant army and on all the lords collectively. The Heilbronn Peasants' Parliament was intended to prepare this reformation, and representatives, invited by the Odenwald and Neckar Valley army, were sent for this purpose by the armies of Swabia, Franconia, and the Upper Rhine. Consultations were broken off, however, because of the defeat of the Württemberg forces at Böblingen by the army of the Swabian League on 12 May.

In preparation for the abortive Heilbronn meetings at least two men composed position papers. One was Friedrich Weigandt, cellar master at Miltenberg, the residence of the electors of Mainz, and a close associate of Wendel Hipler, the head of the Neckar Valley–Odenwald army. Despite this connection, Weigandt stayed in the background in 1525 and did not join the peasants. He did, however, contribute a proposal for the nobles and imperial cities, in view of the forthcoming Heilbronn Diet, and also a fairly unoriginal proposal for the reform of the empire. Weigandt's ideas were hardly representative of the goals of Franconian peasants. Although Wendel Hipler clearly knew of Weigandt's ideas, it is not clear whether he intended to use them as a basis for the Heilbronn meeting. Therefore, Hipler's own "Advisory Plan" for the Heilbronn Diet is a much more important source for obtaining a rounded picture of the program of the Neckar Valley–Odenwald forces. Still, we should not overestimate the representativeness of this "Advisory Plan." After all, the conservative Amorbach Declaration, which did not threaten the basis of the existing political and social order, had already failed to obtain the universal assent of the army.*

If Hipler's "Advisory Plan" was indicative of his social and political thinking, then it cannot be denied that his program was less radical than those of the Swabian, Franconian, and Upper Rhenish troops. Hipler was probably thinking of coordinating all the individual programs, the field ordinances, and the territorial and federal ordinances of the various armies, and he obviously was planning a defensive league binding all the armies together along the lines of territorial defense and mobilization laws. His program did

---

*The Amorbach Declaration was a reform proposal from the Neckar Valley and Odenwald rebels, set forth on May 4, 1525. Its authors included Wendel Hipler, Friedrich Weigandt, and the nobles Götz von Berlichingen and Count Georg von Wertheim.

display one aggressive tendency in aiming at conquering the electorates of Trier and Cologne. Of similar if not even greater weight, however, was his undisguised intention to reach a compromise between rebels and lords. His program remained revolutionary only in that it deprived monasteries of all their sovereign powers. Hipler did not, however, seriously challenge the position of the princes and nobility, especially as he intended to use ecclesiastical lands to reimburse them for their losses of tithe income, indirect taxes, and transfer fines. He accepted the existing relations of emperor and empire, neither questioning the current structure nor advancing any new model. Hipler wanted to restore law and order as soon as possible without running the risk of forfeiting the position the rebels had already achieved. Most peasants were to return to their fields while only a portion remained in arms. That would be possible only if the "Reformation," in the sense of an arbitrated compromise between rebels and lords, could be quickly set up.

Obviously, it was not evident to one of Hipler's mentality that in ruining the clergy economically and politically but simultaneously strengthening the noble hegemony, he was trying to harmonize two irreconcilable principles. If he had really wanted to protect traditional power relations in the forms of princely and noble lordship, he would have had to dissolve the peasant armies. Transforming these armies into political units that would preserve "order, peace, and law" was probably the most interesting idea in Hipler's plan, but it could not be realized within the structure of the old feudal order.

Common to the revolutionary movement in Swabia, Franconia, and the Upper Rhine was the reception of the Twelve Articles and with them the dogmatic establishment of godly law as an unalienable component of the revolution. Godly law fostered supraterritorial organization, or even made it possible to found such an organization, while at the same time it stifled venerable traditions and led the moderate faction beyond the notion of compromises within individual lordships to that of a collective settlement between feudal lords and peasant armies. The revolution in this way overcame the political pettiness of south German lordships, but it by no means finished the task of finding a social and political order for such supraterritorial units. The revolutionary program now had to be extended beyond the Twelve Articles in a way that would complement the victorious advance of the rebels. After they had seized control of Swabia, Franconia, and the Upper Rhine, the resulting vacuum demanded ever more urgently a practical political solution. The initial solution, a crude anticlericalism, limited the utility of the Twelve Articles as a set of basic demands by encouraging negotiations only with the nobility. Eventually, however, the incompatibility between the revolutionary situation and traditional aristocratic rule became clear to the rebels. We must view their platforms and proposals from the perspective of the time before their position was seriously threatened, that is, before the military advance of the Swabian League and the duke of Lorraine of May 10–17 forced the peasant armies to negotiate. From this perspective it is clear that no one really thought of restoring aristocratic rule, for restoration would knock such holes in the corporative and federative structure of the various Christian Associations and armies that they might not be able to survive. If spokesmen failed to draw relentlessly logical conclusions, this is more a proof of their inability to draft definitive, practical political alternatives than evidence of any conciliatory, neutral, or even amicable attitude toward the nobility. This impression is strengthened by the associations' and armies' reactions to the challenge either of integrating their ideas into an empire headed by an emperor or of creating autonomous state structures. Here, too, they displayed indecision and imprecision in their contradictory statements, proof that such bold and untraditional models had not been thought through to their conclusions, or at least that the peasants could not put them down in words. The early modern state, as it was being created in the electoral territories or the duchies, was not a usable concept in Franconia or Swabia because those regions did not know the territorial principality in that form. Imperial free status, which was probably never entirely ruled out, could not relieve the peasant armies of the need to create a stable political order. There were no precedents for the granting of free imperial status although Switzerland could serve as a sort of guide, and it was certainly no accident that the vague models of the state formulated in 1525 along the Upper Rhine and in Upper Swabia were patterned after Switzerland. Wherever such models were lacking, as in Franconia, the revolution basically remained mired in destructiveness.

We may condemn these peasants as uncertain, unable, and unwilling only if we expect of them mature, thoughtful, self-consistent, and well-formulated constitutional proposals. The various attempts to reform the empire throughout the late Middle Ages are the clearest proof that such bold alternatives to the existing system were inconceivable. Neither the bold political theory of Nicholas of Cusa (died 1464) nor the apocalyptic vision of the "Upper Rhenish Revolutionary" * strayed from the sacrosanct ideas of emperor and empire. The Revolution of 1525 actually did go far beyond these previous efforts because it produced the outlines of an alternative: a corporative-federal constitution which grouped together the existing rural and urban communes into armies in Upper Swabia, in southwestern Germany, and in Alsace, giving them real political functions above and beyond their military tasks, and finally federating them in the League of the Christian Association. In this three-tiered state the really creative element was the "army," that supraterritorial military and political institution, which was genuinely original, as the feeble efforts to conceptualize it prove. In contrast, the communal and cooperative foundations grew out of living traditions, while the idea of a league had precedents in the Swiss Confederation, in the late medieval urban leagues, and in the Swabian League. The fact that

*See note on p. 68 above.

political concepts were so much vaguer in Franconia and that peasants there were much readier to negotiate reinforces the conclusion that revolutionary blueprints in 1525 were patterned after real-life models.

Godly law yielded no positive law for the state, and the gospel, no ideal policy. They remained open to interpretation, but the theologians refused to interpret and thus disqualified themselves from the task of forging a unified political ideal for the supraterritorial rebellions. The example of Markgräflerland demonstrates this clearly, for this land followed its own peculiar path, completely without concern for the general movement throughout the German southwest.

The peasants in the districts of southern Baden called Rötteln-Sausenberg, Badenweiler, and Hochberg hoped to replace the margrave's governors and officials with a government of peasants chosen from the territorial "assembly." From their prince they demanded acceptance of the Twelve Articles, as he himself reported to the city of Basel. If he did accept, they were ready to confirm him in the continued possession of his castles and lordships and to recognize him as their lord, with the noteworthy addition that the margrave, and "not His Imperial Majesty, . . . was their lord." [15]

We may pass over for the moment the question of whether Margrave Ernst of Baden reported the goals of the peasants accurately in the truncated form of his petition to the city of Basel (a question all the more troubling since the intelligence reached him in a round-about fashion through his district governor in Rötteln). The intention of these Markgräfler peasants does become clearer, however, if one examines closely the structure of government there. Unlike the peasants elsewhere, the men of Markgräflerland did not have to co-opt the concept of territory and assembly in order to articulate their political demands; for them that concept went back to the fifteenth century and designated corporations of subjects in the three lordships of Rötteln-Sausenberg, Badenweiler, and Hochberg. These groups also held common assemblies that one could designate territorial diets (although this term appears only after 1525). The assemblies already had a considerable range of political authority before 1525. In 1490 they participated in negotiating the succession agreement for Philipp von Hochberg, and in 1503, after the death of Philipp von Hochberg-Sausenberg, they refused allegiance to his widow and daughter and seized his castles because according to them neither was entitled to succeed. In 1509 they were involved in negotiations regarding the recruitment of troops. In 1511, when Margrave Christoph was planning his own succession, the assembly forced him to pass over his favored son, Philipp, and name another son, Ernst. And in 1517 they participated in framing territorial ordinances for the individual lordships.

The demands the assemblies made of Margrave Ernst were therefore a logical extension of their political rights, which they hoped to extend during the uproar of 1525. The peasants had no thought of deposing the margrave, but they clearly intended to separate the so-called upper or southern lordships

(Rötteln-Sausenberg, Badenweiler, and Hochberg) from the margraviate of Baden-Durlach. The assembly's governing council aimed at nothing more nor less than the removal of the (noble) territorial governors and their subordinates while limiting the council's own area of responsibility to the upper lordships, a move that made sense, since Baden-Durlach had no assembly at this time and the upper lordships regarded themselves as a political unit. It appears doubtful, under these circumstances, that the political goal of the Markgräfler peasants should be described as imperial free status, or direct subjection to the emperor.[16] Their supposed reference to the emperor might reflect nothing more than Ernst's worry at the prospect of being subordinated to Habsburg rule, since just ten years before the Peasants' War, the Austrian government in Ensisheim had explicitly claimed sovereign rights over the Markgräfler lordships.

If we are right in seeing the peasants' primary purpose as restructuring their territorial constitution, this confirms once again our finding that clear political conceptions were articulated most readily where peasants had earlier been able to gain political experience at the level of the territorial state. Thus the peasants of Markgräflerland followed more the political ideas of the men from Salzburg, Tyrol, and Württemberg than those common among the other Upper Rhenish peasants.

Inside the Christian associations there was plenty of room for the pursuit of private political visions, but this had a necessarily crippling effect on the revolution, even before the successes of the military counterattack. On the whole, the revolutionaries lacked the firmly fixed goals that might have given them the requisite fervor. When peasants surrendered superior strategic positions without a fight, as the men of Lake Constance and Allgäu did at Weingarten, and when 20,000 unarmed and humiliated peasants left Saverne carrying little white crosses, they were displaying not cowardice (for if that had been characteristic of the peasants, a rebellion would never have broken out) but their own uncertainty. There was uncertainty built into the way the rebels organized and into the consititutional ideas that they developed. Their "democratic principles" not only made decisive military action more difficult but also prolonged their arguments over how radical the rebellion should be. Rarely did the rebels come to any firm agreement concerning the use of godly law as a basis for violence in 1525. We may find this illustrated in the simple fact that the peasants committed almost no atrocities against persons—despite the popular image that has distorted research right down to the most recent times. The persons responsible for this uncertainty, if someone is to be blamed, were the reformers and bourgeoisie, because they refused to lend their swords to the revolution and instead aimed at a compromise where no compromise was possible. The Schappelers, Lotzers, Zells, Bucers, Capitos, Hiplers, and Weigandts sowed what they later refused to reap. Breaking free of the authority of these spokesmen cost the peasants dearly, as they struggled to create a corporative-federative constitution; despite these difficulties they did achieve a respectable new basis for political thought, founded on hopes of establishing a true commonwealth based on brotherly love. Yet wherever the territorial-assembly constitution provided a model that could be adapted to the goals of 1525, as we have seen in the Markgräfler-land, the rebels found this task of political reconstruction much easier.

ALTERNATIVES TO FEUDALISM BASED ON THE EARLY MODERN STATE: THE CONSTITUTION OF TERRITORIAL ASSEMBLIES

Godly law could be anchored immanently in this world, and the gospel could be actualized in the here and now only if society and government were changed. Translating vague yearnings into concrete constitutional and political goals proved easiest (again without assistance from religious reformers) wherever the early modern state with its constitution based on estates provided a political model that could be transformed through the godly law and the gospel. The estates constitution was usable as a model for revolutionary visions of the state because it proved that problems of order in a large territorial state could be solved through the cooperation of the prince and the territorial assembly. Composing an alternate political system involved nothing more than changing the existing constitution to accord with the fundamental objectives of the revolution.

Markgräflerland solved this problem theoretically by resolving the polarity between assembly and prince into an assembly government. Since the governing council had to answer for its policies to the common will of the assembly, there seemed to be sufficient guarantee that the principles of the common welfare, brotherly love, and the godly law would be realized. Salzburg came to a similar solution in its assembly government, although that solution was dependent on a series of prior changes. The assembly had to be transformed from a committee of nobles, clerics, and burghers into a corporation of peasants, miners, and burghers, elected by autonomous communes and thus dependent on them; this would make the power of the state responsible to the common man. Here as elsewhere constitutional reforms were heavily indebted to ideas about the estates and their assembly. If necessary, as in Salzburg, the concept of assembly was completely recast; in fact the powers of the assembly were so expanded that the territorial prince lost all political importance.

It remains to be seen whether the revolution elsewhere used the existing model of the estates constitution, and we will examine Tyrol, Württemberg, Bamberg, Würzburg, and Nearer Austria. In Tyrol, a territory with long traditions of politically successful representation of towns and rural districts, the revolutionary movement remained indecisive because the radical and moderate wings could not unite on any common program. Archduke Ferdinand used shrewd tactics to calm the miners, peasants, and burghers from the Valley of the Inn while forcing the more radical South Tyroleans to negotiate. A territorial diet began in June of 1525 at Innsbruck, and all districts and towns sent representatives, even though these representatives may not always have had the peasants and burghers firmly behind them. After a turbulent beginning, the districts and towns secured the exclusion of the prelates from the diet and established that their program—an expansion of the Merano articles that included the so-called Innsbruck Supplement—would constitute the basic agenda.

No other list of grievances from 1525 was so thorough and detailed as these ninety-six Merano-Innsbruck articles, which were supposed to become the basis of a new territorial ordinance and were therefore very carefully formulated and several times revised. All matters generally covered by the territorial laws of the sixteenth century were here categorized in the form of complaints, running from the law of inheritance to the judicial system, from the agrarian economy to the urban economy to the preservation of law and order.

In characterizing the Tyrolean revolution's goals, we must dispense with an account of the whole panorama of grievances and restrict ourselves to the fundamental social and political concerns. Like the other rebellious regions, Tyrol was united in its anticlericalism, which found expression in the demands that bishoprics and monasteries be secularized to the advantage of the prince, that the clergy be subordinate to rural and urban courts, and that local communities have the right of selecting their pastors. Alongside the expropriation and political dispossession of the clergy the Tyroleans demanded the political disfranchisement of the nobility. Although the nobility's economic position was to remain untouched (except for the effects of the planned reduction of peasant economic burdens), its rights as rulers and its privileged legal status were abolished. In this, the prince was not to be a winner, for the rural and urban districts were to gain in autonomy; they claimed the right of selecting all local officials, leaving the prince the right to control only those offices necessary for the collection and administration of territorial taxes. Thus, the power taken from the clergy and nobility was partitioned between the prince and the rural and urban districts. Eliminating intermediate authorities established a direct relationship between the common man and the prince. The territorial diets retained their mediating function and were even explicitly confirmed as a check on princely policies although final decrees of the diet were binding only if the districts ratified them.

In contrast to the political programs of Salzburg and Württemberg, that of Tyrol failed to offer any clear alternative to the traditional constitution of prince and estates. To be sure, on the local level the rights of the central government were to be restricted, yet at least one ambiguous demand insisted that only "understanding, honorable natives" be appointed to the government, "men who understand our native speech, whether noble, burgher, or peasant." [17] The rebels apparently understood "government" here to mean only the highest judicial courts in Tyrol, as the context of this article makes probable; thus the reform of "government" has to be seen as connected to the many other articles which aimed at improving the administration of justice. The demand that Ferdinand's favorite, Salamanca, and his hangers-on be dismissed is the only indication that the Tyroleans were also concerned with opening up the central offices of government to natives again, and even so, the prince was at liberty to fill his council with men whom he trusted. The shock of revolution did hit the clergy and nobility when the rebels moved to defend the "common good" by easing burdens on the peasant economy, controlling the urban economy more strictly, setting up social welfare institutions (e.g., hospitals), and establishing an improved administration of justice. But Ferdinand used his authority as a sovereign imperial prince to good advantage, knowing well how to appear as the deputy of Charles V even though Charles had already turned Tyrol over to his brother in a series of family treaties. He was no hated ecclesiastical potentate like the archbishop of Salzburg, and he was no outlaw, condemned for breach of the public peace, like Duke Ulrich of Württemberg. Thus he was able to maintain his princely position almost unchallenged even at the high point of the revolution.

In Württemberg barely four weeks elapsed between the beginning of the insurrection and its defeat at the Battle of Böblingen on May 12. Except for a few towns, including Tübingen, whither the Württemberg government under Truchsess Wilhelm von Waldburg retreated, the rebels took over the whole territory. All specific political demands aside, the common objective of town and country was the establishment of the "holy gospel and godly justice." [18] Because the rebels formulated few concrete demands and divided into several political factions, it is difficult to get a grasp of their political goal, one that was just beginning to emerge clearly at the moment of military defeat. The final debate among the rebels was whether to support the exiled Duke Ulrich or the Austrian government or to oppose them both. By examining the concepts they employed, however, we can quickly grasp the goal that united them all despite their individual factions. Soon after coming together the rebels appropriated the title of assembly (*Landschaft*), which had previously been used only for the totality of towns and rural districts as they (together with the high territorial clergy) confronted the prince at the diet. In so doing they claimed the legitimacy of the previous assembly, which had been composed mainly of notables from the district towns, and also the right both to constitute the land itself and to govern the land along with the traditional princely authorities. The notables of the district towns recognized the danger at once, as is shown by the urgent petition of Bottwar and Beilstein to the estates requesting that negotiations with the rebels begin. The "delegates of the assembly" appointed to discuss this proposed that a diet be summoned to settle grievances and that, contrary to previous procedure, representatives from the villages also attend.[19] The peasants however, rejected this idea unless the diet would "take place right here and now." The rebels' counterproposal was not feasible, and indeed it was intended only as a way of saying that traditional diets had lost their credit. All further attempts of the notables to resolve the conflict with a diet ended in failure. Finally, at the end of April and the beginning of May the rebels fixed on "assembly" as a term for all the rebellious districts taken together. Captains proclaimed edicts and ordinances and composed letters of safe-conduct and protection in the name of the "Assembly of Württemberg." [20] Hidden beneath this appropriation of the concept of assembly was a political explosive which the regent of Württemberg, Wilhelm Truchsess von Waldburg, and his cousin Georg took note of by deliberately addressing the rebels harmlessly and colorlessly as "those gathered together from some towns and hamlets of the principality of Württemberg." [21] They insisted on using the concept of assembly in its traditional sense, while Feuerbacher and Wunderer stubbornly responded as "captains of the Assembly of Württemberg." [22]

This fight over terminology clarifies the struggle for legitimacy, which was conducted within definite limits, since the captains of the Württemberg rebels, in contrast to those of Alsace, for example, seldom assumed the title of "government." Although they intended, as they told Elector Ludwig of the Palatinate, "to take over the principality of Württemberg and the Assembly," [23] they were not aiming to destroy all princely authority. On the contrary, the exiled Duke Ulrich of Württemberg was to be restored, [24] although he would have to pay the price of a drastic reduction of his governmental rights by the new assembly. A compromise was to be worked out between him and the new assembly without any interference from foreign armies. If an assembly-dominated constitution as conceived by the rebels had gone into effect after a general amnesty and a settlement of foreign policy complications, [25] it would have brought a decisive constitutional change, for all ecclesiastical lands were to be confiscated by the treasury, thereby eliminating the clergy as a political estate, and destroying an integral part of the constitution. In addition, princely rights were to be reduced to a bare minimum. Alongside the prince there would be a twelve-man regency council, chosen by the assembly and composed equally of peasants, burghers and nobles, who in cooperation with the duke would handle all affairs of government including appointments of all officials. Although the duke was to have the first and last voice, the regency council had the clearly formulated goal of preventing the duke from having "the power to do anything touching the land and its people . . . without their advice and consent." [26] On the other hand, the new constitution left to the diet the actual framing of territorial ordinances, such as one that would guarantee the central demands of the Twelve Articles. The diet, for its part, would have had a new structure, for it would have had to give equal weight to nobles, burghers, and peasants, just as the regency council did. If the electoral principle was to be obligatory on the local level for filling council and judicial posts, then it would certainly have applied to the selection of delegates to the diet. Encrusted old forms of oligarchy, such as the rule of the "notables" in Württemberg, could have been bypassed in this way. Cooperative associations, whether on the communal or the territorial level, were made at least symbolically equal to the territorial regime by requiring district officials, the judiciary, and the council to swear oaths of office to the commune and by requiring forest wardens, the prince's military men, and other officials to take oaths before the assembly.

In the bishopric of Bamberg the rebels' program was even less clearly formulated, and we have to infer it from the actual course of the revolution. Among the sources we can find demands for the secularization of the monasteries and for abolition of the cathedral chapter's role in government as well as for expansion of communal rights. The rebels' behavior, however, provides us with the only grounds for suspecting that ultimately they wanted a constitutional assembly. At the end of April an eighteen-man committee was established to which the bishop named nine delegates and the peasants, the city of Bamberg, and the nobility named three each. The committee was supposed to restrict itself to settling grievances and demands, but only a few days after being constituted, it proclaimed religious edicts, made hunting free for all, and abolished tithes, forced labor services, and servile dues. It thus arbitrarily exceeded its jurisdiction and was well on its way to taking over the functions of a governing council in the bishopric of Bamberg. At the high point of the revolutionary movement, the rebels voiced demands for participation of towns and villages in the choice of a bishop, for the filling of offices by the community, and for appointment of peasants and townsmen as judges to the territorial court; and in the wake of a second uprising the special rights of the nobles were to be set aside in favor of legal equality with the burghers and peasants. This entire development illustrates once more the way that ideas and models of constitutional change spread from region to region.

We find similar ideas in the bishopric of Würzburg. Here, the clergy were to lose their economic and political position, and the bishopric was to be transformed into a secular principality. Although the bishop's rule was not questioned, he was now supposed to rule with a college made up of nobles, burghers, and peasants who were to meet four times a year. Although in Bamberg and Würzburg we can at least glimpse the outlines of a political program which might have resulted in a constitutional assembly, in some territories the ideas of the state were so colorless that they amounted to nothing more than anticlerical emotion. In Speyer and Fulda, for example, the political initiatives included only the transformation of the bishopric and chapter into a secular lordship, the economic and political dispossession of the clergy, and occasionally, the extension of communal autonomy, though the last often did not go beyond selection of pastors. These severe limits are possibly explicable by the fact that in the Palatinate, intersected by a welter of electoral, free imperial, and episcopal territories such as Speyer, the rebels could not remain isolated members of only this or that territory. In the

TABLE 2. LANDS WITH ASSEMBLY CONSTITUTIONS:
STATUS IN 1524/25 AND PROPOSED PROGRAM OF REBELS

	Salzburg		Bamberg	
	1524/25	Program	1524/25	Program
Sovereign	Prince and cathedral chapter	No ruler	Prince and cathedral chapter	Prince and governing council
Governing council	Cathedral chapter	(Nobility) Burghers Peasants (Miners) ↑ *Election*	Cathedral chapter	Bishop [9] Nobility [3] Burghers [3] Peasants [3] ↑
Diet	Nobility Clergy Markets (Communes)	(Nobility) Towns Markets Communes Miners ↑ *Election*	No diet	No diet *Election*
Local officials	Appointed by the ruler	Appointed by governing council with consent of local commune	Appointed by the ruler	Elected by the community

NOTE: Groups in parentheses represent hypotheses rather than textually secure conclusions.

monastic lands of Fulda, too, the rebels joined with other peasant armies from Thuringia. In short, conflicts were not played out solely within the framework of the territorial state, and the need to find a territorial solution was not always so pronounced as in Salzburg, Württemberg, and Tyrol.

As a final example, Nearer Austria also had an estates constitution. As princely subjects, the peasants and townsmen of the Habsburg domain had the right of representation at diets, but the estates model never was the basis of discussion in Sundgau, Alsace, Breisgau, and the Black Forest and never could be because Nearer Austria was not a territory like Tyrol, Salzburg, or Württemberg. The princely interests of the Habsburgs were restricted to the defensive and fiscal capabilities of these peripheral lands. The nobility and clergy had strong positions because there was no princely government or

Table 2—*continued*

	Würzburg		Tyrol	
	1524/25	Program	1524/25	Program
Sovereign	Prince and cathedral chapter	Prince and governing council	Prince and governing council	Prince and governing council
Governing council	Cathedral chapter	Nobility [6] Burghers [6] Peasants [6] ⟰ *Election*	Appointed by the prince	(Nobility) (Burghers) (Peasants)
Diet	Nobility Clergy Towns	(Nobility) (Towns) (Peasants)	Nobility Clergy Towns Rural districts	Nobility Towns Rural districts (Miners) ⟰ *Election*
Local officials	Appointed	No proposal	Appointed by the prince	Elected by the community

unified territorial law to restrain the nearly autonomous rule of nobles and monasteries. Authority here was not a distant prince in Innsbruck or Vienna but the local aristocrat or prelate.

To sum up, the alternatives to the early modern state proposed in 1525 all had a certain uniformity, displayed in Table 2 and traceable to the fact that they were all built on the basis of the unified, dualistic territory with estates (*Ständestaat*). It is nonetheless legitimate to call these alternatives revolutionary because the territory with estates furnished no more than an institutional framework, while existing conditions that organized political rights and duties according to specific legal estates were rejected. The concept of assembly (*Landschaft*), which had hitherto denoted the privileged estates represented in the territorial diets, was taken over by subjects in the strict

Table 2—*continued*

	Württemberg		Markgräflerland (Baden)	
	1524/25	Program	1524/25	Program
Sovereign	Prince and governing council	Prince and governing council	Prince and bailiffs	Prince and governing council
Governing council	Appointed by the prince	Nobility [4] Burghers [4] Peasants [4] ↑ *Election*	Appointed by the prince (Bailiffs)	Peasants
Diet	(Nobility) Clergy District urban elite *(Ehrbarkeit)*	Nobility Burghers Peasants ↑ *Election*	Peasants Town (1)	No proposal
Local officials	Appointed by the prince	Appointed by governing council	Appointed or partially elected	No proposal

sense—that is, by peasants, burghers, and miners. This was the lever they used to topple the social and political order. Everything else was simply the necessary result of this first step: abolishing the economic and political power of prelates; integrating the nobility and clergy into the communal associations as partial corporations within the whole corporate assembly, while taking away their political privileges; changing the composition of the territorial diets. The political expectations of the subjects were important factors in the rebellion, finding expression in theoretical programs wherever peasants already were represented in the diet (as in Tyrol), or where they were on the way to gaining such representation (as in Salzburg), or where they wanted it (as in Württemberg).

This was the step from rebellion to revolution in the larger territories. The grievances that had provoked the crisis were left far behind, hardly relevant any longer to a state with a constituted assembly in which the clergy and nobility had lost their rights to rule. From the peasants' point of view it was the corruption of lordly rule itself that had provoked the uprising, and therefore the removal of noble and monastic lordship got rid of not just specific abuses but the true origin of the abuses as well. If the peasants were to secure the results of their revolution for the long term, however, they would also have to think about the real problems connected with the sovereign territorial prince. Building him into the state with undiminished powers meant running a certain risk, because in the end men would still have to appeal to him for redress of grievances. The immediate consequences of the revolution were supposed to be codified in territorial constitutions in Tyrol, Salzburg, Württemberg, and Bamberg. In these lands the governing committee of the territorial assembly was to serve as a check on princely power, for these committees represented the autonomous bodies of the common man: the rural communes, village communes, urban communes, mining communes, and finally the territorial assembly itself. Creating the sovereign power in a way that combined both the prince and the governing committee of the assembly was normally a compromise solution; although such an arrangement accepted existing institutions, it also freed them from being solely responsible to the prince any longer. Only in Salzburg was the idea of a governing committee from the assembly truly radical, for there the archbishop was to be excluded from all matters of government. In Tyrol, on the other hand, the indefinite proposal for stronger consideration for nobles, burghers, and peasants in the governing council of the prince was extremely conservative, since it did not even question the rights of the sovereign. This could hardly be the last word for the Tyroleans, and in fact, it was Michael Gaismair who pronounced that last word in his Territorial Constitution.

Aside from the peculiarities of this or that political structure, there were some basic elements in the demands of the common man: economic relief for the common man under the slogan of the "common good"; a dissolution of legal and social barriers between the ranks of men under the slogan of "Christian and brotherly love"; a claim of autonomy for the community under the rubric of securing the pure gospel without human additions (to be guaranteed by congregational election of ministers); and a new political and legal order of state associations set on the basis of godly law. The utopians of 1525 tried to bring these elements together in intellectually acceptable, internally consistent systems.

UTOPIAS: THE TOTAL CHRISTIAN STATE

In 1525 the appeal of compelling and consistent revolutionary programs was distinctly limited except in Thuringia. Ideas that went so far beyond the conditions of real life that they would have required the abolition of all social and political traditions failed to achieve general acceptance because the various peasant armies could not agree on the meaning of godly law, but also because revolutionary political ideas often remained enmeshed in the concrete details of the existing estates constitution. A few remarkable projects—those of Michael Gaismair, Balthasar Hubmaier, Thomas Müntzer, and Hans Hergot—escaped the limits imposed by previous experience only by displaying an absolute certainty about the demands of the gospel and the content of godly law and a total refusal to accommodate revolutionary goals to any existing social and political institutions.

Michael Gaismair

Tyrol, having chosen the path of negotiation and compromise, allowed Archduke Ferdinand to beat down one demand after another, and threatened to fall back into all the old patterns of political dependence. Such a relapse would have been especially dangerous for the former subjects of the bishops of Bressanone and Trent, for they had no seat or voice in the Tyrolean diets. Michael Gaismair's Constitution was a response to the disappointing results of the diet, results that were especially disillusioning to the men of Bressanone. Having started as a reformer in the summer of 1525, Gaismair had gradually become a revolutionary by the spring of 1526; his plan for a new social and political order in Tyrol stands as the logical and uncompromising realization of that one basic concern of the whole revolution from Salzburg to Alsace and from Thuringia to Trent, namely, the pure gospel and the common good.[27] The "Assembly" of Tyrol was bound by oath "to seek first the honor of God and then the common good." These were the only axioms necessary for a radical reformulation of society and the state. The "godless people, who persecute the eternal word of God, burden the poor common man, and hinder the common good," were to be rooted out ruthlessly.[28] All privileges were abolished; all legal status differences swept away. Only the society of the common man remained, a homogeneous society differentiated at most according to occupation into peasants, miners, and artisans. This condition of total equality would be produced by demolishing city walls, castles, and fortresses, by concentrating all artisanal occupations at Trent under the supervision of the state, and by distributing manufactured and imported goods through salaried storekeepers appointed by a general bailiff; these measures would prevent usury, unjust prices, and the growth of new social injustices among rich and poor alike.

Unlike proposals elsewhere, here the common good was not thought secure as soon as the nobility and clergy were simply expropriated.[29] Gaismair's plans included a state takeover of the mines, drainage of swamps between Bolzano and Trent, a program to encourage the growing of grain and the raising of cattle, the coordination of viticulture, the removal of all internal tolls and setting up of protective tariffs on imports, and the abolition of all rents.[30] Of the old dues only the tithe remained to support the pastor and the poor, plus a tax for financing state projects if the revenues from the mines did not suffice. The political constitution of this egalitarian, "closed society" remained sketchy. Rural communes and parishes were reconstituted according to economic criteria but were equipped with the traditional functions of justice and administration, which were to be handled by eight elected jurors and one elected judge. The government[31] was to be elected by the miners and by the separate "quarters" of Tyrol, which had developed in the fifteenth century as military and tax districts based on topography. The government served as a court of appeal for the district courts, organized the territorial defenses under four captains and a chief captain, and supervised manufacturing, mining, and relief of the poor. The Christian nature of this government was to be guaranteed by the inclusion of three professors from the theological university, the only university in the land.

Gaismair intended to produce no more than a rough draft. To fill it out, to expand it into a usable constitution, remained a task for everyone, as did the demands for increasing the honor of God and the common weal and for rooting out the godless: "You should all aim at producing a totally Christian ordinance, which in all matters is to be founded on the holy word of God, and you should all want to live to that end." [32] Salzburgers, in their second rebellion of 1526, may have been indebted to Gaismair when they attempted to work out this sort of "Christian ordinance" in the form of a territorial constitution, but the Swabian League drowned this attempt in blood and tears when it conquered the Salzburg peasants.

Balthasar Hubmaier

The Upper Rhine developed its most coherent program in the so-called Draft of a Constitution, which was similar to Gaismair's Territorial Constitution only in its failure to be adopted. It is preserved in the dubious version of an open letter to Duke George of Saxony from Ferdinand's counsellor, Bishop Johann Fabri of Constance, who tried to make Balthasar Hubmaier share the responsibility for the Revolution of 1525 and thus justify his execution.

According to the Draft of a Constitution, the political order was to be based on a league which "the people of each region" joined. The league, the brotherhood, the association, the assembly (all terms used as synonyms), proclaimed an "ordinance . . . according to the word of God," in order to abolish once and for all "the secular lords' fleecing, flaying, mincing, stretching, twisting, and extortion." [33] The draft aimed to achieve this end by challenging the lords to join the association and, if they refused, by tearing the sword from their hands, for they were tyrants, the equals of Herod. The existing princely power (presumably the Habsburg government) would be transferred to an elected sovereign, who would be chosen from among twelve nominees. He would be subject to the control of the assembly, or association, and could be punished by it or even deposed after three punishments. If he resisted or if the former lords opposed their loss of office, they would be punished with secular banishment and, if necessary, with military force "so that the bloodthirsty tyrants may be exterminated."

The Draft of a Constitution was undoubtedly crude; even more than Gaismair's plan, it relied on the association to fill out the details of a constitution along Christian lines, for it settled only the basic questions of choosing and deposing a ruler.[34] But in doing that, it answered exactly the question that the Letter of Articles of the Black Forest peasants and the men of Hegau had left open. It was, as it were, the theoretical basis for a political situation such as that of Alsace under the leadership of Erasmus Gerber before the defeat by the duke of Lorraine. If the Draft of a Constitution had been used to extend the incomplete program of the Christian Association in southwestern Germany to its proper conclusion,[35] it would have established a polity based on the village, territorial, and urban communes; as a "Christian Association" it would have provided itself with a fully autonomous territorial constitution and an elected ruler as head of the league.

We cannot in the end be certain that Hubmaier composed the Draft of a Constitution, especially since it borrowed heavily from Thomas Müntzer. Nonetheless it was not incompatible with Hubmaier's ideas of authority and resistance. Hubmaier had welcomed the alliance of the town of Waldshut with the peasants, thinking that peace, calm, and a Christian way of life would result. In one of his later major works, "On the Sword" (1527), he expressed ideas that were thoroughly compatible with the Draft of a Constitution, since he favored the deposition of "childish or foolish" authorities, although without the use of force. If the rights of authorities were emphasized more in 1527 than one would expect from the author of the Draft of a Constitution, we must remember that in 1527 Hubmaier was concerned to distance himself from the basically hostile attitude of Anabaptists toward the state.

Assuming that Hubmaier did write the Draft of a Constitution and that Fabri transmitted it correctly, we may conclude that it was a hastily composed manifesto, which did at least draw logical conclusions from the revolution along the Upper Rhine but did not transform them into a clearly formulated, practicable model constitution.

Thomas Müntzer

"All things are common" (Omnia sunt communia). This confession, extracted by torture from Thomas Müntzer,[36] marked his program, which he described more closely thus: "Everyone should properly receive according to his need. Any prince, count, or lord who refuses to do this even when seriously warned should be hanged or have his head chopped off."[37] To a certain extent this was the secular side of the revolutionary coin whose legend on the spiritual side demanded "that Christians should all be equals" and that lords who opposed the gospel be driven off and killed.[38]

More than any other revolutionary, Müntzer formulated decisively and logically one conclusion drawn from the Revolution of 1525 that was suggested as far away as Salzburg and Tyrol, the Black Forest and Alsace: the demand that lords be challenged to join the Christian Associations or be banished so as to further the common good. The consistent, radical goals of 1525 articulated in Gaismair's Territorial Constitution and in the Draft of a Constitution were entirely comparable to those of Müntzer.

Müntzer's goals found an organizational or institutional framework in his "Christian League," which, after an early and shaky beginning in Zwickau in 1520–21, had its center and its most vigorous growth in Mühlhausen in 1525. It "included and represented the majority of the people" [39] and was thus very different from Gaismair's Territorial Constitution and the Draft of a Constitution. Müntzer branded the Christian League with his insights and convictions: Men must be led back to Christ through the experience of the cross, which no ecclesiastical institution and no scriptural scholar could provide. The painful experience of the cross, a faith of the spirit, freed man from his creaturely desire for riches, honor, and fame, and allowed him to become one of the elect. So long as creatureliness (which was intrinsically negative) was not conquered by faith, man remained fettered to creaturely authority; in view of the corruption of the world this could mean only the rule of sin. Worldly authority was responsible for the fact that "the poor man's struggle for food keeps him from learning to read." Preachers even told him that he "should suffer the tyrants to flay and scrape him." [40] Thus, rulers with their selfish and unchristian regimes blocked man's access to God, and they were therefore enemies of God.

Truly the world was divided between believers and unbelievers, the followers of an experienced faith and those whose faith was artificial. Only God-fearing believers knew God's will and recognized the unchristian nature of the existing secular order; only they could "preserve themselves from all tyrants." [41] Fear of God conquered tyranny, not by producing an introverted faithfulness that was immunized against the external world, but by destroying tyranny; it had to be eradicated because Müntzer's eschatological expectations held that the process of salvation-history had now been driven so far that the end of the world should be brought about as soon as possible for the returning Christ. This was the conversion of a theology of suffering into a true theology of revolution. The godless must be destroyed; they would be annihilated by the power of God, using the means of the sword, "just as food and drink are a means of living." [42]

The elect were to bear the sword against lords and princes who were not ready to humble themselves, renounce their selfishness, and open up the path to God for men. Their task, the revolution, became the task of the common man. Müntzer's hitherto exclusively theological argument is flimsy here; by connecting the real poverty of the people to "poverty in spirit," in sharp contrast to the wealth and selfishness of the ruling class, he created a very shaky theological scaffold. Still, it was abundantly clear that he had committed himself to the people, to the revolution, to the transfer of power to the people. The clergy and the lords had to be annihilated, for they, like "eels and serpents defiled themselves all in a heap together,"[43] supporting and furthering each other in their unchristian, dissolute, and exploitative selfishness.

Müntzer was clearly indebted to Hubmaier's Draft of a Constitution. If the Revolution of 1525 had become the Red Sea for the German princes, he would have had to employ the draft, since the military victory of revolution would not have meant an immediate victory over all creatureliness. But ultimately, Müntzer was fighting for a world of the last days according to God's plan of salvation, a world whose actual shape could have been communist, communal-democratic, or republican and theocratic.

Hans Hergot

Communist, communal, democratic, republican, and theocratic elements were all blended together in a utopia entitled *On the New Transformation of a Christian Life,* which presented a countermodel to the current world, one that God himself would bring about. Its author wrote: "There are three tables in the world: the first, covered to overflowing with too much food; the second, moderately and comfortably provisioned; and the third, lacking in everything. The people from the overflowing table come and try to take bread from the poorest table, and a fight erupts. God will overturn both the overflowing table and the poor table and approve the moderate table."[44] The suppression of social differences and the removal of the contrast between rich and poor were here set down as the goals of a new order corresponding to God's will. In other words, the "honor of God" and the "common good" became the basic principles of new social and political ordinances. The author of the *New Transformation* used this pair of ideas no fewer than ten times in his brief utopian pamphlet. By using this kind of language the author adopted terminology that had become a verbal symbol for the insurrection in 1525. We cannot be sure that the author was Hans Hergot, as scholars have long assumed, but whoever he was, we can rightly consider his *New Transformation* as essentially connected in content, and maybe even in time, with the Revolution of 1525.

The *New Transformation* was first published in 1527 in Leipzig, but that tells us little about its date of composition, especially since the pamphlet falls into two clearly distinct halves. A first part presents the countermodel to current sociopolitical reality, while the second contains a polemical attack on the political and ecclesiastical powers of the day. The second part was undoubtedly a product of disillusionment after the failure of the Revolution of 1525 and was therefore written after 1525. "Rebellion . . . comes . . . from God's power"; it was "God's wrath" that drove princes and nobles from their castles in 1525, for "even if the emperor had come with all his princes, in a whole year he could not have frightened the nobles as badly as God did in ten weeks." But such proofs of the majesty of God "are worthless," the author complained, "for men say the peasants did it." With resignation he confesses, "I believe that God will never more arouse the peasants to rebel against their lords"; instead, God would arouse the Turks and all the unbelievers, for his judgment was coming "and he will uproot the weeds."

It is noteworthy that the second, polemical and pessimistic half never even mentions the first, utopian and optimistic half. That may help us understand the relation between the two parts, or even the times when they were written. The utopia of the *New Transformation* was formulated without apocalyptic visions, and so it seems possible that the apocalyptic vision of the second part was a result of disappointed expectations, when the utopia did not come to pass. The hopeful visionary became an eschatological preacher of repentance in the last days.

The utopian sketch in the *New Transformation* was drawn with clear, bold strokes. The fundamental idea of the "common good" was to be realized by doing away with property and by abolishing all status relations of superiority and inferiority. In the new, egalitarian sociopolitical order, no one would claim, "This is mine"; and "it is also pointless for anyone to try to maintain his estate." The principles of community of wealth and of social equality have been made real by secularizing the monasteries, by mediatizing* the nobility under the sovereignty of the communal association, and by erasing the legal and economic differences between town and country. Another consequence is that all rents and dues are abolished, even those to the new government, which obtains its bare subsistence from the communes. The economic order combines agrarian and artisanal elements, subordinating them all to the idea of an economically autonomous community in which everyone pursues his occupation to the best of his knowledge and abilities. The author uses the word "field" (*Flur*) to describe this autonomous village. The economic order, oriented to producing a simple sufficiency and based on legal and social equality, had its political reflection in a constitution that was both republican and theocratic (see Fig. 2).

The smallest political unit in the constitution imagined by the *New Transformation* is the "field," or village, each of which has a "house of God," or church; at the head of each church stands a "provider of the house of God" who acts as village chief or mayor. Several fields together make up a "land," whose "lord" and ruler is chosen by the providers of the house of God. This lord, in turn, confirms the providers of the house of God in their

---

*To mediatize means to make subordinate to some superior authority.

**FIGURE 2.   MODEL OF WORLD GOVERNMENT
PROPOSED BY HANS HERGOT**

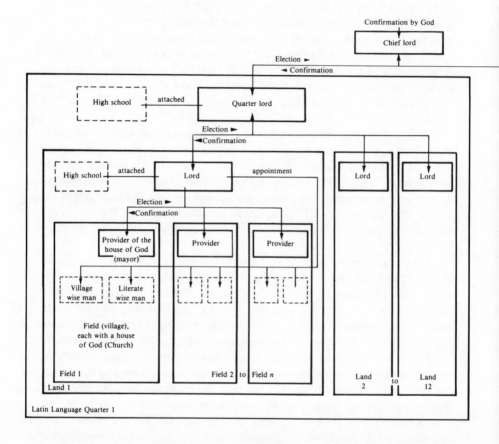

new positions—they may well have been elected by the villages. And the lord also enforces the ethical and religious principles of the common good and the honor of God in the village by mobilizing the village institutions of law embodied in the "village wise man" and the "literate wise man." * The lord also has a "high school," where "the honor of God and the common good will be taught, and where all useful books will be found." Twelve of these lands together constitute a kind of nation, or "quarter," under the rule of a "quarter lord." In close analogy to the land, the quarter lord is elected by the twelve lords, who are themselves confirmed in their positions by him. Finally, there are twelve quarters, four in each tongue (Latin, Greek, and Hebrew). The twelve quarter lords elect a "chief lord" and are in turn confirmed by

*These two officials corresponded roughly to the village officials responsible for economic and for spiritual matters, i.e., to headman and pastor, respectively.

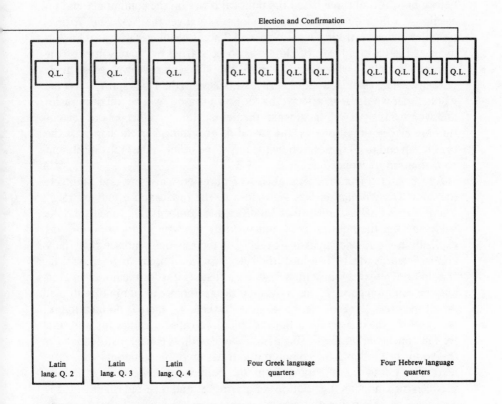

him. The chief lord, for his part, obtains his confirmation from God himself. There are hints of parliamentary institutions, visible, for example, when the rulers at each level consult with their subordinate providers, lords, and quarter lords.

The constitutional arrangements set forth in the *New Transformation* are presented as a global political order. In the biblical words of the author it was based on the model of "one shepherd and one flock." Gone is the idea of two kingdoms with its division of secular and spiritual power, of emperor and pope; gone are Romans 13 ("The powers that be are ordained of God") and Matthew 22 ("Render unto Caesar the things that are Caesar's"). In their place are the principles of a single Christian humanity and of a political order resting on elections, which God sanctions by confirming the chief lord.

The *New Transformation* carries the political ideas developed during the Revolution of 1525 to their intellectually most compelling conclusion. At the basis of its utopian program are the same constitutional ideas as those worked out by Hubmaier and Gaismair. This explains the notable resemblance between the *New Transformation* and the South German constitutional proposals; the author need not have had the actual texts of those proposals before him, for all three based the political order on the community and on elections to fill all governmental positions. Moreover the *New Transformation* also shows a striking resemblance to Thomas Müntzer's ideas. Government at the various levels of state was to be staffed by "pious men of the common people," who would "relieve the villages and towns of all their burdens." The chief lord should pray, "I believe in the Holy Spirit," and the whole order would be so affected by the Spirit that it "will be full of miracles and wondrous signs." Fundamental themes in Müntzer's theology of revolution are evident in all of this: the sword of government in the hands of the people, an end to all oppression by the lords, the belief in the Holy Spirit, and confirmation by wondrous signs.

As we can tell from these parallels to Hubmaier, Gaismair, and Müntzer, the *New Transformation* was very close to the mood and events of 1525. There is one final argument that solidifies and confirms this conclusion. As we have seen, the political order imagined by the *New Transformation* was explicitly a world-encompassing order, but there is one sentence that flatly contradicts this idea: "If a lord [the ruler of a land] needs to go to war, he should be given every third man from each field, if it is for the honor of God and the common good." This is the only clear reference to war in this utopia. At all the other levels of state analogous to the land, there is no mention of war. Neither the quarter lords nor the chief lord calls up armies for war, and we can conclude that the waging of war along with its ethical justification (in the honor of God and the common good) has crept unintentionally into the text. The phrase itself sprang from the context of military negotiations between the Christian Associations or assemblies and their old rulers in 1525. The passage seems directly parallel to the actual practice of the Alsatians under Erasmus Gerber, who, we will recall, recruited every fourth man from each village and planned to rotate his men weekly until the victory of the gospel was secure.

CHAPTER 9

Reformation Theology and Revolutionary Practice

Godly law, as the peasants understood the Bible, paralyzed the old law and custom and thus gave the rebels their first real opportunity to break out of the continuity of medieval legal and intellectual traditions. Insofar as godly law was derived from evangelical preaching and from the Reformation pamphlet, the theology of the Reformation assumes a position of great importance for the revolutionary movement of 1525. To be sure, the peasants were original in giving an imperative urgency to godly law when applied to the conditions of this world, but we do know that the Reformation also provided legitimacy for the peasants' demands. The question rightly arises of whether and to what extent elements of Reformation theology and ethics entered into the revolutionary goals of the rebels.

The names and labels used by the rebels of 1525, together with their forms of organization and their ideas of legitimacy, can be described in two different ways: on the one hand they represented a break away from perverted traditions as they saw them; but on the other hand they were a new departure toward the radical realization of a political and social order corresponding to the will of God. Both sorts of breaks came to expression in the programmatic models of Hubmaier, Gaismair, Müntzer, and Hergot and in the constitutional experiments actually tried in the Christian Associations of Upper Swabia, the Black Forest, Alsace, and Franconia. In all of these cases the feudal system of government was replaced with a republican model, to give it a shorthand description. This new model had the following concrete features: (1) the rural and urban commune was made the basis for all political structures, regardless of whether the state oriented itself toward existing conditions, as in the territorial state with an estates constitution, or created a new federal union of many communes by borrowing the structure of the Swiss; (2) all political offices were to be filled by elections, which had their basis in communal elections; and (3) the constitutional framework of territorial laws was to reflect the demands of godly law.

This last point can be illustrated quickly from the very words and concepts chosen by the rebels: "Christian" associations, "Christian" brotherhoods, "Christian" communities. These words reveal the ethical basis and legitimacy of authorities that now aimed at Christian brotherly love and the common good as central parts of a revolutionary goal that hoped to actualize the law of God.

These generalizations about the rebels' goals, arrived at inductively from many examples, prove once more that actual peasant programs must not be viewed in isolation from the utopian projects, for both were simply expressions of the same basic concern. Of course they differ in that the constitutional projects that I have called utopian succeeded in formulating the concerns of 1525 more logically and coherently than the league ordinances and territorial edicts that arose from political practice. For example, the constitution set up by Erasmus Gerber in Alsace and defended against the criticisms of Strasbourg was burdened by the still undecided political situation. It naturally had a weaker "theoretical" character than, say, the *New Transformation* by Hergot.

The basic outlines of the political program of 1525 make it clear that the insurrection increasingly outgrew the structural limits of political, economic, and social differences. The principles of community, elections, godly law, the common good, and Christian brotherly love neutralized and overwhelmed the particular interests of any group or estate. Adopting these goals and working for their realization was possible for peasants, burghers, and miners alike. If we accept the uncontroversial idea that the Reformation began as a popular movement, then the broad base of the revolutionary movement in 1525 can hardly astonish us. The goal of these programs, after all, was at long last to shape the world exactly according to the will of God, to actualize the message of Christ laid down in the New Testament, and thus to secure eternal salvation. This world and the world to come became more closely intertwined in 1525, and both were anchored in a will of God that stretched out over both "kingdoms"—the spiritual and the secular. This sense of unity corresponded to the mentality of the common man, who could not imagine himself as inhabiting two kingdoms, since he saw himself as undivided. For him the removal of oppression and misery was part of salvation and blessedness.

In 1525 the economic, social, and political concerns of the common man were unmistakably bound up with the arguments and elements of the Reformation. The code word for economic relief was the common good; the slogan for justice was Christian brotherly love; the code word for the best legal order was the godly law; and the slogan for good political order was reliance on the community and on elections. It remains to be seen how all of this was connected to the Reformation and how important the Reformation was for the formulation of these goals.

Despite the fact that the Protestant reformers disagreed among themselves on countless points, there was nevertheless a common "Reformation theology" that stood opposed to the old church. When Luther rejected the magisterial authority of the old church, theology was set free from its axiomatic dependence on dogma and tradition and necessarily reoriented Christian doctrine to Scripture. The recourse to Scripture made possible a whole new theological starting point over against the Roman Church, and thus a "Reformation theology." But turning to Scripture also fostered the rise of many theological systems that grew out of the individual confrontation with Scripture and out of the private religious experience and the social context of each reformer. And so Reformation theology displays a double structure of unity and diversity. The unity can be seen in the fact that all the reformers adopted Luther's basic principles of *sola gratia, sola fide,* and *sola scriptura* (salvation by grace alone, by faith alone, with Scripture the only authority). The diversity came from all the different possible ways of digesting Luther's theology. The structure of Luther's theology was dialectical, after all, and his theological thinking continued to change. We can see the dialectical structure of Luther's theology in such antithetical concepts as *simul iustus et peccator* ("righteous and sinful at the same time"), "grace and judgment," "law and gospel," "the letter of Scripture and the spirit of Scripture." His students and friends gave up these antitheses and usually simplified matters by opting for one side of the balance or the other. The opportunity this gave for theological differences was further strengthened by the only gradual emergence of Luther's theology, unfolding without ever presenting a closed system. Thus, the particular moment a reformer encountered Luther could determine his direction even though Luther's thinking might go on developing in completely original paths.

Aside from the incontrovertible and unquestioned importance of Luther, the theological positions of the other reformers were determined by their own individual confrontations with the theological traditions of the Middle Ages and with the concrete sociopolitical environment. To give just the briefest of summaries, Reformation theology broke down into three main groups: the Wittenberg theologians around Luther; the "Christian humanists" around Zwingli, Oecolampadius, and Bucer; and the "theologians of the Spirit" around Müntzer (Anabaptists and Spiritualists). The circle around Zwingli and Bucer weighted Luther's dialectic between law and gospel toward the law, while Müntzer's group, under the influence of mysticism, weighted Luther's dialectic between the letter and spirit of the gospel toward the spirit.

If we think back on the utopias and the actual programs of 1525, it is clear at first glance that the Wittenberg school of the Reformation would have had nothing to do with such projects. On the other hand, the object of exploiting the gospel to obtain positive law and of bringing the gospel to bear on the political order was closely related to the aims of the Christian humanists in southern Germany. We might be able to tell which of these reformers could have had a decisive influence on the events of 1525 if we could show that the goals of 1525 had some special affinity with the theology and ethics of a particular South German reformer. We must begin this search with the Twelve Articles and the Federal Ordinance of the Upper Swabian armies, which were frequently reprinted in March and April of 1525 and which demonstrably influenced rebel manifestos and platforms throughout the whole area of insurrection. We know now that the authors and editors of these two programs were almost certainly Christoph Schappeler and Sebastian Lotzer. Furthermore, we know that Lotzer was a student of Schappeler's, and that Schappeler himself was without any doubt a disciple of Zwingli.[1] To what extent could the revolutionary movement appeal to Zwingli for support?

In many fundamental theological areas Zwingli and Luther were in agreement. For example, their doctrine of justification used the ideas of grace (*sola gratia*) and faith (*sola fide*) to locate human salvation in the direct encounter between man and God, thereby rejecting categorically the role of the old church as mediator and administrator of grace. On this basis they both developed a new understanding of the congregation, one that logically assumed the existence of Christians who had come of age. This new idea of the congregation found expression in the preaching of the pure gospel, with individual congregations deciding for the new teaching and choosing their own pastors; at least this was the case until both reformers, feeling threatened, fled to the secular authorities, a move that favored the growth of state church structures even at the parish level.

Luther and Zwingli did disagree on christology. "Luther stressed the *revelation* of God [in Christ] while Zwingli stressed the revelation of *God*"; or to put the point another way, "Luther's christology was one of Christmas while Zwingli's was one of Easter or Ascension."[2] For Zwingli the divinity of Christ was in the foreground and his humanity was in the background. This had ethical implications, especially for Zwingli's idea of the state and the ruling authorities. For Zwingli faith in the gospel implied "the decision in favor of a total change of social and political life."[3] In place of the old, unchristian order, Zwingli set up a new concept:

Human doctrine	were to be	*the gospel*
and	replaced	and
selfishness	by	*the common good.*

The gospel and the common good were categories that depended on each other. To bring them into social reality one needed the government. In other words, the punishment of evil men and the protection of the pious were "the will of God" and the task of the state.[4] "Therefore," Zwingli concluded, "all of [the government's] laws should conform to the will of God." To prove the point he cited the Acts of the Apostles: "We must obey God rather than man" (Acts 5:29). From this passage Luther had defended more than merely passive resistance to the state in cases of conscience, but Zwingli extracted a completely different consequence from it. For he immediately concluded,

"Therefore Christian princes need laws that are not opposed to God; otherwise they will not be obeyed, and there will be unrest." Such laws were the only guarantee of internal peace, and they had to correspond to "the law that God has given." The nature of this correspondence can be seen in the following explanation: "Now pay attention. All laws relating to our common neighbor should be grounded in the law of nature. Do unto others as you would have them do unto you, Matthew 7[:12]. Jesus said this even more clearly in Matthew 22[:39-40] 'You shall love your neighbor as yourself.' If there is a law that does not conform to this word of God, it is opposed to God." The natural law and the gospel were thus interrelated, and Zwingli argued that they could ultimately be derived from the same origin: "The law of nature is nothing but the leadership and guidance of God's spirit." Everyone knew from experience, of course, that natural law was not obeyed, that, for example, love of one's neighbor should also imply respect for one's fellow man. Why was this? Because "only the faithful rightly understand the natural law." Christian faith was actually a prerequisite for knowing the natural law; natural law, as part of the order of creation, was an emanation of God's will. But if knowledge of natural law was bound up with knowledge of God, then it followed logically that secular laws and authorities had to be Christian, that is, Protestant. A Christian government was now not just desirable, as Luther thought, but absolutely indispensable. Only when a government took on this Christian character could it follow natural law and fulfill its office as God intended: protecting the good, who don't really need government among themselves; and punishing the wicked, thereby leading them to a knowledge of natural law.

Zwingli would have been no reformer at all had he thought that all the current forms of lordship were basically Christian. And therefore he had to confront the problem of what to do when secular laws did not conform to the natural law as he understood it. His answer was emphatic: "the old laws" needed to be thoroughly checked to see "if they conform to God's law of neighbor and of nature, for they are indeed both laws." This pointed to a possible—indeed, in most cases a necessary—recodification of territorial law. In concrete form this would require the drafting of new ordinances, a process in which the preacher would have a part as the person best qualified to recognize "the leadership and guidance of God's spirit." Zwingli made this point clearly enough: "The most peaceful and God-fearing regime will be found where the word of God is preached most purely." From this he drew the conclusion "that they are nothing but tyrants if they refuse to allow the gospel of Christ to be preached to the people." Thus the office of preacher and the office of magistrate complemented and completed each other. The church was obligated to the state, and the state to the church. It is not surprising, therefore, that when Zwingli discussed the various forms of government, he favored aristocracy in the shape of representative democracy—as was common in the senatorial regimes of Zurich, Bern, Basel, St. Gallen, and

Constance. This preference for a republican model implied a corresponding depreciation of both monarchy and democracy, monarchy because it was always perverted to tyranny, and democracy, perhaps because the rural cantons of central Switzerland rejected Zwingli's Reformation. In short, Zwingli held that constitution to be optimal that merged the ecclesiastical and political communities into one body.

Although there were gaps in this series of arguments and although Zwingli did not construct a perfectly consistent intellectual system, nevertheless if we add up the more important points, we will not fail to draw one striking conclusion. By aiming at a Christianized state, by making natural law normative, in the shape of godly law, and by using the community as his organizing or formal principle for the state, Zwingli created a set of constitutional ideas that were broadly identical with the revolutionary goals of the common man in 1525. Only a few details needed to be specified more clearly to make the agreement perfect. Luther certainly had had no intention of making the legitimacy of a state dependent on its Christian virtue. He left secular ordinances and their historical legal basis as they were. For Müntzer, on the other hand, such secular laws fell out of sight when he concluded that he must prepare for the coming of God. After the breakthrough of the eschaton there would be no more need for worldly laws. It seems evident that here was an affinity between Müntzer's and Zwingli's ideas of a world restored; for if one thinks through Zwingli's political concepts to their conclusion, they too result in the final death of the political order: a Christian government, with the help of preachers, teaches the wicked to be good people; and the good (i.e., the right-believing) had no need of any state.

Zwingli developed his ethics and particularly his ideas of government in his *Sixty-seven Conclusions* and in the *Explanation* of his *Conclusions*. He wrote both works during 1523, before the Second Zurich Disputation of October 1523 at which Christoph Schappeler presided, along with a theologian from St. Gallen and one from Schaffhausen. As a friend of Zwingli's, Schappeler was asked to lead the disputation, and it therefore makes sense to assume that he knew Zwingli's writings and theses. The internal agreement between Zwingli's theory of the state and the revolutionary constitutional ideas of 1525 can thus be explained by the obvious connections between these historical figures. Such conclusions are not entirely astonishing, for they fit well into the broad picture drawn by urban historians, who have shown that the Reformation in southern Germany was inspired much more by Zwingli than by Luther.

In general it can be said that Zwingli was fundamentally oriented to the continuation of this world, that he was not, in other words, so strongly affected by expectations of the end of time as were Müntzer and Luther. This may help us understand Zwingli's vigorous interest in this world and its political order. And for that reason he was useful and interesting to common men whose pragmatism directed them mainly to the concrete changes, the consequences, that flowed from the new religious doctrines. The rebels of 1525, after all, were interested in practical politics from Upper Swabia to Alsace and north to Franconia. The projects sketched by Hubmaier, Gaismair, and Hergot were also intended as practical reforms. Müntzer and the Thuringian rebellion, therefore, were not so much the completion and pinnacle of the Revolution of 1525 as they were just one variation, one possibility, that actually gained a wider footing only after 1525, in the Anabaptist movement.

With these reflections we may hope to have clarified the question of whether the Revolution of 1525 was a mistaken Reformation, whether the peasants falsely understood the central assertions of the Reformation in a "carnal" sense, whether they only wanted to improve their economic and social position under the pretext of the gospel. This interpretation, common ever since the Reformation, assumes that the common man had base and objectionable motives in contrast to the lofty reformers. The only way to keep this interpretation afloat would be to affirm the Lutheran Reformation as the only legitimate Reformation. As soon as one certifies Zwingli and the south German "Christian humanists" as independent reformers—and there can be no doubt of that—then one has to agree that the Revolution of 1525 was an unfolding of the Reformation itself. Just because the reformers could derive their ethics from theological premises and then tell the state how it would have to change is no reason a priori to value their deductive procedure more highly than the thought of peasants. To the contrary. The relatively loose and arbitrary nature of the reformers' arguments is obvious if one considers that from the same theological starting point the dialectical encounter with the real conditions of life could produce completely divergent ethical and political ideas. Although they had begun on the road as companions, by 1525 what did Luther, Zwingli, and Müntzer have in common? At least in their voluminous comments on worldly affairs one searches in vain for common principles.

III

THE CONSEQUENCES
OF THE REVOLUTION:
RESTORATION
AND COOPERATION

Because you behaved so nobly, bravely, and well, and because you helped to restore and maintain the godly, Christian and praiseworthy laws, ordinances, justice, and fairness in Our Holy Roman Empire, and throughout the German Nation, when those laws were attacked and almost abolished, therefore we extend to you our gracious and well deserved thanks.

—Charles V to Georg Truchsess von Waldburg

CHAPTER 10

Efforts at Stabilizing the Empire: The Grievances of the Common Man at the Diet of Speyer, 1526

Every anthology of reports and letters chronicling the massacres of the peasants from Saverne to Frankenhausen, from Leubas to Zell am See, paints such a grim portrait of the vengeful rulers, that the best that could be expected from them was a restoration of the conditions of 1524. Although contemporaries counted the 100,000 dead on the battlefields and gallows, this contrasts queerly with relative nonviolence of the peasantry, except for the killing of the noble garrison at Weinsberg. Burnt-out villages were far more numerous than ruined castles and plundered monasteries. This contrast impressed one contemporary observer, who wrote "that they, the suffering peasants, were torn from the cart harness and are now chained to the singletrees of their wagons." [1] More oppressive servitude—was this the fruit of 1525? [2]

Despite the feudal lords' convincing military victory, the Large Committee established by the Imperial Diet at Speyer in 1526 occupied itself, in obedience to the emperor's directive, with the peasants' grievances. And the committee tried, to the extent that a committee so composed could, to answer the complaints of the subjects. The resulting "Memorial of the Large Committee concerning the Abuses and Burdens of Subjects" was doubtless a product of the more reform-minded estates. Its principal topic was ecclesiastical reform; and it concerned itself only secondarily with grievances of the common man, for at least half its proposals dealt with abuses of ecclesiastical jurisdiction and the cure of souls. The committee's projected reforms to improve the lot of the common man do show that it tried to take into account demands from all parts of the empire, insofar as they were of more than local significance. The Twelve Articles served as the basis of the committee's discussions,[3] but regional complaints, where they were known to members of the committee, seem also to have been considered. The committee's Memorial prefaced its treatment of the Twelve Articles with six points (combining individual points

into larger units) which to some degree correspond to the regional grievances
of subjects in the empire.

The committee recommended that in the future annates no longer be paid
to Rome, as they were overwhelmingly paid by the common man and gave
"cause for rebellion and other forms of disobedience." [4] Consecration taxes
(*Weihsteuer*) (here subsumed under the concept of annates) had indeed been
significant triggers of crisis in many bishoprics and archbishoprics. This had
been true of the dioceses of Salzburg and Basel in the fifteenth century, and
was true of others—Würzburg, Bamberg, Mainz—in the sixteenth. In urging
the abolition of consecration taxes and other dues to Rome without compensation, the committee aimed to relieve the peasants and townsmen, who normally shared the burden of this tax equally.

Being haled before ecclesiastical courts for debt was a widespread object of
peasant grievance, common chiefly on the Upper Rhine during the fifteenth
and sixteenth centuries, above all in the dioceses of Basel, Constance, and
Strasbourg, but also in Salzburg in 1525. The committee aimed to supress this
grievance by proposing to prohibit the appearance of Jews as plaintiffs in
ecclesiastical and secular courts and to prevent the church courts from
punishing civil offenses with excommunication.

Charging parishioners a fee for the administration of the sacraments had
been to varying degrees a cause of resentment in 1525. The committee attributed the evil to the practice of "incorporating" parishes. Incorporation, a
modification of the old proprietary church system, assigned parish incomes
to a chapter, monastery, or hospital, leaving the village pastor only an insufficient salary and more or less forcing him to supplement his income by taking fees for the sacraments. The Committee of the Diet recommended the flat
abolition of such fees for the sacraments and urged that incumbents of incorporated parishes be forced to pay the pastors and curates adequately. The
committee also threw its weight behind the demand, common in 1525, that
the semiclerical stratum be subject to local secular jurisdiction. Against the
custom of some regions that wine growers had to have the tithe-holder's permission before they could begin picking grapes, the committee recommended
that magistrates in such regions fix the time for the grape harvest and thus
assure that wine growers did not have to let their grapes rot on the vines.

To the extent that the Committee of the Diet went beyond these matters[5] to
concern itself with the grievances of the common man, it replied directly to
the Twelve Articles. The committee did not accept the peasants' demand for
the election of pastors but used it instead as an opportunity to grant to the
ecclesiastical and lay princes of the empire any appointments to benefices and
livings formerly reserved to Rome. In doing so it claimed that this would
improve the cure of souls. Rome was chiefly to blame "that many of the
pastors are so ignorant and so uneducated and preach and proclaim God's
word so incompetently that the common man is outraged." The committee
therefore hoped to limit Rome's influence; there was not the slightest inten-

tion, however, of allowing the congregation to take part in the appointment of pastors.[6]

The committee expressed itself much more clearly on the Twelve Articles' economic and social demands. It recommended that the small tithe no longer be imposed where it had not been "paid for as long as anyone could remember." The large tithe, which the peasants wanted, not to abolish, but to employ differently, should continue to be paid in accordance with the law and good custom. The committee's Memorial did not approve the demand for the abolition of serfdom, to be sure, but it did recommend an immediate halt to all further restrictions on liberty and freedom of movement, and recommended that the diet debate whether subjects should not be able to purchase manumission. The estates also recognized the economic burdens of serfdom. Death taxes could threaten a peasant's very existence if—and this was the committee's motive for proposing changes—the lord simultaneously collected a transfer fine. As concrete measures the committee's Memorial proposed the abolition of the death tax or the reduction of death taxes and transfer fines; but in view of the great differences from region to region in servile dues and transfer fines, the committee left the work of providing appropriate decrees to the "circles," thus considerably expanding the powers of these imperial administrative districts.* To the extent that compulsory labor was part of the lord's dues, the Committee's memorial agreed with the Twelve Articles' demand that this exaction should be voluntarily abolished if it was less than one generation old; and during harvest time the lords should demand servile labor services as little as possible.

Where the Twelve Articles had registered complaints against landlordship, the committee advised that the following peasant demands be satisfied: transfer fines should no longer be collected at the death of the lord; and dues in money and in kind should be lowered, "so that farms may yield more." More detailed provisions specified that transfer fines should be collected only on the death of the tenant (and not on the lord's death) and be limited to 3.3 to 5 percent of the farm's assessed worth. In return, annual rents were to be raised slightly, or the dues would be fixed at the customary level, but a transfer fine of 15 to 20 percent might be collected at the tenant's (not the lord's) death.[7]

The committee also spoke unequivocally to the problem of common fields and forests. The fishing waters, woodlots, pastures, and fields, which the rulers had appropriated for game parks or other purposes, had to be restored to the villages; the burden of proof, however, was to lie, not on the lords, as the Twelve Articles had it, but on the villages. The authorities were also to retain powers of control over the commons, chiefly to protect the forests

---

*Six imperial circles had been established in 1500 and expanded to ten in 1512. Originally little more than electoral districts, they became administrative and military districts of some importance in the course of the sixteenth and seventeenth centuries.

against reckless exploitation, whereas the Twelve Articles had wanted the commons controlled by elected village officials. To meet the complaints of crop damages by wild game, the committee proposed to reduce game populations, to permit the peasants to fence their fields and to keep dogs, or to compensate them for damages through reductions in rents and dues.

Finally, the committee's Memorial dealt with the administration of justice by proposing improvements that were much more concretely framed than those in the grievances of the Upper Swabian peasants. No one should be barred from resorting to the courts, the hierarchy of appeals courts should be maintained, which meant that local and village courts were not to be bypassed,[8] and punishments should be reduced.

Referring to the bewildering variety of legal customs in the empire, which made it impossible to draft a set of norms valid in all territories for the relations between subjects and lords, the Large Committee did not propose legislation but rested content with urgent appeals that the lords should treat their subjects in a manner consonant with their "consciences," the "law of God and of nature," and "fairness." To assure greater protection for the peasants from their governments, the committee's Memorial proposed that, in disputes between peasants and mediate territorial nobles and monasteries, the prince's prerogative court of his territorial court should have ordinary jurisdiction; in disputes between subjects and lords with free imperial status, however, the Imperial Chamber Court or the Governing Council would have jurisdiction.

Very little of the material in these proposals found its way into the final edict of the diet. Beyond a few bland formulae recommending that the lords make conciliatory gestures, the diet did nothing. The Swabian League did try repeatedly to promote a more lasting commitment to the proposals of the recess, strongly urging its members to follow the document's guidelines. The Imperial Diet, however, was chiefly interested in finding ways to suppress future revolt and not in eliminating the causes. More positive changes were probably unattainable, because imperial edicts were products of compromise. Nonetheless, the Large Committee's Memorial at the Diet of Speyer shows that the causes of the Revolution of 1525 had been clearly recognized. The proposals aimed at providing at least some relief for the common man and a greater general security of rights. The remedies proposed by the imperial estates were remarkable enough, in that if they had been realized by 1524, the revolution could have been avoided. Its fleeting references to godly and natural law, to fairness, to ancient tradition, and to fair wages placed the committee on the side of a juster social order, but the Committee of the Diet could do nothing more than recommend. Whether and to what degree the proposals became reality lay in the hands of the imperial estates.

Regardless of the incontestable freedom and autonomy of the separate imperial estates, we should not overlook the fact that the vote of the Committee of the Diet and the recommendations of the diet itself marked out a normative framework, no matter how vague, for the resolution of differences between peasants and their lords. The most lasting effect was the attempt to transfer conflicts to the arena of judicial compromise. The governments of the territorial states waged a campaign in the following decades and centuries "to entangle subjects in a complex administrative and legal system, thereby cutting off rebellion at the root, making it impossible as the last resort of social behavior." [9] But this did not fully succeed, as the numerous revolts throughout the empire in the seventeenth and eighteenth centuries make plain.

CHAPTER 11

Resolution of Conflict
in the States
of the Empire

The Large Committee's Memorial at Speyer in 1526 outlined the possibilities for resolution of the conflict. Changes in social and political structures were now out of the question, and the most that might be achieved were reductions of economic burdens, the easing of social tensions, and modest fulfillment of political expectations. The revolution had been thrown back to its starting point: the apathy or stubbornness of the common man and the euphoria of victory or readiness to compromise of the rulers would together decide whether the future would see a total restoration of the status quo or a new cooperation to solve or at least limit conflicts.[1]

THE CITY-STATE

Internal stability was relatively easy to restore in the city-states. In the imperial cities, the quarrel between regime and citizenry generally lost its supraregional significance through the military defeat of the peasants, although some towns had already had order restored by the brutal military action of the Swabian League, which drove insurrectionary elements out of the cities. Stability could easily be restored in the urban territory because the peasant grievances were more restricted here than in other territories, and because the urban regimes themselves recognized the failings of the status quo. Caspar Nützel of Nuremberg made this point, for example, in a letter to Duke Albrecht of Prussia: "The poor, blind, stupid peasants have kicked too hard at the traces in this incompetent rebellion," to be sure, but "no reasonable person can deny that the rulers have improperly, unchristianly, and excessively pulled the hair of the very subjects whom they ought to care for, supervise, rule, and not fleece."[2] The more important city-states, such as Nuremberg, Zurich, Basel, and Memmingen, were even prepared to make significant concessions to their subjects; and where they were not willing, as at Heilbronn, Rothenburg, and Strasbourg, a neighboring imperial estate bent on full restoration was usually to blame.

The cities seem to have been relatively accommodating to the demands their peasants presented to them, as witness the examples of Basel and Memmingen. Even Erasmus of Rotterdam noticed that the cities reacted more reasonably to the challenge of the peasants than did the princes. At Basel during May and June 1525, charters of liberties were drawn up for the districts of Liestal, Waldenburg, Farnsburg, Homburg, Münchenstein, and Muttenz. These acts responded precisely to the districts' grievances by liquidating serfdom, abolishing the small tithe, reducing servile labor obligations and indirect taxes, conceding partial hunting rights, and improving logging rights. Between March 10 and April 3, 1532, however, the communes sent delegates to Basel and gave back their charters—"voluntarily," as the city's regime emphasized. We do not know why the peasants took this step or to what extent political pressure from the urban regime motivated it. Of the concessions made in 1525, the peasants by 1532 had salvaged only their freedom from boundary tithes, freedom of marriage within the urban territory, and the reduction of servile labor obligations.

The city of Memmingen had replied quite positively to its peasants' grievance list, which was nearly identical with the Twelve Articles, and had reserved only the article on the tithe for negotiation with the Swabian League. The abolition of serfdom was not revoked after 1525,[3] and peasants manifestly retained the freedom to hunt and fish; during the sixteenth and seventeenth centuries, moreover, the landlords' dues were not raised again. The peasants did not, however, take advantage of the regime's offer to abolish entry fines if heritable and life tenancies were converted into annual tenancies. Survival took priority over financial relief.

The Memmingen example brings us back to the question of the causes of the revolution. The reaction to Memmingen's regime shows that the causes of unrest could be ameliorated. It was indeed possible to reduce the economic burden on the peasants—in this sense the Peasants' War succeeded at least in some places. But these urban regimes also rejected any far-reaching change in social and political structures, which meant that in a broader sense the revolution failed miserably. On the other hand, throughout Memmingen's hinterland the wide range of village authority and self-government was preserved undiminished during succeeding years and centuries. Here there was no political disfranchisement of the peasantry. The general significance of the Memmingen data nevertheless remains to be demonstrated.

THE PETTY STATE

The concept of the petty state helps us to set those areas apart where free imperial status was the rule and where structures remained more feudal—the

Upper Rhine, Upper Swabia, and Franconia—in contrast to the early modern state with its constitutional dualism of prince and estates. Bridging the chasm between lords and peasants was much harder for the petty states than it was for the imperial cities. For the prelates and nobles, there were memories of their humiliating flight to the imperial cities, their forced alliances with the rebels, and the destruction of their castles and monasteries. For the peasants, there was the brutal behavior of the mercenary armies of Lorraine and the Swabian League, along with the false assurances from the League, from Archduke Ferdinand, and indeed from all the lords. These strains on both sides made even a minimal consensus between rulers and ruled difficult to restore.

Taking first the area where the Twelve Articles originated, one notes a strange contrast between the peasants' moderate behavior in the Upper Swabian regions of revolt and the Swabian League's harsh measures of repression. Here and there, to be sure, a crippling lethargy spread through the peasantry. In many territories, however, the peasants held out stubbornly and continued to refuse dues, taxes, and labor services. They had no intention of adding a political defeat to their military one. "They're just as bad as they ever were," complained the abbot of Schussenried about his peasants; "they let me yell and give me nothing." [4]

The feudal ruling class simply could not ruthlessly restore the pre-1525 forms of domination. When Georg Truchsess von Waldburg—called "Peasant George" and celebrated by King Ferdinand as the military hero of the Swabian League—was filling vacancies in his territorial courts in early 1526, he used the occasion to ask his subjects to submit their grievances to him. Interestingly enough, their grievance list was based on the Twelve Articles; although they did not explicitly demand the abolition of serfdom, they did place serfdom at the head of their list. The peasants asked for a restructuring of relations "according to the laws of God and the emperor." [5] Labor dues should be reduced (in accordance with ancient tradition) to the level which had been customary in the fifteenth century; the tithe—meaning chiefly the small tithe—should be reassessed if not abolished;[6] streams and rivers should be restored to the villages, unless they were leased; there should be free access to the woodlots for isolated farms; lumbering quotas should be increased; there should be limited hunting rights; and recently issued laws should either be abolished or limited in their application. Except for the demand that consumption taxes and the fees for the preparation of leases be lowered, the grievances drew their entire content and part of their argument from the Twelve Articles.

The issue of serfdom, which the Waldburg peasants put at the head of their list and which had been the central demand in the Upper Swabian rebellion, was the first to be dealt with. The traditional form of death tax, requiring a man to pay his best horse and best garment and a woman to pay her best cow and best garment, was commuted to a cash payment graduated according to ability to pay.[7] With this commutation of the servile death tax into a "property tax," serfdom lost its socially demeaning character because no mark of serfdom as such remained. The marriage payment and the ban on marriage outside the lord's jurisdiction were abolished with one exception—that if a man married a serf from elsewhere and continued to live in Waldburg territory, he was obliged to see that she became a Waldburg serf within one year, or else leave the territory. The dissolution of the bond of serfdom was nonetheless affirmed in principle in writing, and manumission was to be available for a relatively small fee. This act gave the Waldburg peasants both the possibility of free movement and the possiblity of living in the Waldburg lands as free men and women.[8]

While the Waldburg concessions concerning serfdom had no time limit, those concerning service obligations and other grievances were limited to ten years, but they were renewed often, some even until well into the eighteenth century. Labor dues were commuted to money payments, based on the ability to pay (or better, on the capacity of the individual farm to produce for the lord). Neither abolished nor commuted, however, were servile hunting services and forced labor on the lord's castles. The harsher special ordinances for the lordship of Wolfegg, specifying the retention of one day's labor each for lumbering, hauling fish, and harvesting grain, clearly survived to meet the household needs of the Truchsess von Waldburg family.

The Waldburgs ruled the largest territory in Upper Swabia, and thus the issues of serfdom and services were fairly satisfactorily resolved for a considerable part of the Upper Swabian peasantry. And it is just this Waldburg settlement which forbids us to speak of the Peasants' War as a total failure. And it was even less so, when we notice that the peasants in the ecclesiastical territories also achieved very positive results.[9] The county of Kempten represents just such a solution.

Meeting in Memmingen in January of 1526 the Swabian League arbitrated a dispute in which the Kempten serfs and tenants forced the prince-abbot to accept a settlement of the grievances they had stubbornly advanced since 1492. The central grievance was serfdom. The peasants wanted to be rid of the prohibition of marriage between serfs and free tenants, and to stop the legal dispossession of free tenants through extorted liens, the deterioration of their inheritance rights, and the increases in taxes and military levies. This Treaty of Memmingen, which endured until the territory was secularized in 1806, granted unrestricted marriage rights between serfs and free tenants, whose children would share according to the old Swabian law the status of the mother and not (as had been the recent practice) that of the less free parent. The treaty stabilized the legal position of individual groups of subjects, because free tenants could no longer be pressed into serfdom. There was also a decided improvement in inheritance rights, or more precisely a reduction of the economic consequences of serfdom and tenancy: the death tax paid by serfs was reduced from one-half the inheritance to a modest cash payment based on the property's value; [10] the payment of the best animal was commuted to cash at 75 percent of the payment in kind; and the exit fine was lowered from 33 percent to 10 percent of the personal property removed from the territory. Finally, the tax burden was fixed at 0.5 percent of the self-assessed sworn value of the property. But serfdom was not abolished. This was a demand that the Kempten peasants had voiced along with the other Allgäu peasants only after they were swept up in the wave of revolutionary events in 1525. Their demands in 1526 coincided neatly with the (still undeveloped) demands they had expressed in January 1525. The economic, social, and legal implications of serfdom were nonetheless so thoroughly ameliorated that we may say that the Treaty of Memmingen fully satisfied the demands of the Kempten peasants. [11]

We cannot generalize on the basis of these cases, which cover barely half the area of Upper Swabia, for they need to be confirmed by other detailed analyses. A general survey does permit us to affirm, however, that Upper Swabia did not experience a worsening of economic conditions, an aggravation of internal village conflicts, or the loss of peasant political rights after 1525. The peasant's economic position improved, in fact, because of the quickening agricultural market during the sixteenth century; internal conflicts lost their edge through greater rights to free movement that flowed from general acceptance of territorial control over serfs; and communal rights were retained, so that in the seventeenth century the peasants still handled all cases except capital crimes "in their rude, half-witted peasant court." [12]

On the Upper Rhine, too, some areas reached settlements which were positive for the peasants. In the lordships of Rötteln-Sausenberg and Badenweiler, a compromise was reached on the basis of the Twelve Articles, mediated by the cities of Strasbourg, Basel, Offenburg, and Breisach. This treaty remained in force for centuries and became a part of the agrarian order and political constitution of Markgräflerland. [13] The installation of pastors was still reserved for the lay patron, but now candidates had to be "pleasing and acceptable to the subjects and parishioners." Subjects' complaints could now lead to the pastor's deposition; and the appointment of a new one was to be decided "by the patron in consultation with the subjects and parishioners." [14] The pastors were now obliged to reside in their parishes and could appoint vicars or chaplains only when the pastors themselves were ill. Monks could no longer be pastors. The small tithe was abolished, [15] though holders of impropriated small tithes could get compensation if they could prove their purchase. The large tithe was now to supply the pastor's needs, thereby placing this burden on the titheholders. Out of respect for conditions in neighboring territories, a nominal serfdom remained; but for the margrave's subjects it was so weakened through the abolition of marriage restrictions and the death tax that it could scarcely be considered a burden. Only a restriction on freedom of movement remained as a memento of serfdom after 1525.

The peasants received the unlimited right to hunt damaging game, such as bears, wolves, and foxes; and they could hunt hares, too, as well as stags, deer, and boar on their own properties. The brooks and other waters were to be restored to the villages from which they had been taken.

Servile obligations newly introduced "within the memory of man" were abolished, new servile labor dues were prohibited, and the lord's obligations in return for customary services were fixed. Tenants had their duties set also: "Before they work for others, subjects must work for their ruler and lord if requested, in exchange for a decent wage."

Tenants still had to pay rents at the customary levels, but they were to be reduced in cases of damages to the property on the basis of amicable agreement between peasant and landlord, or "according to the decision of upright people named by both sides." The so-called perpetual rents, paid by the tenants as a result of capital loans, were declared redeemable. The entry fine, paid in kind in the Markgräflerland, was commuted to cash and became only a symbolic transfer fine, as it was levied at only 0.5 percent of the property's value.[16]

Concerning the administration of justice, the treaty provided that "subjects shall retain the old penalties, as in times past, and justice shall be done at all times according to the legal judgment of the court (using impartial jurors) and uninfluenced by envy, hatred, or favoritism." The treaty also expressly confirmed the courts' creative role in interpreting the law and limited the use of jail to felony cases of high justice.

The settlement for the Markgräflerland thus fulfilled what the Twelve Articles demanded and, in so doing, removed the causes of the rebellion. Only the formal abolition of serfdom and the expansion of communal rights remained unachieved, but these were demands which went well beyond the local grievances. The Treaty of Renchen provided the same settlement (with a few minor changes) for the subjects of Margrave Philip of Baden, the bishop of Strasbourg, the counts of Zweibrücken, Fürstenberg, and Hanau-Lichtenberg, and several nobles and towns in Ortenau. An analysis of it would simply repeat what has already been said. Some have questioned the binding force of this treaty, but it should be noted that the Imperial Aulic Council heard a suit requesting enforcement of the treaty as late as the eighteenth century. This fact speaks for the continued significance of the treaty's provisions long after 1525 and against the thesis that it became a dead letter.

A glance at Switzerland will round out this picture. In Zurich and Bern serfdom was abolished outright. In St. Gallen, though serfdom could not be eliminated, there were slight improvements in the legal administration, a modest tax reduction, and, for some villages, the right to elect their own village headmen. Otherwise, the abbot's rights were confirmed on the basis of ancient tradition. One point deserves special attention, however: by cantonal decision St. Gallen's territorial constitution, then some fifty years old, was considerably expanded and given true "constitutional" character through the decision that all innovations would require the consent of each of the canton's four districts. This meant a partial check on the prince-abbot's sovereign power, assuring the perpetuation of the older customary laws in the form of *Weistümer,* * and offering the peasants some opportunities for political influence; disputes between the monastery and the subjects now had to be settled by the canton's four districts.

We should not overgeneralize on the basis of such treaty agreements even if we do find that satisfactory settlements were achieved in other regions; the petty states of Franconia and Thuringia hardly ever came to such compromises at all.[17] These examples of real solutions in the petty states do show, however, that pre-1525 conditions were not restored everywhere. Indeed, it was found possible to grant some relief to the peasants, just as the original grievances had intended.

THE LARGE STATE

The large state, or more exactly, "the state ruled by prince and estates," possessed in its territorial diet an instrument by which many internal conflicts had already been resolved. Territorial estates flew into action everywhere in 1525—as in Nearer Austria, Würzburg, Ansbach, Salzburg, Württemberg, and Tyrol—proof that the lords believed that the diets were a tested means of stopping the revolt through negotiations and of pulling its fangs with compromises if necessary. The diet could play this role only under two conditions: if the revolt remained confined within the territory, and if the diet retained enough credibility to be trusted by the common man. Such conditions were met only in Tyrol and Salzburg, where the moderate wing of the rebellion sent deputies to the diets. In Franconia the supraterritorial character of the peasant armies wrecked the negotiations with territorial diets; in Württemberg the diet had expended its last ounce of credibility during the "Poor Conrad" rebellion of 1514; and in Nearer Austria the common man immediately ceased to trust the territorial diet when the nobles, prelates, and towns vigorously supported the prince's interest and decided against the city of Waldshut and Balthasar Hubmaier.

In Tyrol the diet opened in June 1525. It was thoroughly dominated by the representatives of the rural and town districts, who were able to exclude the prelates and thereby secure a majority against the nobles. Then, against Archduke Ferdinand's resistance, they pushed through consideration of a grievance list of some 100 articles—the Merano articles expanded by additions from Innsbruck. The product of these tough negotiations was the first great Tyrolean constitution, which appeared in printed form in 1526. The

---

*A *Weistum* was a response from local authorities concerning what the local customary law was in specific cases.

constitution was admittedly a compromise. It was forged against a background of distant summer lightning from the bloody battles in Franconia and nearby Allgäu; and Ferdinand, from his position of tremendous authority, could resolutely reject all radical demands without seriously threatening the diet itself. And so revolutionary demands were buried, article by article, under an avalanche of proposals, counterproposals, and counter-counterproposals. In short, the revolutionary program outlined in the Merano articles, providing as it did for the political disfranchisement of prelates and nobles and for the economic destruction of bishoprics and monasteries, could not be realized. Such a Tyrolean constitution could have spelled the death of the Holy Roman Empire, had the imperial statthalter (Ferdinand) secularized the bishopric of Trent, expropriated the bishop of Freising, and dispossessed the nobility—as the radicals demanded.

The Tyrolean constitution did answer some of the demands of the Merano-Innsbruck articles, giving in either wholly (30 articles) or partly (19 articles) to the common man. Indeed, the Constitution of 1526 was indebted to the grievance lists right down to its wording; the ruling authorities left no mark on the content but succeeded only in introducing some systematic order.

The peasant economy secured considerable relief in Tyrol through the improvement of property rights, the transformation of a 10 percent transfer fee into a larger symbolic "recognition" fee, abolition of servile labor dues that were not demonstrably at least fifty years old, and eradication of certain kinds of tithes. Certain forms of rents were declared redeemable; servile labor services during the wine harvest were forbidden; and extensive fishing rights were granted along with limited hunting rights. Economic relief for the peasants and townsmen—or at least for underprivileged townsmen—weakened the guilds and meant stronger controls on pedlars and merchant companies. The former were forbidden to do business except at fairs and markets, while the latter lost their autonomous jurisdiction and were subjected to price controls. Export and import controls were designed to make food cheaper.

The Tyrolean constitution also provided for an improved administration of justice through simplification of the hierarchy of appeals courts, establishment of state salaries for judges, abolition of special legal immunity for princely officials and noble servants, and restriction of rights of sanctuary for criminals.

Even if this list is not complete, at least it allows no doubt that the year 1525 brought significant improvements for the common man in Tyrol. All the positive aspects of the constitution outlined here were already to be found in the Merano-Innsbruck articles. The natural suspicion that the territorial Constitution of 1526 was nothing more than an ephemeral success, especially since a second Constitution of 1532 explicitly nullified its predecessor, can be shown to be unfounded by comparing the two constitutions. Of seventy-one articles in the 1526 constitution fifty were taken over by the Constitution of

1532 essentially unchanged; fifteen were accepted with greater or lesser modifications; only six were omitted altogether. Admittedly, the towns and districts could not retain all of the gains of 1526, but in general the changes were not important ones. The proof of this does not need to be derived from a minute and exhaustive analysis of the modified articles; rather, it is provided by the behavior of Ferdinand himself. When the committee of the diet and his own councillors laid the draft of the 1532 constitution before him, he hesitated to ratify it. In 1533 he considered cancelling the constitution, but he decided against it because 200 copies had already been printed and sold. The regime even encouraged the districts of Kufstein, Rattenberg, and Kitzbühl to retain their old Bavarian law because it provided more income to the prince than the new constitution did. The regime also forbade the Habsburg lands of Vorarlberg and Nearer Austria, which had no territorial constitutions, to introduce the new Tyrolean one as supplementary law in difficult cases. The Innsbruck regime considered it a special privilege whenever it allowed even a partial introduction of the 1532 constitution into other Habsburg lands. The Habsburg province of Swabia, for example, "bought" the criminal provisions of the Tyrolean constitution by accepting an excise tax.

In the landgraviate of Hesse, which was barely touched by the insurrection, the parallels with Tyrol are astonishing. After the rebellion was crushed on the battlefield, the grievances of town and country were collected and either resolved directly or taken care of in an ordinance of 1526. It is expecially noteworthy that "shortly after the Peasants' War" Landgrave Philipp joined with his "subjects" in a treaty which is unfortunately no longer extant.[18] We do know, however, that this treaty obviously protected the peasants from heavier burdens (placed on them by the nobility) and brought to a standstill the wave of increased oppression that was sweeping the empire.

The outcome in the archbishopric of Salzburg was also comparable to that in Tyrol, though here the settlement of internal conflicts was powerfully influenced and disrupted by Bavarian and Austrian hopes of secularizing the territory. The humiliations experienced by the archbishop at the hands of the Bavarians, the Habsburgs, the Swabian League, and the rebels did not improve his willingness to negotiate. In the summer of 1525 a military stand-off between the rebels and the League troops in Salzburg led to a truce in which the differences between the archbishop and his subjects were to be settled through a territorial constitution. In October 1525, the Salzburg grievances were dealt with for the first time at a special diet of the towns, market villages, rural communes, and mining communes, where some were remedied and recorded in an edict of the territorial diet. Most of the grievances were supposed to be answered in a territorial constitution to be considered at the next diet, which met in March 1526. Although a committee to draft a constitution was established, by November (the time for the next diet) it had still not reached agreement with the archiepiscopal councillors on all points. The estates then decided to publish the results of the current negotiations in the form of an archiepiscopal decree instead of a constitution. For decades this edict took the place of a Salzburg constitution.

The territorial diet's edict of October 30, 1525, and the decree of November 20, 1526, allow us to measure the consequences of the revolution in Salzburg. The clergy were forbidden to charge fees for administering the sacraments; on other religious matters the diet awaited decisions by the imperial diet or a general council. Economic improvements were modest, at least compared with those in Tyrol: a fixed schedule of dues replaced the arbitrarily imposed dues and fees; perpetual rents were reduced; the excise tax was abolished; and prices of foodstuffs were subjected to strict supervision by the state. The peasant, however, had to go to court to defend himself against unjust demands, and he bore the burden of proof if his rights were infringed by his lord. The peasant was thus isolated. Improvements in judicial administration were doubtless even more important than those in the economic sphere. They curbed the district officer's interventions in the jurisdiction of the rural communes, sorted out the overlapping claims of different kinds of courts, restored the hierarchy of appeals courts, fixed the payment of court officials, and relieved the district communes of some costs.

The Salzburgers tended to emphasize ancient tradition and were therefore more strongly concerned for restoration than the Tyroleans were, though here, too, it was admittedly left to the common man to make of these edicts what he could. The 1525 edict of the territorial diet and the archbishop's decree of 1526 repeatedly urged him to complain to the prince against the arbitrary actions of wardens, judges, and landlords, and even to defend his just claims against the prince himself by appealing to the privy council. Between the poles of success or failure for the Revolution of 1525 Salzburg thus achieved a balance that should probably be seen as favorable to the peasants.

Graubünden provides an example of especially deep structural changes in the wake of the Revolution of 1525.* Although their constitution was unique, it more resembled that of the prince-and-estates form than it did the traditional, patrimonial petty state, and thus Graubünden can be considered here. Building upon massive pressure from the rebellious subjects of the bishop of Chur, the League of Ten Jurisdictions, the Gray League, and the League of God's House approved the Ilanz articles of 1526, which called for a reduction in tithes and rents and for the removal of the bishop and all other clergy from governmental positions. The legal basis for this demand was slight indeed, both because the bishop and the cathedral chapter had been excluded from the deliberations and because the usual ratification by the districts did not take place. According to the constitution of the Rhaetian leagues such documents as the Ilanz articles required the bishop's seal for full legality

*Graubünden (the Grisons) was a federation of three alpine leagues (the League of God's House, the Gray League, and the League of Ten Jurisdictions) composed of communes and feudal lords and associated with the Swiss Confederation since 1496.

because the bishop was both head of the League of God's House and one of the heads of the Gray League. Naturally, neither the bishop nor the chapter recognized the articles, but they could not prevent severe damage to and restrictions on episcopal authority. After the Peasants' War, for example, the bishop's court lost its role as highest appellate court. From 1526 on, the Upper Engadine independently elected its chief magistrate without any governmental interference; and everywhere villages and towns took over primary jurisdiction, relinquishing it again to the prince-bishop only when they discovered that the costs of judicial administration were higher than its revenues. In 1537 came the Engadine's abandonment of the old religion and the dissolution of the monasteries in the city of Chur. The League of God's House, worried by the existence of a legitimate bishop living in exile and by the cathedral chapter's refusal to surrender its political rights, strove for a permanent, legally safe-guarded relationship between regime and subjects. Thus in 1537/38 the bishopric's rights to govern were sold off for ridiculously low compensation: the subjects in Greifenstein bought their freedom from episcopal power for 2,300 gulden, and those of the Puschlav, for 1,200 gulden; and the districts of Lugnez, Ilanz, Grub, and Flims followed suit. Episcopal rule was thereby reduced to a shadow of its former self. In 1541 it was with perfect safety that the League of God's House agreed to the election of a Catholic successor to the exiled Bishop Ziegler. The League's peasants—and not the cathedral chapter—dictated the terms he had to swear before taking office. The new bishop had to confirm the unalterability of all existing political and ecclesiastical relationships and to approve retroactively the recent sales of episcopal rights. Although most of the sovereign powers of a territorial prince had been destroyed, a vestige did remain because, after the bishop and chapter had sworn to the election agreement, the League's peasants generously granted them the right to sit and vote once more in the assemblies of the League of God's House. The humanist Fabricius was right when he asserted: "There is no other republic in the world today like ours in Rhaetia." [19]

The alpine regions' post-1525 gains in the administration of justice, economic stability, and communal and regional autonomy apparently had no parallels in Franconia and Thuringia. The rulers there did nonetheless try to bring some lasting relief to their tense relations with their subjects. If we take just one example—the developments in the Rheingau after 1525—it is clear that the peasants' total defeat at the hands of the Swabian League and the consequent suspension of all rights were not permanent. [20] The territorial ordinance of 1527, secured from the elector of Mainz through an embassy from the Rheingau, altered the pre-1525 situation only in doing away with the election of local councillors in favor of cooptation with princely approval and in making mayors more responsible to the electoral viceregent. The suspension of rights declared by the Swabian League was formally lifted in 1545.

CHAPTER 12

Results of Revolution:
The Territorial Constitution

In July 1526, exactly one year after the last battle in Upper Swabia, the peasants of Weissenau appeared before their abbot and demanded that he negotiate a contract; otherwise they would "pay him neither rent, fine, nor fee, nor would they perform any labor service." "Because of this," moaned the prelate to the abbot of Weingarten, "we are once more considering calling together all the serfs to tell them that we are willing to negotiate their grievances. This is our will." [1] Such negotiations, whatever they might do to satisfy grievances, were politically explosive if they resulted in a contract, because the ruler's political counterpart was no longer the village commune but the entire body of subjects—a territorial assembly (*Landschaft*). Negotiating a contract did more than just promote associative meetings at the territorial level; it institutionalized such meetings in the form of the territorial assembly, which, as a legal corporation, could go to court to enforce such contracts if necessary.

Kempten supplies empirical verification for the thesis that the territorial assembly, the political corporation of all subjects, was the child of the Revolution of 1525. Two copies of the Treaty of Memmingen (1526) were sealed and distributed to the abbot and to his subjects, the assembly. The territorial assembly's vigilance and precautions carefully preserved this document, which served to protect the Kempteners' hard-won rights of 1525–26 in countless seventeenth- and eighteenth-century suits. The assembly's participation in the assessment and collection of taxes, a concession wrung from the abbey in 1526, became the stimulus for a continuous institutional strengthening of the corporation of subjects. In the early nineteenth century a Bavarian government official could regard the assembly's powers as covering "not only collection of taxes, revision of their apportionment, and conservation of the tax base, but also legislation, public finance, and even the constitution of government." [2]

Kempten was by no means the last standard-bearer of a lost cause. To the lords' military *touché*, the Kempteners answered with a political *en garde*. Territorial assemblies of the Kempten type survived in many other Upper Swabian territories, as in Ochsenhausen, Schussenried, the prince-bishopric of Augsburg, and the Habsburg province of Swabia. Others developed during the seventeenth century, as in the territories of the imperial city of Rottweil and the abbey of Rottenmünster.

Moreover, Upper Swabia was not a lonely island of peasant political rights in a sea of subjection and arbitrary princely authority. The Markgräflerland preserved its assembly-constitution and even expanded it decisively during the seventeenth century, when no taxation was permissible without the assembly's consent, and no new laws could be put into effect without its consultation. In Graubünden, communal autonomy survived; and the League of God's House preserved its new political rights intact. The Tyrolean peasants continued to sit in the territorial diet and on its committees, which voted and administered taxes, drafted territorial laws, and issued military regulations. In Salzburg, representatives of the rural districts sat in the territorial diet, though not continuously, at least into the second half of the sixteenth century. New territorial corporations even emerged after 1525, as in the Markgräflerland of Baden and the prince-bishopric of Basel.

The corporately constituted state of the sixteenth to the eighteenth century realized in weakened form one of the demands of 1525: that the common man ought to be part of the territorial estates alongside the nobles, the clergy, and the towns. Wherever this cause won out, we cannot say that there the lords crowned their military conquest with political victory. In states with a constitutional assembly of estates—which at least during the sixteenth century, meant throughout the southern parts of the empire—princely authority did not amount to much. The prince in his governance was still bound to the active consent of the common man. Only later, during the formation of the absolute state, did the prince succeed in freeing himself from that consent. The process of perfecting the territorial state then moved in patterns which expelled the common man from public life, sometimes in the seventeenth century, sometimes in the eighteenth; but in many places—especially in the quietistic, archaic small states of the German southwest—this was never the case. The evidence for Upper Germany thus refutes the thesis that the lost Revolution of 1525 was linked causally to the structure of the absolute state; and it is doubtful that this thesis is valid for any part of the entire area of the revolution.

CHAPTER 13

The State Seizure of the Communal Reformation

Since it was the Reformation that gave revolutionary force to the rebellion of 1525, the Reformation itself could hardly remain unaffected by the peasants' military defeat. The most noticeable effect was a new concern for religious discipline on the part of the rulers. In the imperial abbey of Buxheim, a Carthusian house near Memmingen, for example, the abbot issued a new fundamental law in 1553. Its introduction stressed new rules about religion, laying various fines on those who stayed away from mass or left church before it was over, gossiped during mass, made fun of the pastor, violated the laws governing fasting, or refused Communion. The rules themselves were a direct response to the peasants' neglect of religion, or at least of the church, and were not just commonplaces which crept more or less unintentionally into the territorial constitution. This is clear from the disproportionately high fines imposed: tithe refusal, for example, was punishable by ten gulden, the price of two or three cows.

The many new constitutions and police ordinances issued after 1525 confirm this impression, for they devote much attention to religion. Many foreshadow the Buxheim ordinance and reveal a general lack of popular interest in religion. These and similar sources support the view that after 1525 peasant attitudes towards "the Reformation were indifferent, if not hostile." [1] Though often attacked, this hypothesis has never been convincingly refuted. [2] Instead it has recently received support from the ranks of ecclesiastical historians, one of whom writes: "Not only were the peasant revolts lost, but also the entire Reformation as a joint enterprise of laymen and clergy." [3] At first glance, the strongest remaining argument against the thesis that 1525 marked the end of the "people's Reformation" would seem to be the communal character of the reform movements in the north German cities. [4] This, however, is a weak argument, because these movements had no geographical links with the main areas of revolution, nor did they affect the peasantry.

183

The thesis of 1525 as the turning point in the history of the Reformation thus remains a fascinating notion, not least because it has so stoutly resisted all the strenuous efforts to refute it. In itself, of course, the thesis is not terribly original, nor is it now seriously disputed. In fact, the Marxist idea that with 1525 the "people's Reformation" became a "princes' Reformation" parallels the idea of Western historians that 1525 divides "the period of the 'Reformation movement' from the era of 'Protestantism.' " [5] Thomas Müntzer expressed a similar idea in his *Apology and Answer to the Spiritless, Soft-Living Flesh at Wittenberg;* Luther and his movement, Müntzer claimed, had openly become tools of the princes. We therefore need to ask whether 1525 really marks the transformation of the German Reformation into a movement controlled and shaped by the state.

One case which bears on this question is that of Lower Alsace, where the various imperial estates came to an agreement at Hagenau after the peasants had been crushed. Its ninth article touched the religious question:

> Concerning the preachers and parishes in the diocese of Strasbourg, every ruler ought to take care to see that the parishes are supplied with pious, honorable priests who preach only the holy gospel and the epistles clearly and without human additions, and who admonish subjects to act with brotherly love, to uphold the honor of God, and to obey the secular ruler. Priests should all receive an adequate living either from the tithe or from another source; and the ruler should dismiss anyone who misbehaves.[6]

By means of this stipulation, later overruled, the regime of Strasbourg sought both to protect the new doctrine legally and to calm the peasants, but the article also shows just what function would be expected of the gospel in the future: to promote brotherly love, the honor of God, "and obedience to secular authority." [7] Corresponding to this change, the sources now say nothing of the community's right to elect the pastor, who was to be appointed and dismissed by the ruler. The ruler, too, and not the community, now decided what was right doctrine. This example does support the generalization that "the Peasant's War paved the way from the vital communal Christianity of early Lutheranism, whose most characteristic expression was the demand for the free election of pastors, to the inflexibility of the established territorial church." [8] Be that as it may, under the impact of the Revolution of 1525 Luther, Melanchthon, Brenz, and others called for new church regulations to be issued and enforced by the lay rulers. This demonstrable "turn towards a rulers' Reformation" entailed a "politicization" of the Reformation.[9] The first glimmering of this development appeared at the Imperial Diet of Speyer in 1526 in the conscientious objection to enforcing the Edict of Worms; it grew stronger in the "Protest" (whence "Protestantism") of some princes and imperial free cities at Speyer in 1529; and it culminated in the confessional division of Germany at Augsburg in 1530.

The communal Reformation and the rulers' Reformation were so deeply interrelated that the princes' Reformation was in some respects just the counterpart of the people's Reformation. At first the Reformation was a communal movement, and we can avoid the vagueness of the term "people's Reformation" by referring instead to the "communal Reformation." Evangelical doctrine gripped urban and rural communities alike, and the lay community claimed the right to decide right doctrine, a position expressed both in the interconfessional disputations and in the demand for the right to appoint and dismiss pastors. This movement clearly gained force from the reformers' view of man, which stressed the autonomy of the individual and thus fostered a society based on the communal principle. Reformation theology declared the Christian to be of age and thus suggested general human equality, at least in relation to God. Because the conferring of divine grace became a private event between God and man, the church became obsolete as a mediator of salvation and grace. The communal Reformation thus created an area of common interest between town and village. When this ecclesiastical community turned to politics, it became revolutionary because the equality of Christians before God turned into the equality of men among themselves. The church's loss of *raison d'être* made the clergy superfluous and disrupted at least in principle the established social hierarchy. Thus, the Reformation's dependence on community erased the barriers between urban and rural communities, between burghers and peasants.

The communal Reformation's program now swelled with revolutionary ideas. By turning toward the secular realm, it became involved with social and economic demands that had been piling up in the towns and on the land for decades. The Christian humanists of south Germany, whose practical-minded reform theology encompassed secular laws and the secular order, intended to improve the life of this world according to the demands of the gospel. At that point the communal Reformation became fully revolutionary.

Now the princes had to take over the Reformation. Only if they could bring it under political control could revolt be eliminated root and branch. They had to shear the Reformation of its revolutionary components, which they did by denying the communal principle as a mode of Christian life both in theory and in practice. With help from the theologians, the rulers tried to restore their own legitimacy by turning the gospel squarely against the common man. The Bible, they said, required not new secular laws but submission to established authority. And so the center of the Reformation shifted towards Wittenberg, where Luther had always held this very position; and the Christian humanists of the south no longer found any room for their program in the Holy Roman Empire.

The communal Reformation and the rulers' Reformation could not be made compatible or even brought creatively together. The proof of this is a glance at the history of the Anabaptists. They sought to save a remnant of the communal Reformation by withdrawing from the realm of this world; but the rulers mercilessly exterminated them.

CONCLUSION

The Revolution
of the Common Man

Our final task is to test the conceptual validity of our empirical interpretation of the Peasants' War as a revolution of the common man. To do this we must, on the one hand, weave our hypotheses together into a general thesis and, on the other, compare our findings with the general theory of revolutions.

If we integrate our results into an overarching, coherent interpretation, we get the following general thesis: the Peasants' War was an effort to overcome the crisis of feudalism through a revolutionary transformation of sociopolitical relations. The revolution's agent was not the peasant as such, who appeared as the central figure only in the initial stage, when grievances and demands were being formulated, but the common man. The revolution's social goal was, to put it negatively, the abolition of all rights and privileges specific to particular social groups; or, to put it positively and in the language of 1525, the goals were "the common good" and "Christian brotherly love." From these social goals arose the revolution's political goal: in the petty territories, to form a corporative-federal state; in the large territories, to form a constitution based on a territorial assembly (*Landschaft*). These two political forms drew their rationale entirely from the gospel and the communal principle of election. The revolution's military defeat, however, led to a stabilization of the pre-1525 sociopolitical system. This was achieved through general economic relief for agriculture almost everywhere, through stronger guarantees of justice, and through a stabilization and institutionalization of the peasants' political powers; but it was also achieved through the ruler's suppression of the communal Reformation.

The *causes, goals,* and *consequences* of the revolution can be defined more precisely in terms of the revolution's own history as seen in terms of cause and effect. The *causes* of the Peasants' War had economic, social, political, and religious-legal dimensions.

1. The decades before 1525 witnessed a relative economic decline in the average farming operation because of several interrelated, though regionally varied, factors, such as population movements, the revival of servile dues, restrictions on the use of resources, and higher taxes. Their net effect was to lower the income of the average farm.
2. These economic trends necessarily stimulated simultaneous social crises within the family and within the village. Contrasts grew between rich and poor, as did the size of the rural lower class. Many elementary needs could no longer be met, partly because of restrictions on the freedoms to marry and to move about. Village autonomy was also pruned back.
3. The political expectations of peasants rose in many parts of the region from Salzburg to Alsace and from the Palatinate to Tyrol, especially because in the decades before 1525 the peasants came to constitute a house in the territorial diet or a part of the territorial assembly.

Relative economic depression, growing tensions within family and village, and rising political expectations were elements that varied from region to region; but in every area of revolt they came together to produce similar results. The relation between lord and peasant was overstrained, and the perversion of agrarian feudalism through the loss of its ethical content had become obvious.[1] Further,

4. There was the religious-legal dimension to the revolt's causes. A strong, if not the strongest, pillar of feudalism was the force of legitimacy, which impelled the peasants to present only such grievances as could be justified by law. So long as they felt themselves bound by the legal principle of ancient tradition, the peasants confined their actions within the old territorial boundaries and limited them to attacks on the lords' "innovations." They could not complain at all about problems caused by such exogenous factors as overpopulation. When, however, the ancient tradition was replaced by the religious-legal principle of the godly law, the effect was liberating and even revolutionary. Under the godly law, the peasants' needs could be expressed as morally justified demands.

The one fixed *goal* of the peasants, the implementation of the godly law and of the gospel as its concrete expression, opened up the established social and political order to radical change. This basic goal also expanded the revolutionary appeal from the peasantry alone to all common men; the protest could now be escalated from mere demands to the settlement of demands through force, and the state of anarchy could give way to a vision of an alternative sociopolitical order.

Through the preachers the godly law and the gospel migrated from town to countryside, changing the Peasants' War into a revolution of the common man. Already burghers, peasants, and miners had some real interests in common, with similar agricultural problems (for example, between the agricultural workers of the petty towns and the rural wage-workers), similar tax burdens (such as military and episcopal consecration levies), and the same encroachments by rulers into the communal autonomy of towns, villages, and mining districts. But the common longing for a more just and more Christian world fortified these common interests.

Rulers now became the major enemies of peasants, townsmen, and miners, either because they blocked access to the gospel, or because, in the case of evangelical rulers, they opposed the common man's interpretation of the godly law and the gospel. This led to the seizure of castles and monasteries. As the gospel and its corollaries—"godly law," "the common good," and "Christian brotherly love"—were put into practice, the clergy were dispossessed of their economic position and political power, while the nobles, whose position often remained quite murky, were bound more tightly into the new communal federations and robbed of their political privileges. Thus, both in principle and in fact, the common man became the shaping force of society and the state.

Something was surely needed to fill the power vacuum created by the revolution in both the theoretical and the practical realms. This something was a program, which, either established in principle or arising from practice, could move well beyond simple lists of grievances. Based on the existing institutions of the territorial states, the political programs evolved by the revolution moved flexibly towards two alternatives. The regions of petty territories—Swabia, the Upper Rhine, and Franconia—developed the idea of the corporative-federal constitution. Its corporative basis was formed by autonomous village and urban communes now bound together in "armies," which became political rather than chiefly military bodies. These armies federated voluntarily into "Christian Associations" without surrendering their individual "sovereignties." The federations approximated in size the duchy of Württemberg or the Swiss Confederation. The larger territories, on the other hand, developed constitutions based on an assembly of peasants, citizens, and miners. Although the new order retained the old institutional framework of local communes, territorial diet, the standing committee of the diet, the central regime, and prince, the assembly principle replaced the structure of separate legal estates. In 1525 "assembly" meant the total body of rebels in a territory. The autonomous village, mining, market, and urban communities elected envoys to the diet, which then established a joint regime with the prince.

The *consequences* of the Peasants' War were shaped in two ways by its revolutionary character and its military defeat. Military defeat made further revolutionary changes impossible, but it did not destroy the chance of reform. (1) In south Germany the rulers' insecurity, as witnessed by the committee's report to the Imperial Diet of Speyer in 1526, and the peasants' stubborn opposition led to long-term cooperation between lords and peasants within the bounds of a constitutional assembly. There was no general restoration of the nobility. Instead, the established system was stabilized through the greater integration of the peasants into the system, and this, of course, further diminished the rights of the old privileged classes. (2) Stabilization also required the neutralization of revolutionary elements, elements derived at least in part from Reformation theology and further developed by the common man. The Reformation, therefore, had to be shorn of its power to create social and political disruption, something the rulers achieved by taking the Reformation away from the communities and making it a matter of state.

I have used the term "the Revolution of the Common Man" for an empirically derived interpretation of the events of 1525. The term betrays something of the difficulty, native to the historian's task, of finding adequate modern language for historical conditions. The pair "revolution" and "the common man," for example, unites a modern scholarly concept with one taken directly from the sixteenth-century sources. That I couple them together, of course, means that I believe they form a usable definition. If we may name rebel movements after the rebels, as in the "bourgeois" and "proletarian" revolutions, then the Revolution of "the Common Man" is the proper expression for 1525. It remains to be seen if we might rightly call this movement a "revolution." In its own day it never acquired a universally acceptable name, for all the common expressions—"Peasants' War," "tumult," "disturbance," "rising"—came from the rulers and ruling classes and were therefore polemical, loaded terms with relatively little precise meaning.

What are revolutions? Hannah Arendt, to begin with a frequently cited definition, writes that only where

> this pathos of novelty is present and where novelty is connected with the idea of freedom are we entitled to speak of revolution. . . . Violence is no more adequate to describe the phenomenon of revolution than change; only where change occurs in the sense of a new beginning, where violence is used to constitute an altogether different form of government, to bring about the formation of a new body politic, where the liberation from oppression aims at least at the constitution of freedom can we speak of revolution.[2]

Samuel P. Huntington lays more stress on change in political institutions when he defines revolution as "the rapid and forceful destruction of existing political institutions, the political mobilization of new social groups, and the creation of new political institutions." [3] Hans Wassmund's recent survey of current definitions of revolution sums up as follows:

> We should properly call "revolution" only a change in the political organization, the social and economic structures, property ownership, and the principles of political legitimacy which meets the following conditions: it must occur after an acute, prolonged crisis in one or more of the state's traditional

patterns of stratification (class, status, or domination); it should be supported by a mass movement; it should be carried through by force; and it should be ideologically oriented towards the ideals of progress, emancipation, and freedom. Finally, it should be both rapid and radical.[4]

The common elements in these three definitions are a mass basis, the use of force, and new ideas of a future state and society. By such standards the revolt of 1525 easily qualifies as a revolution. We must recognize, however, that although there is some agreement among those who study revolutions empirically, "there is anything but unanimity about the concept of revolution." [5] There is nonetheless a consensus that "revolutions are a form of sociopolitical change; they pose a challenge of force to existing conditions; and they aim to disrupt the continuity of development." [6] Some elements in this definition remain uncertain, and we must seek greater precision. Perhaps we can clarify matters by contrasting revolutions to other forms of action based on discontent and resistance, and also by applying elements from the theory of revolution to the problems of the causes and goals of revolutions.[7]

The Peasants' War is frequently interpreted as a rebellion or revolt. A revolt, to be sure, is characterized by the use of force, but its posture is purely one of resistance, and it lacks the ability to innovate. The feeling that current conditions are unbearable expresses itself more or less in outbreaks of rage against those deemed, rightly or wrongly, responsible for things as they are.[8] Chalmers Johnson has tried to distinguish between rebellions and revolutions. For him rebellion is a spontaneous act of force by "normal people" who oppose existing conditions, while revolution is the act of rebuilding a shattered society according to a plan or vision (an ideology) of a more perfect and more just society.[9] By Johnson's criteria, the Peasants' War should undoubtably be called a revolution rather than a rebellion because of the new ideas it created of society and the state, based ideologically on the gospel.

We can ascertain more precisely the usefulness of the concept of revolution for 1525 if we ask how the various theories of revolution handle the problems of causes and goals. Ever since revolution has been studied, the question of causes has been controversial. Karl Marx construed as causal components the contradiction between forces of production and productive relations, exploitation, and increasing class conflict. His analysis competed with that of Alexis de Tocqueville, who thought that revolutions were favored by a general improvement in the lot of the masses and by the relative weakness of governments. Crane Brinton's roster of causes of revolution combines elements from Marx with others from Tocqueville: class antagonisms, the regime's inability to adapt to new conditions, economic prosperity, and lessened security for established elites.[10] Significant here is the fifth category mentioned by Brinton, a change in the function of the intellectuals, who withdraw their loyalty from the established system and critically pose new alternatives.[11] James C. Davies believes that Marx's and Tocqueville's ideas are actually compatible. For him, revolutions are "most probable when a period of steady economic and social growth is followed by a short, severe recession." [12] This unleashes discontent and disappointment, which bring together social groups whose objective economic positions normally keep them apart.

Such theories are important and have attracted vigorous debate right down to the present. They are also often accompanied by propositions of a lower level of generalization. Hans Wassmund has classified these propositions into five preconditions of revolution:

(1) *economic*—long-term growth interrupted by short-term recession, mounting poverty, and great differences in income levels;

(2) *social*—rapid rise and fall of social classes and groups, deceleration and acceleration of the circulation of elites;

(3) *psychological*—discrepancy between expectation and fulfillment, a feeling of insecurity;

(4) *intellectual*—critical social philosophies, alienation of the intellectuals; and

(5) *political*—an incompetent, divided, and oppressive regime. [13]

We cannot treat here the question of whether these studies of revolution have provided an adequate basis for a general theory. Their theories of causation, however, definitely run parallel to the hypotheses set forth in this study of the events of 1525. [14]

The goals and programs, the alternative constitutions, and the new ideas of legitimacy of 1525 were all formulated during the revolt itself and were not available at the beginning. Any attempt to reject, on this ground, the claim of 1525 to be a revolution runs against the most detailed analysis yet done of the course of revolutions. Rex D. Hopper has developed a four-phase model of revolutions, in which goals are clearly formulated during phases two and three, but not at the very beginning. [15] With regard to the general goal of revolutions, Isaac Kramnick argues that they aim "to transform society in the light of theoretical principles which flow from a kind of vision of an ideal order, that is, an ideology." [16] Dealing more precisely with the functions of ideology in revolutions, Mostafa Rejai adds that ideology rationalizes and justifies the grievances and demands of the rebels, it offers alternative values and visions of society, and it legitimizes acts of revolution. [17] According to Samuel P. Huntington, who defines revolution simply as "the extreme case of the explosion of political participation," the alternative conception of society must lead to the creation of institutions which are adaptable, complex, autonomous, and coherent, precisely in order to guarantee political participation. [18] Thus, to adopt Ralf Dahrendorf's paraphrase of Brinkmann, revolution makes yesterday's criminality into today's legality. [19]

The political plans of 1525, the corporative-federal and the assembly-based constitutions, assured mass political participation through the electoral principle and through the new legitimacy created by the "ideology" of the gospel. Thus the godly law, formerly rejected by the ruling classes as illegal, became a new legality.

The marks by which scholars define revolutions can therefore be applied to the Peasants' War of 1525 without doing violence to them and without selecting only the points that seem especially applicable. One can deny the revolutionary quality of 1525 only by arguing that the concept of revolution properly applies only when the word itself appears in history with its full, modern meaning. If, however, we accept these events as a revolution of the common man, then the implications reach far beyond 1525. Drawing the connection between 1525 and the great European revolutions emphasizes, paradoxically, the evolutionary process of European history. To emphasize the ideological meaning of the Reformation, on the other hand, enhances the social dimensions of the movement which began at Wittenberg. It also brings the German Reformation closer to the socially creative and politically active movement of Calvinism.

Such suggestions obviously require much more discussion than can be given them here, nor are they central to our task of definition. What the use of the concept of revolution expresses here is the conviction that the movement of 1525 was not just a series of inexplicable, individual actions on a level of no more than regional significance. Rather, what happened in 1525 was a deliberate movement, proceeding on a rational course and with challenging ethical claims, for human self-realization.

APPENDIX 1

The Twelve Articles

THE JUST AND FUNDAMENTAL ARTICLES
OF ALL THE PEASANTRY
AND TENANTS OF SPIRITUAL AND TEMPORAL POWERS
BY WHOM THEY THINK THEMSELVES OPPRESSED

To the Christian reader, the peace and grace of God through Jesus Christ.

The Antichrists.

Fruits of the New Gospel.

Reply of the Articles. Apology for the Articles. Rom. 1

There are many antichrists who, now that the peasants are assembled together, seize the chance to mock the gospel, saying, "Is this the fruit of the new gospel: to band together in great numbers and plot conspiracies to reform and even topple the spiritual and temporal powers—yes, even to murder them?" The following articles answer all these godless, blasphemous critics. We want two things: first, to make them stop mocking the word of God; and second, to establish the Christian justice of the current disobedience and rebellion of all the peasants.

First of all, the gospel does not cause rebellions and uproars, because it tells of Christ, the promised Messiah, whose words and life teach nothing but love, peace, patience, and unity. And all who believe in this Christ become loving, peaceful, patient, and one in spirit. This is the basis of all the articles of the peasants (as we will clearly show): to hear the gospel and to live accordingly. How then can the antichrists call the gospel a cause of rebellion and of disobedience? It is not the gospel that drives some antichrists and foes of the gospel to resist and reject these demands and requirements, but the devil, the deadliest foe of the gospel, who arouses through unbelief such opposition in his own followers. His aim is to suppress and abolish the word of God, which teaches love, peace, and unity.

Rom. 11, Isa. 40
Rom. 8, Exod. 3
and 14, Luke 18

Second, it surely follows that the peasants, whose articles demand this gospel as their doctrine and rule of life, cannot be called "disobedient" or "rebellious." For if God deigns to hear the peasants' earnest plea that they may be permitted to live according to his word, who will dare deny his will? Who indeed will dare question his judgment? Who will dare oppose his majesty? Did he not hear the children of Israel crying to him and deliver them out of Pharaoh's hand? And can he not save his own today as well? Yes, he will save them, and soon! Therefore, Christian reader, read these articles diligently, and then judge for yourself.

These are the Articles

THE FIRST ARTICLE

1 Tim. 3, Titus 1,
Acts 14, Deut. 17,
Exod. 31, Deut. 10,
John 6, Gal. 2

First of all, we humbly ask and beg—and we all agree on this—that henceforth we ought to have the authority and power for the whole community to elect and appoint its own pastor. We also want authority to depose a pastor who behaves improperly. This elected pastor should preach to us the holy gospel purely and clearly, without human additions or human doctrines or precepts. For constant preaching of the true faith impels us to beg God for his grace, that he may instill in us and confirm in us that same true faith. Unless we have his grace in us, we remain mere, useless flesh and blood. For the Scripture clearly teaches that we may come to God only through true faith and can be saved only through His mercy. This is why we need such a guide and pastor; and thus our demand is grounded in Scripture.

THE SECOND ARTICLE

As the whole
Epistle to the
Hebrews says.

Ps. 109, Gen. 14,
Deut. 18, Deut. 12

Second, although the obligation to pay a just tithe prescribed in the Old Testament is fulfilled in the New, yet we will gladly pay the large tithe on grain—but only in just measure. Since the tithe should be given to God and distributed among his servants, so the pastor who clearly preaches the word of God deserves to receive it. From now on we want to have our church wardens, appointed by the community, collect and receive this tithe and have our elected pastor draw from it, with the whole community's consent, a decent and adequate living for himself and his. The remainder should be distributed to the village's own poor, again with the community's consent and according to need. What then remains should be kept in case some need to be called up to defend the country; and then the costs can be met from this reserve, so that no general territorial tax will be laid upon the poor folk.

Deut. 26

1 Tim. 5, Matt. 10, 1 Cor. 9

A Christian offer.

Wherever one or more villages have sold off the tithe to meet some emergency, those purchasers who can show that they bought the tithe with the consent of the whole village shall not be simply expropriated. Indeed we hope to reach fair compromises with such persons, according to the facts of the case, and to redeem the tithe in installments. But wherever the tithe holder—be he clergyman or layman—did not buy the tithe from the whole village but has it from ancestors who simply seized it from the village, we will not, ought not, and do not intend to pay it any longer, except (as we said above) to support our elected pastor. And we will reserve the rest or distribute it to the poor, as the Bible commands. As for the small tithe, we will not pay it at all, for the Lord God created cattle for man's free use; and it is an unjust tithe invented by men alone. Therefore, we won't pay it anymore.

Luke 6, Matt. 5

One shouldn't take anything from another.

Gen. 1

THE THIRD ARTICLE

Isa. 53, 1 Pet. 1, 1 Cor. 7

Third, it has until now been the custom for the lords to own us as their property. This is deplorable, for Christ redeemed and bought us all with his precious blood, the lowliest shepherd as well as the greatest lord, with no exceptions. Thus the Bible proves that we are free and want to be free. Not that we want to be utterly free and subject to no authority at all; God does not teach us that. We ought to live according to the commandments, not according to the lusts of the flesh. But we should love God, recognize him as our Lord in our neighbor, and willingly do all things God commanded us at his Last Supper. This means we should live according to his com-

Rom. 13, Wis. 6, 1 Pet. 2

Deut. 6, Matt. 4

Luke 4, Luke 6

Matt. 7, John 13
Rom. 13
mandment, which does not teach us to obey only the
rulers, but to humble ourselves before everyone. Thus we
should willingly obey our elected and rightful ruler, set
over us by God, in all proper and Christian matters. Nor
Acts 5
do we doubt that you, as true and just Christians, will
A Christian offer.
gladly release us from bondage or prove to us from the
gospel that we must be your property.

THE FOURTH ARTICLE

Fourth, until now it has been the custom that no com-
Gen. 1, Acts 10,
1 Tim. 4, 1 Cor. 10,
Coloss. 2
moner might catch wild game, wildfowl, or fish in the
running waters, which seems to us altogether improper,
unbrotherly, selfish, and contrary to God's Word. In
some places the rulers protect the game to our distress
A Christian offer.
and great loss, for we must suffer silently while the dumb
beasts gobble up the crops God gave for man's use,
although this offends both God and neighbor. When the
Lord God created man, he gave him dominion over all
A Christian offer.
animals, over the birds of the air, and the fish in the
waters. Thus we demand that if someone owns a stream,
lake, or pond, he should have to produce documentary
proof of ownership and show that it was sold to him with
the consent of the whole village. In that case we do not
want to seize it from him with force but only to review
the matter in a Christian way for the sake of brotherly
love. But whoever cannot produce adequate proof of
ownership and sale should surrender the waters to the
community, as is just.

THE FIFTH ARTICLE

As in shown in the
first chapter of
Genesis.
Fifth, we have another grievance about woodcutting,
for our lords have seized the woods for themselves alone;
and when the poor commoner needs some wood, he has
to pay twice the price for it. We think that those woods
whose lords, be they clergymen or laymen, cannot prove
ownership by purchase should revert to the whole community. And the community should be able to allow in an
orderly way each man to gather firewood for his home
and building timber free, though only with permission of

the community's elected officials. If all the woods have been fairly purchased, then a neighborly and Christian agreement should be reached with their owners about their use. Where the woods were simply seized and then sold to a third party, however, a compromise should be reached according to the facts of the case and the norms of brotherly love and Holy Writ.

Officials should see that this does not lead to denuding the woods.

A Christian offer.

THE SIXTH ARTICLE

Rom. 10

Sixth, there is our grievous burden of labor services, which the lords daily increase in number and kind. We demand that these obligations be properly investigated and lessened. And we should be allowed, graciously, to serve as our forefathers did, according to God's word alone.

THE SEVENTH ARTICLE

Luke 3, 1 Thess. 4

Seventh, in the future we will not allow the lords to oppress us any more. Rather, a man shall have his holding on the proper terms on which it has been leased, that is, by the agreement between lord and peasant. The lord should not force or press the tenant to perform labor or any other service without pay, so that the peasant may use and enjoy his land unburdened and in peace. When the lord needs labor services, however, the peasant should willingly serve his own lord before others; yet a peasant should serve only at a time when his own affairs do not suffer and only for a just wage.

THE EIGHTH ARTICLE

Matt. 10

Eighth, we have a grievance that many of us hold lands that are overburdened with rents higher than the land's yield. Thus the peasants lose their property and are ruined. The lords should have honorable men inspect these farms and adjust the rents fairly, so that the peasant does not work for nothing. For every laborer is worthy of his hire.

THE NINTH ARTICLE

Isa. 10, Ephes. 6,
Luke 3, Jer. 26

Ninth, we have a grievance against the way serious crimes* are punished, for they are constantly making new laws. We are not punished according to the severity of the case but sometimes out of great ill will and sometimes out of favoritism. We think that punishments should be dealt out among us according to the ancient written law and the circumstances of the case, and not according to the judge's bias.

THE TENTH ARTICLE

As above, Luke 6

A Christian offer.

Tenth, we have a grievance that some people have seized meadows and fields belonging to the community. We shall restore these to the community, unless a proper sale can be proved. If they were improperly bought, however, then a friendly and brotherly compromise should be reached, based on the facts.

THE ELEVENTH ARTICLE

Deut. 18, Matt. 8
Matt. 23, Isa. 10

Eleventh, we want the custom called death taxes totally abolished. We will not tolerate it or allow widows and orphans to be so shamefully robbed of their goods, as so often happens in various ways, against God and all that is honorable. The very ones who should be guarding and protecting our goods have skinned and trimmed us of them instead. Had they the slightest legal pretext, they would have grabbed everything. God will suffer this no longer but will wipe it all out. Henceforth no one shall have to pay death taxes, whether small or large.

CONCLUSION

Because all the
Articles are
contained in
God's Word.

Twelfth, we believe and have decided that if any one or more of these articles is not in agreement with God's Word (which we doubt), then this should be proved to us from Holy Writ. We will abandon it, when this is

*"Great Mischief" (Grosser Frefel) was the technical term for serious crimes.

A Christian offer. proved by the Bible. If some of our articles should be approved and later found to be unjust, they shall be dead, null, and void from that moment on. Likewise, if Scripture truly reveals further grievances as offensive to God and a burden to our neighbor, we will reserve a place for them and declare them included in our list. We, for our part, will live and exercise ourselves in all Christian teachings, for which we will pray to the Lord God. For he alone, and no other, can give us the truth. The peace of Christ be with us all.

APPENDIX 2

The Upper Swabian Grievance Lists and Their Evaluation

The evaluation of the Upper Swabian grievances of 1525 rests on lists from the following sources (the name in parentheses after the place name is the modern administrative district [Kreis] in which the place is located):

(1) The peasants of the Baltringen army who were subject to nobles: Achstetten (Biberach), Altbierlingen (Ehingen), Erolzheim, Walpershofen, and Binnrot (Biberach), Pfänders (Biberach?), Unterroth (Biberach), Öpfingen-Griesingen (Ehingen), Edelbeuren (Biberach), Bronnen (Biberach), Ellmannsweiler (Biberach), Risstissen (Ehingen), Warthausen (Biberach), Bach (Ehingen?), Bussmannshausen (Biberach), Untersulmetingen (Biberach), and the seigneury of Stadion (Ehingen).

(2) The peasants of the Baltringen army who were subject to abbeys: Schemmerberg-Altheim (Biberach), seigneury of Rot an der Rot (Biberach), Sulmingen-Maselheim (Biberach), seigneury of Ochsenhausen (Biberach), Höfen (Biberach), Alberweiler (Biberach), Rottenacker (Ehingen), Attenweiler (Biberach), Oggelshausen-Tiefenbach (Saulgau), Unterroth (Biberach, Illertissen?), Oberholzheim (Biberach), Mietingen (Biberach), seigneury of Gutenzell (Biberach), Mittelbiberach (Biberach), and Äpfingen (Biberach).

(3) The peasants of the Baltringen army who were subject to hospitals and towns: Röhrwangen (Biberach), Langenschemmern (Biberach), Burgrieden-Bühl-Stetten (Biberach), Baltringen (Biberach), Streitberg (Biberach?), Baustetten (Biberach), and hospital seigneury of Biberach.

(4) Southern Upper Swabia: seigneury of Schussenried (Ravensburg), seigneury of Kisslegg (Wangen), Rappertsweiler (Tettnang), peasants of the Lake Constance army (Tettnang-Lindau).

(5) Allgäu and Bavarian Swabia: Memmingen villages of Woringen, Dickenreishausen, Hitzenhofen, Hart, Buxheim, Steinheim, Memmingerberg, Ungerhausen, Holzgünz, Lauben, Frickenhausen, Arlesried, Dankelsried, Betzenhausen, Dassberg, Erkheim, Gottenau, Unterreichau, Wespach,

Brunnen, Amendingen, Boos, Pless, Buxach, Volkratshofen, Priemen, Westerhart; seigneury of Kempten; Martinszell (Kempten); the *Tigen* of Rettenberg (Sonthofen); the *Tigen* of Marktoberdorf; Weicht (Kaufbeuren); Wiedergeltingen (Mindelheim?); and Langenerringen (Augsburg?).

These grievances lists are printed by Franz, *Der deutsche Bauernkrieg: Aktenband,* nos. 24, 26a–e, g–i, k, m–r, 28, 30, 31; Franz, *Quellen,* nos. 28, 34b, h, 35, 36, 40, 56; Baumann, *Akten,* nos. 58, 62, 104, 133; Vogt, "Correspondenz Artzt," nos. 34, 47, 55, 59, 67c, 880, 882, 883, 885–87, 890–92, 895, 898a, 900, 903.

The following schema has been used to classify each demand or grievance that appears more than once:

I. Religion
   A. New gospel
   B. Election of pastors
   C. Church and religion in general

II. Landlordship
   A. Reduction of dues in event of poor harvests
   B. Rents
      1. Too high
      2. Increased
      3. Other
   C. Deterioration of legal status of tenures
   D. Entry fines
      1. Too high
      2. Increased
      3. Other
   E. Services
      1. Abolish
      2. Too high
      3. Increased
   F. Right to alienate farms

III. Servility
   A. Freedom from serfdom
   B. Restriction of serfdom
   C. Recognition fines
   D. Exogamous marriage
   E. Death taxes
   F. Servile dues
      1. Abolish
      2. Too high
      3. Increased

  G. Deterioration of tenants' legal status
  H. Freedom of movement
  I. Inheritance rights

IV. Local jurisdiction
  A. High and low justice
  B. Refusal of justice
  C. Judicial administration
  D. "Foreign" courts
  E. Increases in fines
  F. Legislative practice
  G. Communal power of command
  H. Election of communal "officials"
  I. Communal "employees"
  J. Other

V. Tithes
  A. Abolition of the small tithe
  B. Abolition or restriction of large tithe

VI. Commons and forests
  A. Timber rights
  B. Communal waters
  C. Fishing rights
    1. Free
    2. Free with limitation
  D. Pasturage rights
  E. Hunting rights
  F. Damages by wild game
  G. Commons, general
  H. Other

VII. Services not otherwise classifiable

VIII. Taxes
  A. Military taxes
  B. Unspecified taxes
  C. Excise taxes
  D. Other

Any attempt to quantify these grievances meets certain methodological problems, some of which are discussed in the notes to Chapter 3. The basic problem is that the entire material—54 grievance lists containing about 550 individual grievances—is none too large for statistical analysis. The distribution of the lists within Upper Swabia is quite uneven: 39 from the villages of the Baltringen army, but only 15 from the entire remainder of Upper Swabia (including Allgäu and modern Bavarian Swabia). This statistical problem is made worse when we classify the grievances from the villages according to the type of lord; for example, in the Baltringen region, although villages subject to abbeys and those subject to nobles are about equally represented (15 and 17, respectively), we have grievance lists from only 7 villages subject to towns and hospitals. Another difficulty stems from the fact that some lists represent the grievances of individual villages, while others contain those of whole seigneuries with as many as 20 villages each. Moreover, the language of the lists creates certain difficulties. When one article says that rents are too high and another says that they have increased, they may be describing the same situation, or they may not. Finally, the date of composition can be crucial. The earlier the date, the more a grievance list expresses local conditions; those formulated during March already betray the influence of other grievance lists and even of the Twelve Articles. Such problems can be solved to a large degree through a scheme of classification which breaks down the mass of grievances into the largest possible number of regional and subject categories and which thus permits a cautious answer to various sorts of questions.

When dealing with Swabian material, the numbers and percentages presented throughout this book are based on all the available written grievance lists from Upper Swabia. Individual articles are counted; but a multiplication of the grievances submitted by the peasants of a seigneury by the number of known villages in the seigneury (some of which, as in the county of Kempten, are fictitious), in order to compensate for the accidents of survival of lists, would confuse the picture more than it would help. Much more helpful to this investigation is an emphasis on the point of origin of the grievances. This can be illustrated by an example. The grievances of the subjects of abbeys in the region of the Baltringen army make up 17 lists, among them one list for the entire 26 villages of the seigneury of Ochsenhausen. If the Ochsenhausen grievances are multiplied by 26 and (adding the other 16) the total is put at 42, then the percentages of occurrence of individual articles remain nearly constant, providing one groups them in larger units. Taking the 17 lists (counting Ochsenhausen as one list), 94.11 percent complain about serfdom; taking 42 lists (counting Ochsenhausen as 26), the figure is 97.67 percent. Only when particular complaints are isolated do significant differences appear: by the first reckoning, 41.17 percent contain grievances against the death tax of one-half the estate; by the second reckoning, as much as 74.42 percent contain such grievances—an increase which derives from the unusually high death tax in Ochsenhausen, where besides the best animal and best garment, there was a large cash fine, amounting to 5 percent of the value of real and personal property.

Notes

INTRODUCTION

1. L. von Ranke, *Deutsche Geschichte im Zeitalter der Reformation,* 2:165.
2. F. Engels, *Der deutsche Bauernkrieg,* p. 409.
3. W. Zimmermann, *Allgemeine Geschichte des grossen Bauernkrieges,* 1:5 ff.
4. S. Skalweit, *Reich und Reformation,* p. 179.
5. M. Steinmetz, "Die frühbürgerliche Revolution," p. 43.
6. G. Franz, "Die Führer im Bauernkrieg," p. 1.
7. G. Franz, *Der deutsche Bauernkrieg,* 9th ed., p. ix, a formulation he left unchanged from the first through the ninth edition.
8. The term "Poor Conrad" refers specifically to a rebellion in Württemberg in 1514 and more generally to the poor.
9. M. M. Smirin, *Deutschland vor der Reformation,* pp. 47, 50, 74, 92 ff.
10. Steinmetz, "Die frühbürgerliche Revolution," pp. 45 f.
11. G. Vogler, "Marx, Engels, und die Konzeption," pp. 197 ff.
12. Steinmetz, "Die frühbürgerliche Revolution," p. 53.
13. Vogler, "Marx, Engels, und die Konzeption," p. 193.
14. G. Franz, *Der deutsche Bauernkrieg,* 1st ed., p. 468.
15. Franz, "Die Führer im Bauernkrieg," p. 2.
16. Franz, *Der deutsche Bauernkrieg,* 9th ed., p. 299, and see pp. 280–300. Franz modified his views in a little-known article, "Folgen des Bauernkriegs—noch heute spürbar?" *Die Landwirtschaftliche Berufschule* 18 (1968):1 ff. See, however, G. Franz, *Geschichte des deutschen Bauernstandes,* pp. 145 ff., where he repeats without correction or qualification his opinion of 1933. For possible antecedents of this view, see F. Schnabel, *Deutschlands geschichtliche Quellen,* p. 199, and F. L. Baumann, *Akten,* p. iii.
17. A. Waas, *Die Bauern im Kampf,* p. 259.
18. H. Rössler, "Über die Wirkungen von 1525," esp. p. 111.
19. Steinmetz, "Die frühbürgerliche Revolution," pp. 44, 54.
20. Vogler, "Marx, Engels, und die Konzeption," p. 189.
21. See the massive bibliography by Ulrich Thomas listing over 500 titles published since 1974. This work renders all citations of additional bibliography superfluous.
22. The East Germans produced, for example, an impressive *Illustrierte Geschichte der deutschen frühbürgerlichen Revolution,* by A. Laube, M. Steinmetz, and G. Vogler. G. Vogler also published the fascinating little book, *Die Gewalt soll gegeben werden dem gemeinen Volk.*
23. R. Wohlfeil, "Der Speyrer Reichstag," p. 8.

24. See, e.g., J. Bücking, "Der 'Bauernkrieg' . . . als sozialer Systemkonflikt," where the term is used without any explanation. Sabean's critique is in his "Der Bauernkrieg—ein Literaturbericht," p. 228.

25. H. Rosenberg, "Der deutsche Bauernkrieg in sozialgeschichtlicher Perspektive," pp. 9, 16, 13. This work exists only in manuscript, but Prof. Rosenberg has kindly lent me a copy to be incorporated in this second edition of my book.

26. Ibid., pp. 17–18.

27. Ibid., p. 24.

28. Ibid., p. 26.

29. Ibid., p. 27.

30. Ibid., p. 29.

31. Ibid., p. 31.

32. Ibid., pp. 14–15.

33. For some of Endres's works, see Works Cited.

34. There are a number of excellent studies. See the bibliography for the works of Blaschke, Czok, Laube, Schwarze, and Straube; and for Alsace see the essays in Wollbrett, *Guerre des Paysans.*

35. D. Sabean, "Der Bauernkrieg—ein Literaturbericht," p. 228.

36. H. Wunder, "Der samländische Bauernaufstand," p. 151; J. C. Stalnaker, "Towards a Social Interpretation of the German Peasant War," p. 38; J. Bücking, "Der 'Bauernkrieg' . . . als sozialer Systemkonflikt," p. 168.

37. Fundamental is the study of E. Wolf, *Peasants,* p. 91. But see also the older work of A. Chayanov, *The Theory of Peasant Economy.*

38. T. Shanin, "The Nature and Logic of Peasant Economy"; idem, *The Awkward Class,* pp. 81 ff.

39. E. Wolf, *Peasant Wars,* pp. 290 ff; H. A. Landsberger, *Latin American Peasant Movements,* p. 36; idem, *Rural Protest,* p. 21.

40. D. Sabean, "Markets, Uprisings, and Leadership," pp. 17 ff., "The Communal Basis of Pre-1800 Uprisings," and "German Agrarian Institutions."

41. J. C. Stalnaker, "Towards a Social Interpretation of the German Peasant War," p. 36.

42. Especially H. Wunder, "The Mentality of Rebellious Peasants."

43. R. Scribner, "Is There a Social History of the Reformation?" p. 494.

44. R. van Dülmen, *Reformation als Revolution,* pp. 63–168.

45. H. A. Oberman, "The Gospel of Social Unrest," p. 50.

46. H. Cohn, "Anticlericalism"; idem, "Reformatorische Bewegung."

47. M. Brecht, "Der theologische Hintergrund"; G. Maron, "Bauernkrieg."

48. R. W. Scribner, "The Reformation as a Social Movement," where one will also find references to Scribner's earlier attempts at the same project. See also the impressive contribution of T. A. Brady, *Ruling Class, Regime, and Reformation.*

CHAPTER 1

1. The origins of the Twelve Articles are no longer controversial. See the summary of G. Franz, "Entstehung der Zwölf Artikel." Quotations from the *Twelve Articles* are from the critical edition by A. Götze, "Die Zwölf Artikel," pp. 9–15.

2. See below, Chapter 10.

3. "Great Mischief" did not belong to the area of competence of the high judge, as was common in other parts of Germany; it meant, rather, the penalties for specific infractions that were usually tried before the low court of the village. "Great Mischief" included penalties between 10 lb. heller and 10 shillings heller. According to the 1498 judicial ordinance of Ersingen, "great mischief" was defined as follows: "Item: if someone strikes another, making

him lame or crippled, or wounds him so that one has to bandage or sew up the wound, the person committing such a crime shall be fined 13 lb. 5 shillings heller."

4. Here and hereafter the concepts of "feudal" and "feudal lords" are intended as simple abbreviations for awkward and long-winded circumlocutions. In a work dealing with only the fifteenth and sixteenth centuries it makes sense to use "feudal" for no more than the economic, social, and political relations between lord and peasant. "Feudal" laws in this system are therefore the rights of landlordship, of mastery over serfs, and of lower jurisdiction, with all of the special laws that flowed from that jurisdiction. "Feudal lords" are nobles and prelates but not corporations such as hospitals and cities.

5. There are virtually no statistics to measure the importance of tithes. C. Heimpel calculated that for the hospital at Biberach between 1517 and 1526 the annual payments of seigneurial dues came to 2,653 double hundred-weights of grain, while the tithes amounted to 1,598 double hundred-weights. Figures from the abbey of Ochsenhausen for 1522 show that tithes were just as important as dues:

	Dues (in malters)	Tithes (in malters)
Rye	526	361
Spelt (German Wheat)	43	334
Oats	737	397
Barley	0	26

6. The abbess of Lindau set down the annual income for her noble convent at a miserable 400 gulden.

7. The fact that priests had occasionally been elected elsewhere does not disprove the revolutionary character of this demand in 1525.

8. In current research on the Peasants' War, the Twelve Articles are usually presented as a moderate program for reform. Franz describes them as "serious, well-founded reform proposals, which were feasible," (G. Franz, Der deutsche Bauernkrieg, 1st. ed., p. 200). For Smirin the articles were "no program of social upheaval" because they left "untouched the foundations of feudal law and of the whole social order" and especially because they used "godly law as a radical principle" only for "religious and ecclesiastical changes" (M. M. Smirin, Volksreformation, pp. 401 and 516 ff.).

CHAPTER 2

1. What follows is based on an analysis of the grievance lists of Upper Swabia, which are described in Appendix 2. There, too, is a discussion of the problems met in trying to quantify them.

2. It was Günther Franz's great innovation in the study of the Peasants' War to have begun evaluating the grievance lists as indicators of peasant consciousness. See Franz, Der deutsche Bauernkrieg, 1st ed., pp. vi–vii.

3. If individual grievances are classified by content, eliminating purely semantic differences, the Baltringen grievances vary from those of all of Upper Swabia by an average of only about 3 percent. Services, for example, are targets of 51.28 percent of the Baltringen articles and 50 percent of the Upper Swabian ones; the figures for grievances against taxes are 28.21 percent and 29.63 percent; against the large tithe, 41.03 percent and 40.74 percent; and against entry fines, 64.10 percent and 61.11 percent.

4. An evaluation of the importance of services runs into special difficulties because the lists do not always distinguish clearly among those arising from landlordship, from serfdom, and from jurisdictional rights. Unspecified grievances against services occur in half of all lists, and some of them must have been directed against servile obligations.

5. A full 50 percent of the peasants complained against unspecified services, while 5 percent specify services due the landlord, and 15 percent specify services due masters of serfs.

6. About 10 percent of the individual grievances in local lists cannot be usefully classified—for example, those demanding free sale of goods, precise definition of seigneurial rights in the commons, the abolition of restriction of the obligation to maintain hunting dogs, etc.

7. The local articles only suggest restoration or expansion of communal rights (22 percent), meaning mainly the communal power to issue orders (18 percent).

8. Previous scholars have been content merely to add up the causes, based on the Twelve Articles. See the summary by Franz, *Der deutsche Bauernkrieg,* 9th ed., pp. 113–27; and more recently E. Walder, "Der politische Gehalt der Zwölf Artikel." The Twelve Articles and the Swabian demands as a whole were interpreted as revealing a conflict between territorial sovereignty and communal autonomy, thereby lacing the entire question into a narrowly political corset. Innovative approaches first appeared with Sabean's *Landbesitz.*

9. Some marginal additions aside, this section is based on the following Upper Swabian seigneuries: the abbeys of Schussenried, Weingarten, Ochsenhausen, Rot, and Kempten, and the lands of the counts of Montfort and the Truchsesses of Waldburg. The largely uniform results attest the validity of the general picture offered here.

10. In the Waldburg seigneury of Zeil enserfment was a prerequisite to securing land, so that around 1500 all the subjects were serfs; but treaties from the year 1526 suggest that around 1500 there was still a limited right of movement in the other Waldburg seigneuries. The process by which formerly free peasants were integrated into the ranks of the serfs is especially clear from the Zeil materials. Despite relatively fragmentary documentation we can see from the charters that before 1525 many free peasants became Waldburg bondsmen, chiefly through exogamous marriages to Zeil serfs. Two-thirds of the documents on serfdom before 1525 are receptions of free peasants into bondage (Waldburg-Zeil'sches Gesamtarchiv Schloss Zeil, Archivkörper Zeil, Urkunden 24, 28, 29, 49, 51, 53, 58–60, 62, 64, 68, 69, 73, 85–87, 90, 92–96, 100, 101, 109, 114, 135, 140, 145, 159, 161, 165b, 172, and 176). Surprisingly enough, there are hardly any data about serfdom in the neighboring Waldburg seigneury of Wurzach. See P. Blickle, *Kempten,* pp. 200 f.; and F. L. Baumann, *Geschichte des Allgäus,* 2:626; Joseph Vochezer, *Geschichte des fürstlichen Hauses Waldburg,* 2:630 ff.

11. Emperor Sigismund (1410–37) forbade all subjects and cities of the empire to give refuge to persons in various categories of bondage. In 1431 the abbey of Rot secured a privilege that its serfs, tenants, and subjects could not be admitted as citizens. In 1479 the abbey of Ochsenhausen received a privilege that, upon request, all imperial cities and other powers had to return the abbey's serfs. In 1434 and 1496 the emperor forbade the city of Kempten to extend its protection over the serfs and tenants of the abbey of Kempten.

12. Müller *(Spätformen der Leibeigenschaft,* pp. 10 ff.) notes that in the Alemannic regions permission to marry, which derived from domanial and servile rights, fell into disuse very early. The need for the lord's consent to marry was the exception everywhere by the fourteenth century.

13. Hauptstaatsarchiv Stuttgart, B 486, U 154.

14. This shows how wrong the older literature was to interpret the article on serfdom (art. 3) as a demand for the abolition of the mere "concept" of serfdom.

15. According to the calculations of David Sabean, *Landbesitz,* pp. 59, 82, in the region around Weingarten no more than one tenant farmer in three was able to produce surpluses for market.

16. See the summary by David Sabean for the region of the Twelve Articles, *Landbesitz,* p. 86; and Blickle, "Bäuerliches Eigen im Allgäu." Peasant allods are very difficult to detect in the sources, especially in this early period, because they usually show up only when they were sold to abbeys, nobles, towns, hospitals, or townsmen or when mortgaged to nobles, clerics, and burghers. Tax books, which are a real help for the modern period, are nonexistent for the fifteenth century.

17. Because of this sort of research is extremely time-consuming, only the material for one abbey (Rot an der Rot) has been analyzed. For references to the Memmingen region see Blickle, *Memmingen,* pp. 351–55.

18. Even today we still do not know where the Upper Swabian imperial cities obtained the raw materials they needed for making linen and fustian. In the feudal rent book for the villages of Memmingen there is no mention of flax dues before 1525, but by the second half of the sixteenth century this due was paid by all peasant holdings. Flax dues were also unknown in Weingarten. This could mean that the cloth producers, whose production was doubtless greater in 1400 than in 1550, obtained their raw materials directly from the peasants, that is, from peasant allods. In protecting the processing of flax and hemp, the judicial and village ordinances from the fifteenth century prove that peasants did raise fiber crops.

19. Exact and quantifiable statements are extremely hard to formulate because of scanty sources before 1525. One has to be content with outlining the main tendencies and trends.

20. At the end of the fifteenth century and at the beginning of the sixteenth, sales of allodial estates and of inheritance rights became common, as a result of the peasants' economic troubles. It was in this way that the abbey of Rot acquired quite a sizeable territory.

21. The calculation depends on the assumption that yields per acre were roughly the same in southern and northern Upper Swabia. Using the yields calculated by Sabean *(Landbesitz,* p. 57), one finds that in Mietingen peasants harvested 328.01 kg. of oats per hectare and had to pay dues of 98.28 kg.

22. So far as I have been able to determine, in the Memmingen area only one feudal lease (1474) inserted the claim that the landlord could increase dues even during the period covered by the contract. Otherwise, all feudal leases agreed that dues could not be increased during the life of the contract.

23. As an example of the relative stability of rents, a farm in Betzenhausen is here presented. In the fifteenth century the landlords were citizens of Memmingen; in the sixteenth century dues were paid to the Unterhospital in Memmingen.

	1474	1486	1494	1574
Size of farm				
Arable*	30	30	———	35
Meadow†	15	15	———	17
Dues				
Rye‡	6M	6M	6M 4Q	6M 4Q
Oats‡	3M	3M	3M 4Q	3M 4Q
Hay money	4 lb. h.	4 lb. h.	4 lb. 7 sh. h.	5 lb. 7 sh. h.
Hens	1	1	1	2
Other Fowl	6	6	6	6
Eggs	150	150	150	150
Flax				4 lb.

*In jauchert.
†In days' work.
‡In malters (M) and quarters (Q).

24. Generally speaking, feudal leases and agreements do not reveal the size of farms, and only in a few cases can one consult records of the arable. But one can be certain that a farm's size has remained constant only in cases where the documents clearly state that a certain peasant had taken over a farm of unchanged size—a very unusual statement.

25. The problem was probably as old as landlordship itself and was solved differently from one case to the next. Thus, in 1425 the abbey of Rot was ordered by arbitration to grant its subjects in Haslach a reduction of dues because of crop failure and war.

26. See below, pp. 50–51.

27. Timber was floated downstream on the Danube, Iller, Wertach, Aitrach, Schussen, and other rivers as well.

28. For the territory governed by the imperial city of Memmingen only one feudal lease (for a farm in an area to be cleared, in Betzenhausen) provided that the tenant was entitled to sell five cords of wood annually. Through a contract in 1512 the peasants of the sovereign abbey of Kempten and of the prince bishop of Augsburg succeeded in asserting their rights to obtain and sell timber and to use the woods for pasture. Still, in 1525 the men of Kempten complained that they were forbidden to sell wood. Occasionally the sale of wood was explicitly prohibited in feudal leases, as in 1474 on a farm in Betzenhausen. As early as 1456 the peasants of Mietingen, near Baltringen, were forbidden to sell wood from the communal forest. This was also the case at Mähringen and in the abbeys of Söflingen and Ochsenhausen.

29. Village ordinances and contracts lead one to suspect that before 1500 peasants could sometimes use the lords' woods whenever they needed and wanted to, as in the case of the subjects of the abbey of Weissenau in Ummendorf. A privilege of Emperor Sigismund (1410–37) for the abbey of Rot forbade its subjects to cut timber in the forests of the abbey.

30. We can observe this process in detail in the abbey of Rot. Peasants had to satisfy their needs first from woods belonging to their farms or from common woods; the abbey's own restricted forests were open to use only if peasants did not have their own woods, common woods, or woods that they rented. In 1396 the abbey tried to abolish these rights but, after arbitration, had to concede them to the peasants of Zell. During the fifteenth century the abbey exercised a right of supervision over all sorts of forests, claiming that it had to prevent plundering of the woods. At the same time peasants were forbidden to sell timber even from their own woods. And finally, in 1456 peasant rights to woodland pasture were restricted, with landed peasants being allowed to pasture four pigs, and cottagers, only two. Collecting acorns and beech nuts was now punished with fines.

31. This was proclaimed in an edict of 1445. These money payments varied from 5 shillings heller (for a handcart?) to 1 pfund heller (for a team and wagon?). One pfund heller was roughly the same as the annual hay-dues owed by a whole farm to its landlord.

32. It can be shown that villages were well aware of this problem as early as the fifteenth century, and to the extent that they controlled the communal woods, they undertook conservation measures similar to those imposed by the princely policy.

33. The statistical breakdown is as follows: 80 percent of the subjects of nobles and 70.58 percent of monastic subjects complained of forest policies, while 57.14 percent of urban and hospital subjects complained. With the complaints against restrictions on grazing rights, the breakdown is 60 percent, 41.17 percent, and 28.56 percent, respectively.

34. Noble subjects: 53.33 percent; monastic subjects: 66.67 percent; urban and hospital subjects: 14.28 percent.

35. Noble subjects: 33.33 percent; monastic subjects: 35.29 percent. Villages belonging to towns and hospitals did not complain of fishing restrictions at all.

36. In trying to calculate days of compulsory labor and of services with precision, one encounters difficulties because one cannot tell in each case whether the services demanded would require only half a day or even more than one day. For instance, the provisions for Alleshausen state: "On account of service due, henceforth every peasant of Alleshausen and Brachsenberg having four horses shall annually provide three horses along with mine; and a peasant with three horses shall provide two; and one with two horses shall provide two as well. And they shall ride and work up to half a mile away, to where the lands of the lord of Marchtal extend. And anyone having only one horse shall annually provide a cord of wood or pay four kreutzers instead; and anyone with no horse at all shall also provide annually a cord of wood or four kreutzers; and this wood shall be set aside in a rack especially for this purpose just as other neighbors keep their own." The peasants from the lordship of Argen (subject to the counts of Montfort) performed four days of service at Lake Constance and were obliged further to harvest and cut hay one day each, to transport five wagonloads of wood to their lord's house, to attend their lord for two days, and to make two trips to transport hay and grain from the fields to storage.

37. Only 2.56 percent of the Baltringen articles and 1.85 percent of all the articles from Upper Swabia complained of the excise.

38. Taking into account all of Upper Swabia, 18.75 percent of noble subjects and 10.0 percent of urban subjects complained of military taxes, compared to 50.0 percent of monastic subjects.

39. Complaints about restrictions on communal self-government or demands for an increase in communal rights account for 25.93 percent of the grievance articles. Complaints about the administration of justice were recorded in 53.70 percent of the articles.

40. Monastic regions: 29 percent; noble regions: 20 percent.

41. Burghers, hospitals, and towns were able to secure a foothold in the country mainly at the expense of the lower nobility, who were becoming progressively poorer. Nobles were willing to sell off lands first, but they held on to rights of lordship (jurisdiction, rights of command) as long as possible.

42. The preamble to the seigneurial ordinance of Söflingen of ca. 1495 (P. Gehring, *Nördliches Oberschwaben*, pp. 213, 538).

43. F. L. Baumann, *Akten,* no. 62.

44. Although serfs could not be freely sold, they changed lords when their farm was sold. In such cases the documents of sale often asserted the right of serfs to continue farming the land and prohibited any changes in their burdens and rights.

45. This explains the jurisdictional difficulties which the Swabian League was unable to solve. Was it the lord of high justice or of low justice who was the local lord? Was it the landlord or the lord of high justice who had sovereignty in taxation and in military matters?

46. We have only approximate ideas of the development of population in the Upper Swabian imperial cities during the fourteenth and fifteenth centuries but we have examples that permit us to estimate the general growth of population. The population of Ravensburg, despite many plagues, rose from 1,500 in 1300 to 3,500 in 1380, and to 4,500 in 1500. In Ulm it rose from 4,000 in 1300 to 7,000 in 1345, to 9,000 in 1400, to 13,000 in 1450, to 17,000 in 1500, and to 19,000 in 1550.

47. As early as 1486 the estates of the Swabian League agreed not to tolerate in their lordships any serfs owned by fellow estates-members.

48. At about the same time the population figures from the imperial cities turn downward. Until recently it has been common to attribute this downturn to economic stagnation in the cities. Scholars have not yet examined the possibility, however, that restrictions on the freedom of movement of peasants may have helped cause this development. As far as we know, only Ulm consciously shut itself off from the surrounding countryside in the fifteenth century.

49. Even if one rejects this train of thought as speculative, the prohibition on freedom of movement would remain a sufficient explanation for the overcrowding in the villages. Indeed, my argument cannot avoid speculation because there are no detailed studies of the distribution of allods and land held in tenure from a lord during the fifteenth century.

50. The source for 1450–80 lists only the serfs of Ottobeuren, while the source for 1548 lists all the "subjects" living within the boundaries of the lower court's jurisdiction, but it does include their various masters. A proper comparison, therefore, can only count the serfs of Ottobeuren. The situation is complicated by the fact that during the period in question serfs were exchanged between lordships. This might have produced an artificial increase in the numbers of Ottobeuren serfs, although it is worth noting that Ottobeuren was not really very interested in exchanging serfs or in the institution of serfdom as a whole. It is also unclear whether or not both lists are complete, which might be something one could check with archival records in Munich.

51.   The condition of the sources makes it necessary to compare the number of women with the number of children. Since not all women had children, the family sizes mentioned should be corrected upwards.

52.   By 1548 the population in the large enclosed villages was obviously reacting by controlling births; as the following table makes clear:

	1450–80			1548		
	Women	Children	Children per woman	Women	Children	Children per woman
Attenhausen	24	74	3.08	48	109	2.27
Benningen	21	51	2.43	62	155	2.50
Hawangen	53	201	3.79	104	225	2.16
Frechenrieden	24	81	3.38	52	122	2.35
Egg	12	51	4.25	32	65	2.03
Sontheim	28	84	3.50	46	139	3.02
Ottobeuren	52	132	2.54	52	118	2.27

53.   The tithe on livestock was not common in Upper Swabia so far as I can see, at least with respect to small domestic animals like poultry and goats. Perhaps lords were able to take advantage of this lucrative source of extra income only by collecting heriots.

54.   H. Decker-Hauff, *Die Chronik der Grafen von Zimmern,* 2:272.

55.   Baumann, *Akten,* no. 62, p. 55.

56.   G. Franz, *Der deutsche Bauernkrieg: Aktenband,* p. 150.

57.   Hauptstaatsarchiv Stuttgart B486 U207 and Stiftungsarchiv Memmingen 58/3 and 4.

58.   We can demonstrate the presence of the following at imperial diets: Weingarten from 1460 on; Salem from 1471; Marchtal, Ochsenhausen, Rot, Schussenried, and Weissenau from 1497; and Buchau from 1501 on.

59.   P. Herrmann, *Zimmerische Chronik,* 2:533.

CHAPTER 3

1.   Special problems attach to the evaluation of this group of articles. See Baumann, *Akten,* p. 208. Appended to the grievances of the subjects as a whole are local articles from individual villages and districts. The latter are excluded from this statistical evaluation in order not to skew the larger picture. This analysis is therefore based on only five grievance lists: (1) Winzeln-Hochmössingen (Herrmann, *Zimmerische Chronik,* 2:354 ff.); (2) the seigneuries of Stühlingen and Lupfen (Baumann, *Akten,* pp. 188–208); (3) the seigneuries of Fürstenberg (omitting the regional grievances of Lenzkirch, Löffingen, Rötenbach, Reiböhringen, Döggingen, Unadingen, Waldau, Neustadt, and the valleys of Bregenbach, Hammereisenbach, Schönenbach, Langenbach, Linach, Urach, Schollach, Langenordnach, and Viertäler), plus Vöhrenbach, Rudenberg, Schwarzenbach, Langenordnach, Schollach, Schönenbach, and Hausen vor Wald (ibid., pp. 209–24); (4) Göschweiler (ibid., pp. 225 f.); and (5) Brigtal (ibid., pp. 96 f.).

2.   The five lists are naturally too small a basis for a schematic statistical analysis, so that the percentages are only approximate. Including the local lists yields very different figures but illustrates the same tendencies.

3.   Depending on how one classifies them, 30–40 percent of the articles concern financial burdens on the farms. The figure for Baltringen is 71.79 percent.

4.   For Hegau-Black Forest, 20–24 percent; for Baltringen, 5.13 percent.

5. The figures on serfdom vary so widely, depending on how one classifies the articles, that here we can supply only estimates based on the classification used for the five basic lists. About 30–40 percent demand the abolition of serfdom here, while the figure for Baltringen is 82.05 percent.

6. The complaints from the two regions compare as follows:

	Hegau-Black Forest	*Baltringen*
Marriage restrictions	ca. 70%	15.38%
Death taxes	ca. 80%	33.33%
Labor dues	20–23%	12.82%

7. Free movement, ca. 35 percent; inheritance rights, ca. 50 percent. Of course, the grievance about inheritance rights could just as well be incorporated into articles against the death tax. The problem was in any case more prominent in the Hegau-Black Forest grievances than in the Baltringen ones.

8.

	Hegau-Black Forest	*Baltringen*
Complaints against communal administrators	ca. 50%	10.26%
Complaints against village employees	ca. 20%	10.26%

9.

	Hegau-Black Forest	*Baltringen*
Wood	ca. 60%	66.67%
Commons	ca. 15%	12.82%
Fishing rights	ca. 50%	20.51%
Hunting rights	ca. 45%	12.82%
Damages by wild game	ca. 30%	2.56%

10.

	Hegau-Black Forest	*Baltringen*
Labor dues, general	80–82%	51.28%
Military taxes	ca. 50%	28.21%
Taxes, general	ca. 75%	10.26%
Excise on foodstuffs	ca. 50%	2.56%

11. The twenty-four articles are reprinted by H. Schreiber, *Der deutsche Bauernkrieg,* pt. 2, p. 197, no. 324; and by Franz, *Der deutsche Bauernkrieg: Aktenband,* p. 207, no. 73. Here is the reference to the fact that the House of Austria never held serfs (the text actually says that Habsburg subjects on the Upper Rhine were now in danger of enserfment).

12. Collating the order of the Sundgau-Upper Alsatian articles with that of the Twelve Articles; art. 1 (Sundgau-Upper Alsace) = art. 1 (Twelve Articles); art. 2 = art. 2; art. 3 = art. 3; art. 4 = art. 4; art 5 = arts. 5–7; art. 6 = art. 8; art. 7 = art. 9; art. 8 = art. 10; art. 9 = art. 11; art. 24 = art. 12.

13. W. Vogt, "Correspondenz," no. 226b.

14. Franz, *Quellen,* p. 50, no. 8.

15. Ibid., p. 301.

16. Ibid., p. 306.

17. Ibid., pp. 308 f. (art. 23), which refers to the excise on foodstuffs *(Ungeld).*

18. H. Wopfner, *Quellen,* presents the local, regional, and territorial grievance lists. A quantitative analysis similar to the one we have made of the Upper Swabian lists cannot be offered here, as the ca. 130 local documents would take too much work. Then too, the majority of the local documents were composed after the Merano-Innsbruck articles and could simply ignore those matters already covered in the general grievance lists. In weighing the grievances it is helpful to reach back to the decades before 1525, when the peasants frequently submitted such lists (analyzed by Macek, *Tiroler Bauernkrieg,* p. 69). Macek's analysis enables us to gain a rough weighing of the causes of the Tyrolean revolt, for the 343 articles occur with the following frequencies:

1. New dues; cash exactions and repeated increases in same	73
2. New tolls, duties, etc.	52
3. Violations of the commons and of freedom of the woods, pastures, and waters; hunting restrictions	49
4. Arbitrary and corrupt behavior of wardens and other officials	31
5. Damages by wild game and by hunters	24
6. Labor dues and increases in same	19
7. Taxation levels; debts for taxes	15
8. Dues to the church	15
9. Violations of traditional rights and customs	12
10. Ecclesiastical abuses	10

19. Fully a quarter of the Merano-Innsbruck articles are concerned in some way with landlordship.

20. The territorial assembly of St. Gallen further complained about properties being bought up and placed in mortmain, which raised peasants' taxes; they also objected to restrictions on the commons and to servile labor dues. The analogous body in Thurgau complained of the excise tax on food and drink and of the confiscation of farms in capital cases (thereby dispossessing the surviving children).

CHAPTER 4

1. The concept of territorial serfdom is better than the traditional idea of local serfdom because it indicates more clearly that serfdom was used as an instrument of territorial policy in a distinct interest sector above the local level.

2. H. Wopfner, *Die Lage Tirols,* p. 73.

3. W. Müller, *Spätformen der Leibeigenschaft,* pp. 32 ff., provides evidence on confiscation for all of southern Germany. These confiscations include only what was taken from the heirs, not the penalties. During the later Middle Ages, marriage outside the lord's jurisdiction was punished with confiscation (e.g., in Lindau, Allerheiligen, Weitenau, and Constance), with additional annual fines in cash or kind, and with nonrecurring money fines from 3 gulden up to 100 lb. For the Saarland, where conditions were similar to those in Upper Swabia, see I. Eder's work on the Saarland customaries, *Die saarländischen Weistümer.*

4. Quoted from F. Martini, *Das Bauerntum,* p. 251.

5. Historians of agriculture have until now concerned themselves chiefly with questions of agrarian organization, largely because the materials for statistical analysis are so fragmentary and so difficult to use. Although we have nothing for Germany comparable to E. Le Roy Ladurie, *Les paysans de Languedoc,* Sabean's *Landbesitz* has shown that such work can be done in Germany.

6. E. Kelter, "Die wirtschaftlichen Ursachen," pp. 670–81, notes that even the market-oriented peasant had to sell his produce at less than market value, because he could not freely select his marketplace. The cities' and princes' ability to store grain could ruin the peasant even in times of short harvests. Little is known about the peasants' ability to trade in grain; but see G. Franz, "Die Geschichte des deutschen Landwarenhandels," pp. 30 ff. Individual peasant families who were wealthier than average appear in many chronicles and were to be found in all territories. For Alsace, see F. Rapp, "L'aristocratie paysanne."

7. The basic studies are Sabean, *Landbesitz,* and F. Pietsch, "Die Artikel der Limpurger Bauern." Pietsch shows that the transfer fines originally were fixed at the symbolic payment of a measure of wine, but by 1520 they had climbed to 15 percent of the property's value. Risking an extrapolation, this could come to 20 or 30 times the annual rent; and if we assume an average tenure of 20–30 years, this would mean an increase of 100 percent.

8. David Sabean's thesis that the conflict between peasant and cottager provided a motive for the Peasants' War has made a strong and favorable impression. At the basis of this thesis, however, is the concept of peasant society (with groups distinguished according to their degree of involvement in the market); unfortunately, the usefulness of this concept has not yet been shown empirically. Sabean found only two relevant examples in the region he studied, and even they are contested.

9. Stadtarchiv Memmingen, 14/1.

10. H. W. Eckardt, *Herrschaftliche Jagd,* p. 78.

11. The leases sometimes fixed the wood-cutting rights, setting a maximum to be cut, but they did not yet specify a money payment.

12. Fred Graf, "Die soziale und wirtschaftliche Lage," pp. 149–157, presents evidence indicating that fishing was probably very important to the peasants. The restriction of usage rights, documented by Graf, corresponded to the upward movement of prices.

13. A. Hauser, "Bäuerliche Wirtschaft," p. 173, calculates that in Switzerland the average farm had three to four cows.

14. In the Salem territory the number of persons obliged to pay taxes rose about 15 percent between 1488 and 1505, according to H. Baier, "Zur Bevölkerungs und Vermögensstatistik," p. 197.

15. By 1491 Tyrol already had laws against begging; and Bavaria had one by the end of the fifteenth century. Imperial legislation on begging began in 1497.

16. In the suits conducted by the city of Zurich against those who illegally sought mercenary service abroad, returning soldiers asserted that poverty compelled them. See W. Schnyder, *Die Bevölkerung der Stadt und Landschaft Zürich,* p. 110, R. Wackernagel, *Humanismus und Reformation,* p. 376.

17. O. Pickl has shown that in Styria the labor intensity was especially high (4.03–5.20 persons per farm) where there was no alternative employment in the mines (in the iron mining center of Mürzzuschlag the average was only 2.74 persons per farm). Persons under twelve years of age are not included in these figures, which means that the average family size in Styria, a region hit hard by feuds and Turkish raids, was considerably higher than this. See Pickl, "Arbeitskräfte und Viehbesatz," p. 147.

18. G. Oestreich, *Geist und Gestalt,* pp. 5 f.

19. G. Oestreich, "Verfassungsgeschichte," p. 361.

20. The financial exigencies of territorial policy require further research. The connections between the consolidation of the state and the rise of taxation have been especially well demonstrated for Saxony and the Palatinate. Thus, the growth of the bureaucracy in Saxony during the sixteenth century was financed only through the substantial incomes from the mines (Oestreich, "Verfassungsgeschichte," p. 407). The consolidation of territorial sovereignty in the Palatinate cost 520,000 gulden (G. Landwehr, "Die Bedeutung der Reichs- und Territorialpfandschaften").

21. We can no longer speak of a general reception of Roman law in the agrarian sector. For recent views of this legal problem, see F. Wieacker, *Privatrechtsgeschichte,* p. 119, and H. Conrad, *Deutsche Rechtsgeschichte,* 2:339–43.

22. Wopfner, *Quellen,* p. 39.

23. The legal distinctions among village, association, commune, etc., need not be discussed here. In what follows "commune" (*Gemeinde*) means any sort of locally or regionally limited rural association possessing political functions, regardless of whether it refers to a village or to a larger district containing several villages, hamlets, or no nucleated settlements. *Gericht* and *Hauptmannschaft* are two common names for such associations.

24. It must be conceded that this increase was partly due to the growth of literacy.

25. See esp. Wieacker, *Privatrechtsgeschichte,* pp. 63 ff., 118. Of course, legislation is not synonymous with Roman law, whose minimal importance for the Peasants' War was long ago established by A. Stern, "Das römische Recht und der deutsche Bauernkrieg."

26. The fact that this emancipation is known only through written documents has made it seem that it came about at the will of the lords rather than at the demand of associative organizations, which is clearly wrong.

CHAPTER 5

1. *Deutsche Reichstagsakten,* jüngere Reihe, 1:843 f., no. 378.

2. Even though the Stühlingen revolt of 1524 resembled in its course and structure the risings elsewhere in 1525 (see Franz, *Bauernkrieg,* 1st ed., pp. 158–81), I do not believe that it should be regarded as the beginning of the Peasants' War, for two reasons. First, the peasants appealed only to the old law for legitimation. Second, in this way they allowed themselves to be forced into a legal solution to their grievances. This revolt thus belongs with the older revolts and uprisings and does not mark any general breakthrough to a new type.

3. This conclusion is not contradicted by the example of the Bundschuh risings on the Upper Rhine, which in their conspiratorial, elitist, and radical character differed essentially both from the Peasants' War and from the other early revolts.

4. Franz, *Bauernkrieg,* 1st ed., p. 184.

5. Ibid.

6. See Appendix 2 for the material on which this is based. This evaluation is based only on the individual articles. In the preamble the articles were sometimes based as a whole on the old law (7.69 percent) or on the godly law (12.82 percent), while individual articles referred less often to godly law and more often to the old law.

7. Vogt, "Correspondenz," no. 83.

8. See the opening statement of the Twelve Articles in Appendix 1.

9. Stadtarchiv Memmingen, 341/6 (draft), of which the final version is printed by Baumann, *Akten,* pp. 120, 126, no. 108. [The Senate's ironical remark alluded to the Twelve Articles (art. 1) and meant that the Senate wanted the same power to accept or reject tenants that the villages wanted to accept or reject pastors.—TRANS.]

10. Schreiber, *Der deutsche Bauernkrieg,* pt. 3, pp. 25–31, no. 382.

11. Franz and Fuchs, *Akten,* 2:91.

CHAPTER 6

1. According to G. Franz, *Bauernkrieg,* 1st ed., pp. 220 f., and H. Buszello, *Der deutsche Bauernkrieg,* p. 59. It is quite possible that Lotzer obtained his draft from somewhere in the Upper Rhineland, but his dependence on such a source has not yet been strictly proved. It is noteworthy, however, that in Basel there are manuscript versions of a federal ordinance that are identical even in the smallest details with the so-called Lotzer draft.

2. Because of a lack of detailed sources, it is still unclear whether the quasi-political units within the Christian Association, such as the "whole common assembly" of Kempten, were to have much of a role in keeping political order.

3. G. Franz, *Quellen,* p. 180, no. 44.

4. Individual, smaller subunits could, however, be much more active when it came to alienating servants from their lords and persuading nobles to join the association.

5. Franz, *Quellen,* pp. 295, 297, no. 94.

6. This implies that the cathedral chapter was to be stripped of its privileges and that abbeys were to be placed under the government of the assembly.

7. Landesarchiv Salzburg, Landschaft, Kasten II, instruction to Ferdinand on organizing the estates, March 1526.

8. Landesarchiv Salzburg, Geheimes Archiv XI/5, vol. 21.

9. W. Vogt, "Correspondenz," no. 738.

10. Except for Marxist research the literature on the Peasants' War has not paid much attention to this question at all. Only E. Kelter, "Die wirtschaftlichen Ursachen," emphasizes this point explicitly.

CHAPTER 7

1. This entry in the senate records is printed in W. Schlenck, *Memmingen,* p. 18.

2. Ibid., p. 16.

3. Ibid., p. 30.

4. M. Brecht, "Der theologische Hintergrund"; W. Schlenck, *Memmingen,* p. 32. During the first half of 1523 Schappeler was in Switzerland for an extended period. Vadian recommended him to Zurich, and Zwingli tried to attract him to a preachership in Winterthur.

5. Stadtarchiv Memmingen 341/4, the city of Memmingen to Konrad Peutinger, 27 February 1524.

6. The following account is based on Stadtarchiv Memmingen 341/4, "Hernach volgt alle handlung . . .," written on 13 July 1524.

7. The villages here described as belonging to imperial cities belonged actually in the main to the hospital but also to a lesser extent to townsmen. There were extremely few that belonged directly to the imperial city itself.

8. F. L. Baumann, *Akten,* pp. 119 f. no. 107. The Baltringen army used exactly these words in a letter to the city of Ehingen (ibid., p. 131, no. 119).

9. Demands for the election of pastors and for communion under both species had previously been voiced only by the village of Steinheim (Baumann, *Akten,* p. 36).

10. W. Vogt, "Correspondenz," p. 36.

11. Ibid., nos. 159, 161, 166, 178, 209, 224, 356, 380. The following cities were involved in such efforts to attain compromise: Constance, Lindau, Memmingen, Ravensburg, Kempten, Biberach, Kaufbeuren, Isny, Wangen, and Leutkirch—i.e., nearly all of the imperial cities of Upper Swabia.

12. Vogt, "Correspondenz," no. 159.

13. Ibid., no. 386; Ulm wrote to Nuremberg with the same fear (ibid., no. 431).

14. H. Virck, *Politische Correspondenz,* p. 113, no. 199. Strasbourg itself regarded the preachers as "not the smallest cause" of the rising of the common man (Archive de la ville de Strasbourg, AA 1982, fol. 99).

15. Virck, *Politische Correspondenz,* pp. 144 ff., no. 201.

16. Ibid., pp. 120 f., no. 212; pp. 124 f., no. 221.

17. Archive de la ville de Strasbourg, AA 386, fols. 33–48 verso.

18. Virck, *Politische Correspondenz,* p. 161, no. 286.

19. Ibid., p. 161, no. 287.

20. M. von Rauch, *Urkundenbuch,* 4:28, no. 2785.

21. Ibid., pp. 34 ff., no. 2794.

22. Ibid., p. 59, no. 2816.

23. Ibid., p. 64, 2824.

24. O. Rammstedt has labeled these three phases: (1) protest, (2) articulation of protest, (3) institutionalization of the articulated protest. See his article "Stadtunruhen." The quotations are from pp. 252 and 256.

25. H. Decker-Hauff, *Die Chronik der Grafen von Zimmern,* 2:271.

26. O. Merx, *Akten,* pp. 121 f.

27. K. Czok, "Zur sozialökonomischen Struktur," p. 65.

28. Bayerisches Hauptstaatsarchiv München, Abt. I, Allgemeines Archiv, Kriegsakten 73, fol. 58.

29. Vogt, "Correspondenz," no. 801, reads the first four words quoted here as "countryside in the mines," which makes no sense in the context of this source.

30. Ibid.

31. K. H. Ludwig, "Bergleute," p. 36.

32. G. Franz, *Bauernkrieg,* 1st ed., p. 416; the latest summary is in M. Bensing, *Thomas Müntzer.*

33. This is true from Sartorius (1795) through Oechsle (1830), Zimmermann (1841), and Franz (1933), to Buszello (1969).

34. G. Franz, *Quellen,* pp. 235, no. 68; 370 f, no. 122; p. 426, no. 140.

35. Virck, *Politische Correspondenz,* p. 211, no. 364.

36. *Abrede unnd entlicher vertrage,* fol. A1.

37. Quoted by J. E. Jörg, *Deutschland in der Revolutions-Periode,* pp. 96 f.

38. Vogt, "Correspondenz," no. 202.

39. Quoted in H. Bornkamm, *Luther,* p. 331.

40. H. Wopfner, *Quellen,* p. 52, and even more clearly on pp. 191 f.

41. Vogt, "Correspondenz," no. 406.

42. Following the edition of H. Buszello in *Der deutsche Bauernkrieg,* p. 165.

43. This is the sphere to which R. H. Lutz, in *Wer war der gemeine Mann?,* thinks the term should be confined. In his attempt to sharpen the concept, for example, he excludes servants and dishonorable people. Aiming an attack at my interpretation, his thesis seems strikingly simple at first sight: the common man was the guildsman in the city and the peasant in the village. In other words, the common man was the fully legal member of an urban or rural community. Unfortunately, the thesis is not persuasive because one cannot equate the legal concept of "member of a community" (*Gemeindsmann*) with the political concept of the "common man" (*Gemeiner Mann*). Verbal constructions analogous to common man are, e.g., the common good, common (Catholic) Christendom, and the common penny (i.e., a general tax). These phrases all point to something general, not to anything tied to a concrete political or social body, such as a town or village. In this regard the work of H. M. Maurer, "Der Bauernkrieg als Massenerhebung," is important, for it shows with statistical material that the insurrection was indeed all-encompassing, at least in the sense that the majority of able-bodied men took part in it (pp. 256 ff.).

CHAPTER 8

1. Even if the committee of the assembly acted as government and appointed judges and administrators, this did not violate the electoral principle, at least in the sense that the territorial diet and assembly committee were elected from the communes, if we may generalize from the practice of 1525. The right demanded by the Twenty-four Articles to have a say in the appointment of judges was thus not eliminated. Otherwise this demand reflects an earlier draft of the program.

2. Diehl has shown that the term *gemeiner Nutzen,* "common good," occurs in South Germany in the late Middle Ages and that it covered the political goals of the lower classes. In 1525 the concept gained a greater dignity by being called the "Christian common good." The likely connections between the terms "common good" and "common man" need closer attention.

3. H. Buszello, in his *Bauernkrieg*, p. 68, suggests that "freeing" could have implied the abolition of all intermediate authorities, and he goes on to use this possibility as one of the supports for his argument that the German southwest was aiming at a status directly subject to the emperor.

4. Printed in G. Franz, *Quellen*, p. 235, no. 68.

5. "For before we subject ourselves to this government again, from which we expect no good of any kind, we would rather all go under, using our last energies and giving up our goods . . . because we are sure and certain that the lords will not keep faith, honor, and trust with us, regardless of their pretty words" (J. Strickler, *Eidgenössische Abschiede*, 4, sec. 1:686).

6. Ibid.

7. Our trust in the document may be strengthened by the fact that Freiburg possesses a manuscript draft of the Federal Ordinance. The state archive in Basel also possesses a manuscript version that is closely related to Lotzer's draft. Ms. C. Ulbrich-Manderscheid of Saarbrücken has also given me a copy of a transcription of the Federal Ordinance found in the holdings of the abbey of St. Blasien; it is identical with the Upper Swabian published version of 7 March. See above, Chap. 6, n. 1.

8. H. Virck, *Correspondenz*, pp. 127 f., no. 230.

9. Ibid., pp. 161 f., no. 289.

10. The terminology used by the sources is vague. In order to say anything conclusive here, it would probably be necessary to consult the originals of documents published only in summary form by Virck. Then one might be able to determine if these names implied functional differences.

11. Scholars have not yet seriously considered the extent to which the military organization could have been the framework for a political organization as well. If one takes this possibility seriously, one gains a much clearer notion of the goals than one can glean from the few programmatic statements that happen to have survived.

12. Article 1 of the "Articles to be sworn . . .," Virck, *Correspondenz*, p. 182.

13. Private wealth was thus diminished not just by destroying castles and lowering dues as is claimed by G. Franz, *Der deutsche Bauernkrieg*, 9th ed., p. 183, and Buszello, *Bauernkrieg*, p. 39.

14. Franz, *Der deutsche Bauernkrieg*, 1st ed., p. 311.

15. H. Schreiber, *Der deutsche Bauernkrieg*, pt. II, pp. 85 f., no. 216.

16. This idea, which is common throughout the literature, is based on just one passage. See Franz, *Der deutsche Bauernkrieg*, 9th ed., p. 138; and Buszello, *Bauernkrieg*, pp. 70 f.

17. H. Wopfner, *Quellen*, p. 53.

18. G. Franz, "Kanzlei der württembergischen Bauern," pp. 92 f., no. 20; 96, no. 28; 98, no. 35; 99, no. 38; 100, no. 39; 100 f., no. 40; 103, no. 44; 283, no. 57; 304 f., no. 90. Without any apparent reason, Franz describes this as a "secularization" of the concept of godly justice *(Der deutsche Bauernkrieg,* 1st ed., pp. 355 f.).

19. Each district was to send six deputies to the diet—three from the town (one each from court, senate, and commons) and three from the district villages.

20. Franz, "Kanzlei der württembergischen Bauern," pp. 99, no. 36; 107, no. 51; 282, no. 55; 284, no. 59; 287, no. 65; 291, no. 74; 294, no. 80.

21. Ibid., pp. 292 f., nos. 76 and 77.

22. Ibid., p. 294, no. 80; see also p. 106, no. 50.

23. Ibid., p. 100, no. 40.

24. Ibid., pp. 297 f., nos. 85 and 86. The letter sent by the rebels to the Swabian League on April 30 (ibid., p. 106, no. 50) has been taken by Buszello, *Bauernkrieg*, p. 77, and probably also by Franz, *Der deutsche Bauernkrieg*, 1st ed., p. 357, as proof that there was a party of

Habsburg sympathizers among the rebels. In my view this was nothing more than a politic (and empty) confirmation of imperial sovereignty. The Württembergers were concerned only to distinguish themselves from the rebels elsewhere. Buszello's interpretation here confuses the empire with the Habsburgs. The letter in question spoke only of the emperor, not of Archduke Ferdinand, who was the territorial ruler of Württemberg at the time.

25. They intended a reconciliation with Bavaria, the emperor, and the Swabian League and a solution of financial problems.

26. Franz, "Kanzlei der württembergischen Bauern," p. 298.

27. Nearly all general treatments of the Peasants' War offer a description of the contents of Gaismair's plan and an interpretation; see A. Waas, *Bauern,* pp. 253 f.; Franz, *Der deutsche Bauernkrieg,* 1st ed., pp. 261-64. L. Zuck, *Christianity and Revolution,* pp. 20-24, gives an abbreviated version in English. Here we shall content ourselves with referring to the recent and divergent books by Angermeier, Macek, and Seibt (see Works Cited). Scholars have overlooked the interesting work of H. Michaelis, "Bedeutung der Bibel," pp. 87-129, which examines in detail the concept of the justice of God in Gaismair's Constitution and works out Old Testament tendencies in Gaismair's state.

28. Franz, *Quellen,* p. 285.

29. Together with other, widely accepted reasons, this conclusion was drawn from the argument that clerical wealth should be used to care for the poor and noble wealth for meeting judicial costs.

30. Contrary to J. Macek, *Der Tiroler Bauernkrieg,* p. 371, it appears that article 13 must be interpreted to mean that rents were to be abolished or, at most, collected for one more year and used for defensive purposes. Otherwise Macek, pp. 370-75, gives a correct account of the contents and a convincing interpretation of them.

31. "Ruling council" (*Regiment*) and "government" (*Regierung*) seem to have been interchangeable concepts in Michael Gaismair's Constitution. Thus, in article 11 the governors (*Regenten*) for the ruling council (*Regiment*) were to be elected from all the districts. F. Seibt, *Utopica,* p. 85, interprets the ruling council as a "territorial parliament." In my estimation, however, Gaismair was no longer thinking in the categories of the corporate state at all. His constitution has neither diet nor parliament.

32. Franz, *Quellen,* p. 285.

33. Ibid., pp. 231-34.

34. It remains unclear whether the previous lords, by being made part of the league, were to lose their political rights. The draft contradicted itself on this point, but it may not have in its original version, for the original was distorted by the obviously biassed Fabri.

35. It seems to me that several features point to the fact that the Draft of a Constitution has specifically Upper Rhenish conditions in mind: they include the emphasis on excommunication, the frequent use of the terms "fleecing and flaying," and the remarkable hitherto unnoticed parallels with the rough copy of a constitution for the Markgräflerland (Baden) peasants. See above, pp. 135-36. No one has yet proved that Hubmaier had close connections with Markgräflerland, but it is known that Margrave Ernst of Baden tried to act as an intermediary between Waldshut (where Hubmaier was active) and the Habsburgs. These efforts, however, came before the Draft of a Constitution was composed.

36. There is still no end to the controversy over how seriously this statement should be taken. For the latest assessment, see W. Elliger, *Müntzer,* p. 797.

37. G. Franz, *Müntzer,* p. 548.

38. Ibid.

39. M. Bensing, "Idee und Praxis," p. 469.

40. Franz, *Müntzer,* pp. 275 and 463.

41. Ibid., p. 411.

42. Ibid., p. 261.

43. Ibid., p. 256.

44. This and the following quotations are all drawn from the text of the *New Transformation*, in Laube and Seiffert, *Flugschriften*, pp. 547-57.

CHAPTER 9

1. But see M. Brecht, "Der theologische Hintergrund," which argues that "Schappeler's contribution to the Upper Swabian Peasants' War appears to have been made from a Lutheran basis" (p. 44). This conclusion is grounded in the suspicion that Schappeler was mainly influenced by Lazarus Spengler of Nuremberg, a well-known follower of Luther. Brecht's evidence is a comparison of the argument of the Twelve Articles (by Schappeler) and the *Reply and Solution to Several Supposed Arguments* (by Spengler). The strength of this comparison may be doubted. G. Vogler, "Zwölf Artikel," p. 213, also concludes on the basis of content that Luther's influence on the introduction to the Twelve Articles was small. For the established facts see G. Locher, *Die Zwinglische Reformation*, pp. 33, 132, 501. A strong argument for the orientation of Memmingen toward Zwingli is the nomination of Simprecht Schenck to the ministry of Our Lady's Church (January 11, 1525). Until then, Schenck had been the chaplain at Meilen on the Lake of Zurich, and the Zurich Senate tried to keep Schenck in Meilen by intervening directly in Memmingen. See E. Schenck, *Simprecht Schenck*, pp. 9-10, 12-13. Schappeler's ties with Zwingli have recently been proved with new arguments by J. Maurer, *Prediger im Bauernkrieg*, pp. 386 ff.

2. G. Locher, "Grundzüge der Theologie Zwinglis," pp. 209, 213.

3. Ibid., p. 180.

4. This and the following quotations are all drawn from the thirty-ninth article of Zwingli's *Explanation of the Conclusions*. I follow the text of Zwingli, *Hauptschriften*, 4, pt. 2:112-23.

CHAPTER 10

1. According to Anshelm, the Bernese chronicler (printed by Franz, *Quellen*, p. 582, no. 202).

2. The thesis of political emasculation was most recently argued in greater detail by Franz and Waas, but a search for the data behind their arguments finds only a vacuum. Franz strings together examples covering scarcely a tenth of the area of insurrection but claims that they are representative (Franz, *Der deutsche Bauernkrieg*, 9th ed., p. 297); Waas's originality is limited to the Middle Rhenish region (see Waas, "Die grosse Wendung," pp. 458-69).

3. The "Memorial of the Large Committee concerning the Abuses and the Burdens of Subjects," dated August 18, 1526, was edited by Ranke from a Frankfurt copy, in *Deutsche Geschichte*, 6:32-54; extracts appear in Franz, *Quellen*, pp. 593-98. I have checked Ranke's edition against a contemporary copy in the archive of the Germanisches Nationalmuseum in Nuremberg. The memorial itself never mentions the Twelve Articles, but the order of topics makes it certain that they were used in preparing it. The Memorial's recommendations (Ranke ed., pp. 49-51) correspond in their order to articles 2-9 of the Twelve Articles. Article 1 is treated at the beginning of the Memorial (p. 34) in connection with appointments to pastorates; article 11, on the abolition of the death tax, which was not in any logical or systematic position in the Twelve Articles, is handled on p. 50; and article 10, which demands restitution of the common meadows and fields, is treated only indirectly in the larger context of common rights.

4. "Concerning annates," in the Memorial (Ranke ed., pp. 34 f.).

5. The Memorial deals with a few points which appear marginally or not at all in the grievances, such as overcrowding of the villages by Jews and mercenary soldiers, the subjects' duty to participate in local self-help judicial actions, and the costs of the tithe courts. In Tyrol we find the demand that servitors whom the ruler had granted immunity from taxes should nonetheless be forced to pay when they shared communal usage rights. In each case the committee's Memorial proposed reforms (under the rubric "Food," Ranke ed., pp. 52 f.).

6. "That Rome provides incompetent persons to parishes and pastorates" (Memorial, Ranke ed., p. 34).

7. Ibid., p. 50. The Memorial assumed that the farms were leased on heritable tenures, and it intended an extension of inheritance rights to unmarried sons. Like the Twelve Articles, the Memorial envisaged a new regulation of dues, though by the ruler and not by the community.

8. The Memorial expressly recommends that subjects should not be cited in the first instance before the high court at Rottweil or other imperial courts. The connection with grievances from the Upper Rhine is clear, so this article may be attributable to the influence of Strasbourg's envoy.

9. Schulze, "Die veränderte Bedeutung sozialer Konflikte," p. 298. V. Press also supports this thesis in "Der Bauernkrieg als Problem der deutschen Geschichte."

CHAPTER 11

1. The unanimity regarding the failure of the Peasants' War has meant that its consequences have been treated only in a general, comprehensive way. Owing to the complicated state of the sources, exhaustive treatment of the theme can proceed only by examples. This requires a brief explanation. We can estimate the consequences of the Peasants' War only if we look beyond the year 1525, that is, if we investigate individual cases of how serfdom further developed and whether the development can be connected with 1525. In other words, we need careful investigations of political and agrarian history for the sixteenth century, especially for the Middle and Upper Rhine.

2. G. Franz, *Der deutsche Bauernkrieg: Aktenband,* p. 384, no. 196.

3. In any case, serfdom played no role in the free cities' territories. See P. Blickle, *Memmingen,* pp. 411 ff. The hospital's few serfs who were still on the rolls in the eighteenth century were probably acquired after 1525.

4. H. Günter, *Gerwig Blarer,* p. 67, no. 95.

5. The reference to the law of God meant the abolition of serfdom.

6. The grievance list mentions the following as subject to the small tithe: bees, foals, calves, chickens, geese, ducks, hogs, onions, beets, herbs, peas, beans, flax, and hemp.

7. The assessment of the death tax in cash according to the size of holding (whether allod or tenancy) is detailed in Waldburg-Zeil'sches Gesamtarchiv Schloss Zeil, Archivkörper Wurzach 196, which shows that men were assessed twice as much as women.

8. The rather ambiguous documentation seems to say that serfs who owned their land (of whom there were many in the Waldburg lands) or who wanted to move to estates of other landlords within the territory could buy their freedom. Manumission was apparently not possible on the Waldburg demesne lands. Manumission fees were 3 gulden for men and 4 gulden for women upon emigration. If former serfs wanted to remain in the territory, the fee was doubled. In either case the real property continued to be taxed, though no exit fine was collected on personal property.

9. The Waldburg example seems to have served as a model throughout Upper Swabia, but more detailed studies are needed (though see Günter, *Gerwig Blarer,* p. 77, nos. 119 f.; pp. 91 f., no. 144). In the *Tigen* of Rettenberg-Sonthofen (prince-bishopric of Augsburg) the serfdom question was settled as in the Waldburg lands. The death tax of best animal was commuted to a cash payment: for 50-100 lb., 1½ gulden; for 100-300 lb., 3 gulden; for 300-500 lb., 4 gulden; for 500-800 lb., 5 gulden; for 800-1,000 lb., 6 gulden; and for more than 1,000 lb., 10 gulden. For the best garment 1 lb. was charged regardless of the property's value. (Hauptstaatsarchiv Munich, Hochstift Augsburg Urk. fasc. 173, dated September 1, 1525.) Franz, *Der deutsche Bauernkrieg: Aktenband,* p. 163, no. 28, prints the five demands of the

Augsburg subjects (February 1525): abolition of the death tax, abolition of serfdom (freedom to marry, freedom of movement), abolition of services for foreign lords, freedom to hunt and fish, and redeployment of the tithe.

10. One-half gulden on 100 lb.

11. Similar on the whole to the Treaty of Memmingen, but less favorable to the subjects in detail, was the draft of the Treaty of Martinszell, which covered only the subjects of the small Martinszell district of the Kempten (printed by A. Weitnauer, *Die Bauern des Stifts Kempten, 1525/26,* pp. 9–20).

12. P. Gehring, *Nördliches Obers...,* p. 547.

13. K. Hartfelder, "Urkundliche Beiträge," pp. 419–35.

14. The quotations are meant to be easily comparable with the Twelve Articles.

15. The document also calls it the *Etterzehnt* ("kitchen-garden tithe"); the tithe applied to hemp, flax, beans, peas, lentils, wood, beets, cabbage, and fruit, and also livestock (horses, calves, hogs, chickens, geese, sheep, and goats).

16. Properties worth less than 20 gulden were exempt; those worth up to 100 gulden paid, at most, ½ gulden; and sums paid by properties of greater value were correspondingly higher.

17. One exception was the abbey of Waldsassen in the Upper Palatinate. In May 1525, the territorial administration was transferred to a regime of the territorial assembly (*Landschaft*), which was composed of the noble *Landvogt,* two representatives of the town of Tirschenreuth, and two envoys of the assembly (peasants). There was also a concurrent "Committee of the General Assembly," to which each territorial district sent two elected delegates. Born of political unrest, the body fell victim to new unrest in 1529. It is not clear whether the concessions made in 1525—abolition of the small tithe, free usage of the territorial forests, abolition of death taxes, freedom to hunt on one's own property, reduction of servile dues—were preserved. (H. Sturm, *Tirschenreuth,* pp. 96–101.)

18. E. Franz, "Hessen und Kurmainz in der Revolution 1525," pp. 631–32.

19. Quoted from O. Vasella, "Bauernkrieg und Reformation in Graubünden," p. 1.

20. I refer especially to the Rheingau because it has been used in previous works as a decisive support for the thesis that peasants were disfranchised after their rebellion. Cf. A. Waas, *Bauern,* pp. 243–44; and G. Franz, *Der deutsche Bauernkrieg,* 1st ed., pp. 385–86, 477.

CHAPTER 12

1. H. Gunter, *Gerwig Blarer,* pp. 91 f., no. 144.

2. Staatsarchiv Neuburg, Regierung 3065a.

CHAPTER 13

1. G. Franz, *Der deutsche Bauernkrieg,* 9th ed., p. 299.

2. P. F. Barton, "Variationen zum Thema," p. 125, argues that the thesis voiced by Franz and others is a "historical cliché . . . which Franz Lau has unmasked as one of the most dangerous distortions, even falsifications, of history." But for his part, Barton produces only one inadequate reference to Upper Austria (ibid., pp. 136–42).

3. J. Maurer, *Prediger im Bauernkrieg,* p. 246.

4. The reference here is to Franz Lau's well-known study, "Der Bauernkrieg und das angebliche Ende der lutherischen Reformation als spontaner Volksbewegung."

5. B. Moeller, *Deutschland im Zeitalter der Reformation,* p. 101. A. G. Dickens, *The German nation and Martin Luther,* pp. 195 ff., writes in a similar vein, though touching only on urban conditions.

6. W. Gunzert, "Zwei Hagenauer Abschiede," p. 169.

7. Maurer, *Prediger im Baurenkrieg,* pp. 263 ff., points out that after 1525 the clergy favorable to the Reformation clearly emphasized obedience to the ruler.

8. Franz, *Der deutsche Bauernkrieg,* 9th ed., p. 298.

9. G. Maron, "Bauernkrieg," p. 333; H. J. Hillerbrand, "The German Reformation and the Peasants' War," p. 107.

CONCLUSION

1. The concept of feudalism employed here covers the economic, social, and political relations between landlords, serfmasters, and holders of jurisdiction, on the one side, and the peasants, on the other. When the rights of lordship combined landlordship, mastery over serfs, and jurisdictional rights (which was often the case in south Germany), then we may indeed call the state "feudal." But when these rights were divided, as in the territories constituted into estates, the concept should only be used as defined above and not applied to the state because the new forms of public finance (taxes) and administration (bureaucracy) placed the territorial state outside the limits of the feudal system. The concept also does not fit the association of emperor and empire in the fifteenth and sixteenth centuries, the so-called "feudal monarchy." My use of this concept is very close to the French notion of "féodalité." See *L'Abolition de la "Féodalité",* 2 vols. (Paris, 1971).

2. H. Arendt, *On Revolution,* pp. 27–28.

3. S. P. Huntington, "Modernisierung durch Revolution," p. 94.

4. H. Wassmund, *Revolutionstheorien,* p. 42.

5. R. Tanter and M. Midlarsky, "Revolution: Eine quantitative Analyse," p. 135. There are similar formulations in von Beyme's introduction, *Empirische Revolutionsforschung,* pp. 20 ff., esp. p. 24; and Wassmund, *Revolutionstheorien,* p. 16.

6. Wassmund, *Revolutionstheorien,* p. 27.

7. Because the events of 1525 form a failed revolution, we will not consider the category of consequences in the theories of revolution.

8. C. Johnson, *Revolutionary Change,* pp. 135–43; and see M. N. Hagopian, *The Phenomenon of Revolution,* p. 12.

9. C. Johnson, *Autopsy on People's War,* p. 8.

10. C. Brinton, *The Anatomy of Revolution,* pp. 27–64.

11. Ibid., pp. 39–49.

12. J. C. Davies, "Eine Theorie der Revolution," p. 186.

13. Wassmund, *Revolutionstheorien,* p. 51.

14. Compare the first three points here with the first three points under the category "causes" above.

15. R. D. Hopper, "Der revolutionäre Prozess," pp. 149–68.

16. I. Kramnick, "Reflections on Revolution," p. 31.

17. M. Rejai, *The Strategy of Political Revolution,* pp. 33 ff.

18. S. P. Huntington, *Political Order in Changing Societies,* p. 266.

19. R. Dahrendorf, "Über einige Probleme der soziologischen Theorie der Revolution," p. 178.

Works Cited

Abel, Wilhelm. *Agrarkrisen und Agrarkonjunktur: Eine Geschichte der Land- und Ernährungswirtschaft Mitteleuropas seit dem hohen Mittelalter.* 2nd ed. Hamburg, 1966.

L'Abolition de la 'Féodalité' dans le monde occidental: Toulouse, 1968. 2 vols. Paris, 1971.

Abrede unnd entlicher vertrage zwischen den Samlungen zweyer hauffen in Orttnaw vor Offenburg, und zwischen Bühel und Steinbach, uffgericht zuo Renchen uff Ascensionis domini Anno 1525. Strasbourg, 1525.

Angermeier, Heinz. "Die Vorstellung des gemeinen Mannes von Staat und Reich im deutschen Bauernkrieg." *Vierteljahrschrift für Sozial- und Wirtschaftsgeschichte* 53 (1966):329–43.

Arendt, Hannah. *On Revolution.* New York, 1963.

Baier, Hermann. "Zur Bevölkerungs- und Vermögensstatistik des Salemer Gebiets im 16. und 17. Jahrhundert." *Zeitschrift für die Geschichte des Oberrheins* 68 (1914):196–216.

Barton, P. F. "Variationen zum Thema: Bauernkrieg und Reformation." In Bernd Jaspert and Rudolf Mohr, eds., *Traditio—Krisis—Renovatio aus theologischer Sicht: Festschrift Winfried Zeller,* pp. 125–42. Marburg, 1976.

Baumann, Franz Ludwig. *Geschichte des Allgäus.* 3 vols. Kempten, 1883–94; reprinted, Aalen, 1971–73.

———, ed. *Akten zur Geschichte des deutschen Bauernkrieges aus Oberschwaben.* Freiburg i. Br., 1877.

Bensing, Manfred. "Idee und Praxis des 'Christlichen Verbündnisses' bei Thomas Müntzer." *Wissenschaftliche Zeitschrift der Karl-Marx-Universität Leipzig* 14 (1965): 459–71.

———. *Thomas Müntzer und der Thüringer Aufstand.* Berlin, 1966.

Beyme, Klaus von, ed. *Empirische Revolutionsforschung.* Opladen, 1973.

Blaschke, Karlheinz. *Ereignisse des Bauernkriegs 1525 in Sachsen. Der Sächsische Bauernaufstand 1790. Karten mit erläuterndem Text.* Abhandlungen der sächsischen Akademie der Wissenschaften zu Leipzig, Philologisch-historische Klasse, vol. 67, pt. 4. Berlin, 1978.

———. *Sachsen im Zeitalter der Reformation.* Gütersloh, 1970.

Blickle, Peter. "Bäuerliches Eigen im Allgäu." *Zeitschrift für Agrargeschichte und Agrarsoziologie* 17 (1969): 57–78.

———. *Kempten: Historischer Atlas von Bayern.* Teil Schwaben, vol. 6. Munich, 1968.

———. *Memmingen: Historischer Atlas von Bayern.* Teil Schwaben, vol. 4. Munich, 1967.

Bornkamm, Heinrich. *Martin Luther in der Mitte seines Lebens: Das Jahrzehnt zwischen dem Wormser und dem Augsburger Reichstag.* ed. Karin Bornkamm. Göttingen, 1979.

Brady, Thomas A. *Ruling Class, Regime, and Reformation at Strasbourg, 1520–1555.* Leiden, 1978.

Brecht, Martin. "Der theologische Hintergrund der Zwölf Artikel der Bauernschaft in

Schwaben von 1525: Christoph Schappeler und Sebastian Lotzers Beitrag." *Zeitschrift für Kirchengeschichte* 85 (1974): 174–208.

Brinton, Crane. *The Anatomy of Revolution.* 3rd ed. New York, 1965.

Brunner, Otto. *Land und Herrschaft: Grundlagen der territorialen Verfassungsgeschichte Österreichs im Mittelalter.* 6th ed. Darmstadt, 1970.

Bücking, Jürgen. "Der 'Bauernkrieg' in den habsburgischen Ländern als sozialer System-konflikt." In Hans-Ulrich Wehler, ed., *Der Deutsche Bauernkrieg, 1524–1526,* pp. 168–192. Göttingen, 1975. Translated in Scribner and Benecke, *The German Peasant War of 1525,* pp. 160–73.

Buszello, Horst. *Der deutsche Bauernkrieg als politische Bewegung mit besonderer Berücksichtigung der anonymen Flugschrift an die Versamlung gemayner Pawerschafft.* Berlin, 1969.

Chayanov, A. V. *The Theory of Peasant Economy.* Homewood, Ill., 1966.

Cohn, Henry J. "Anticlericalism in the German Peasants' War, 1525." *Past and Present,* no. 83 (May 1979), pp. 3–31.

———. "Reformatorische Bewegung und Antiklerikalismus in Deutschland und England." In W. J. Mommsen, ed., *Stadtbürgertum und Adel in der Reformation,* pp. 309–29. London, 1979.

Conrad, Hermann. *Deutsche Rechtsgeschichte.* 2 vols. Heidelberg, 1966.

Czok, Karl. "Zur sozialökonomischen Struktur und politischen Rolle der Vorstädte in Sachsen und Thüringen im Zeitalter der deutschen frühbürgerlichen Revolution." *Wissenschaft-liche Zeitschrift der Karl-Marx-Universität,* Gesellschafts- und Sprachwissenschaftliche Reihe 24 (1975), pp. 53–68. Translated in Scribner and Benecke, *The German Peasant War,* pp. 84–97.

Dahrendorf, Ralf. "Über einige Probleme der soziologischen Theorie der Revolution." In Urs Jaeggi and Sven Papke, eds., *Revolution und Theorie,* I: *Materialien zum bürgerlichen Revolutionsverständnis,* pp. 169–80. Frankfurt, 1974.

Davies, J. C. "Eine Theorie der Revolution." In K. von Beyme, ed., *Empirische Revolu-tionsforschung,* pp. 185–204. Opladen, 1973.

Decker-Hauff, Hansmartin, ed. *Die Chronik der Grafen von Zimmern.* Vol. 2. Stuttgart, 1967.

Dickens, A. G. *The German Nation and Martin Luther.* Glasgow, 1976.

Diehl, A. "Gemeiner Nutzen im Mittelalter." *Zeitschrift für württembergische Landesge-schichte* 1 (1937): 296–315.

Dülmen, R. van. *Reformation als Revolution: Soziale Bewegung und religiöser Radikalismus in der deutschen Reformation.* Munich, 1977.

Eckardt, Hans Wilhelm. *Herrschaftliche Jagd, bäuerliche Not, und bürgerliche Kritik: Zur Geschichte der fürstlichen und adeligen Jagdprivilegien vornehmlich im südwestdeutschen Raum.* Göttingen, 1976.

Eder, Irmtraud. *Die saarländischen Weistümer: Dokumente der Territorialpolitik.* Saar-brücken, 1978.

Elliger, Walter. *Thomas Müntzer: Leben und Werk.* Göttingen, 1975.

Endres, Rudolf. *Adelige Lebensformen in Franken zur Zeit des Bauernkrieges.* Würzburg, 1974.

———. "Der Bauernkrieg in Franken." *Blätter für deutsche Landesgeschichte* 109 (1973): 31–68. Translated in Scribner and Benecke, *The German Peasant War,* pp. 63–83.

———. "Zünfte und Unterschichten als Elemente der Instabilität in den Städten." In Peter Blickle, ed., *Revolte und Revolution in Europa,* pp. 151–70. Munich, 1975.

Engels, Friedrich. *Der deutsche Bauernkrieg.* In *Marx-Engels Werke,* vol. 7, 39 vols. Berlin, 1956–.

Franz, Eckhart G. "Hessen und Kurmainz in der Revolution 1525: Zur Rolle des früh-modernen Staates im Bauernkrieg." In Hermann Bannasch and Hans-Peter Lachmann, eds., *Aus Geschichte und ihren Hilfswissenschaften: Festschrift für Walter Heinemeyer zum 65. Geburtstag,* pp. 628–52. Marburg, 1979.

Franz, Günther. "Aus der Kanzlei der württembergischen Bauern im Bauernkrieg." *Württembergische Vierteljahrshefte für Landesgeschichte* 41 (1935):83–108, 281–305.

———. *Der deutsche Bauernkrieg.* 1st ed. Munich, 1933.

———. *Der deutsche Bauernkrieg.* 9th ed. Darmstadt, 1972.

———. "Die Entstehung der *Zwölf Artikel* der deutschen Bauernschaft." *Archiv für Reformationsgeschichte* 36 (1939):195–213.

———. "Folgen des Bauernkriegs—noch heute spürbar?" *Die landwirtschaftliche Berufschule* 18 (1968):1 ff.

———. "Die Führer im Bauernkrieg." In G. Franz, ed., *Bäuerliche Führungsschichten in der Neuzeit,* pp. 1–15. Büdingen, 1974.

———. *Geschichte des deutschen Bauernstandes vom frühen Mittelalter bis zum 19. Jahrhundert.* Stuttgart, 1970.

———. "Die Geschichte des deutschen Landwarenhandels." In Günther Franz, Wilhelm Abel, and G. Cascorbi, eds., *Der deutsche Landwarenhandel.* Hanover, 1960.

———, ed. *Der deutsche Bauernkrieg: Aktenband.* Munich, 1935; 2nd ed., Darmstadt, 1968.

———, ed. *Quellen zur Geschichte des Bauernkrieges.* Darmstadt, 1963.

———, ed. *Thomas Müntzer. Schriften und Briefe. Kritische Gesamtausgabe unter Mitarbeit von Paul Kirn.* Gütersloh, 1968.

———, and Walter Peter Fuchs, eds. *Akten zur Geschichte des Bauernkriegs in Mitteldeutschland.* Vol. 2. Jena, 1942; reprinted, Aalen, 1964.

Fuchs, Walter Peter. "Der Bauernkrieg von 1525 als Massenphänomen." In Wilhelm Bitter, ed., *Massenwahn in Geschichte und Gegenwart,* pp. 198–207. Stuttgart, 1965.

———. "Das Zeitalter der Reformation." In Bruno Gebhardt, ed., *Handbuch der deutschen Geschichte,* 2:1–104. 9th ed. Stuttgart, 1970.

Gehring, Paul. *Nördliches Oberschwaben.* Württembergische ländliche Rechtsquellen, vol. 3. Stuttgart, 1941.

Gothein, Eberhard. "Die Lage des Bauernstandes am Ende des Mittelalters." *Westdeutsche Zeitschrift für Geschichte und Kunst* 4 (1885): 1–22.

Götze, Alfred, ed. "Die Zwölf Artikel der Bauern 1525: Kritisch herausgegeben." *Historische Vierteljahrschrift* 5 (1902): 1–33.

Graf, Fred. "Die soziale und wirtschaftliche Lage der Bauern im Nürnberger Gebiet zur Zeit des Bauernkrieges." *Jahresbericht des Historischen Vereins für Mittelfranken* 56 (1909): 1–162.

Günter, Heinrich, ed. *Gerwig Blarer, Abt von Weingarten, 1520–67: Briefe und Akten.* Vol. 1. Stuttgart, 1914.

Gunzert. W. "Zwei Hagenauer Abschiede von 1525." *Elsass-Lothringisches Jahrbuch* 17 (1938): 164–71.

Hagopian, M. N. *The Phenomenon of Revolution.* New York, 1975.

Hartfelder, Karl. "Urkundliche Beiträge zur Geschichte des Bauernkriegs im Breisgau." *Zeitschrift für die Geschichte des Oberrheins* 34 (1882): 393–466.

Hassinger, Erich. *Das Werden des neuzeitlichen Europa, 1300–1600.* Braunschweig, 1959.

Hauser, A. "Bäuerliche Wirtschaft und Ernährung in der Schweiz vom 15. bis 18. Jahrhundert." *Zeitschrift für Agrargeschichte und Agrarsoziologie* 19 (1971): 170–89.

Heimpel, Christina. *Die Entwicklung der Einnahmen und Ausgaben des Heiliggeistspitals zu Biberach an der Riss von 1500 bis 1630.* Stuttgart, 1966.

Hermann, Paul, ed. *Zimmerische Chronik urkundlich berichtet von Graf Froben Christof von Zimmern und seinem Schreiber Johannes Müller, nach der von Karl Barack besorgten zweiten Ausgabe.* 4 vols. Meersburg-Leipzig, n.d.

Hillerbrand, Hans J. "The German Reformation and the Peasants' War." In Lawrence P. Buck and Jonathan W. Zophy, eds., *The Social History of the Reformation,* pp. 106–36. Columbus, Ohio, 1972.

Hopper, Rex D. "Der revolutionäre Prozess." In Urs Jaeggi and Sven Papke, eds., *Revolution und Theorie,* I: *Materialien zum bürgerlichen Revolutionsverständnis,* pp. 149–68. Frankfurt, 1974.

Huntington, Samuel P. "Modernisierung durch Revolution." In K. von Beyme, ed., *Empirische Revolutionsforschung,* pp. 92–104. Opladen, 1973.

———. *Political Order in Changing Societies.* 3rd ed. New Haven, 1969.

Johnson, Chalmers. *Autopsy on People's War.* Berkeley, 1973.

———. *Revolutionary Change.* Boston, 1966.

Jörg, Joseph Edmund. *Deutschland in der Revolutions-Periode von 1522-1526, aus den diplomatischen Correspondenzen und Original-Akten bayerischer Archive.* Freiburg, 1851.

Kelter, Ernst. "Die wirtschaftlichen Ursachen des Bauernkrieges." *Schmollers Jahrbuch für Gesetzgebung: Verwaltung und Volkswirtschaft im Deutschen Reiche* 65 (1941): 641–82.

Kramnick, Isaac. "Reflections on Revolution: Definition and Explanation in Recent Scholarship." *History and Theory* 11 (1972): 26–63.

Lamprecht, Karl. *Deutsche Geschichte.* Vol. 5. Freiburg, 1894.

Landsberger, H. A., ed. *Latin American Peasant Movements.* London, 1979.

———, ed. *Rural Protest: Peasant Movements and Social Change.* London, 1974.

Landwehr, Götz. "Die Bedeutung der Reichs- und Territorialpfandschaften für Aufbau des kurpfälzischen Territoriums." *Mitteilungen des Historischen Vereins der Pfalz* 66 (1968): 155–96.

Lau, Franz. "Der Bauernkrieg und das angebliche Ende der lutherischen Reformation als spontaner Volksbewegung." *Luther-Jahrbuch* 26 (1959): 109–34. Excerpted in Kyle Sessions, ed., *Reformation and Authority,* pp. 94–101. Lexington, Mass., 1968.

Laube, Adolf. "Der Aufstand der Schwazer Bergarbeiter 1525 und ihre Haltung im Tiroler Bauernkrieg, mit einem Quellenanhang." *Jahrbuch für Geschichte des Feudalismus* 2 (1978): 225–58.

———. "Zum Problem des Bündnisses von Bergarbeitern und Bauern im deutschen Bauernkrieg." In Gerhard Heitz, Adolf Laube, Max Steinmetz, and Günter Vogler, 'eds., *Der Bauer im Klassenkampf,* pp. 83–110. Berlin, 1975.

———, and Hans-Werner Seiffert, eds. *Flugschriften der Bauernkriegszeit.* Berlin, 1975.

———, Max Steinmetz, and Günter Vogler. *Illustrierte Geschichte der deutschen frühbürgerlichen Revolution.* Berlin, 1974.

Le Roy Ladurie, Emmanuel. *Les paysans de Languedoc.* 2 vols. Paris, 1966.

Locher, Gottfried W. "Grundzüge der Theologie Huldrych Zwinglis im Vergleich mit derjenigen Martin Luthers und Johannes Calvins." In Gottfried Locher, *Huldrych Zwingli in neuer Sicht: Zehn Beiträge zur Theologie des Zürcher Reformators,* pp. 173–274. Zurich, 1969.

———. *Die Zwinglische Reformation im Rahmen der europäischen Kirchengeschichte.* Göttingen, 1979.

Ludwig, Karl-Heinz. "Bergleute im Bauernkrieg." *Zeitschrift für Historische Forschung* 5 (1978): 23–47.

Lütge, Friedrich. *Geschichte der deutschen Agrarverfassung vom frühen Mittelalter bis zum 19. Jahrhundert.* 2nd ed. Stuttgart, 1967.

Luther, Martin. *Werke.* Weimar, 1883–.

———. *Works.* Ed. H. Lehmann and J. Pelikan. St. Louis, 1955–.

Lutz, Heinrich. "Der politische und religiöse Aufbruch Europas im 16. Jahrhundert." In Golo Mann, ed., *Propyläen Weltgeschichte,* 7: 25–132. Berlin, 1964.

Lutz, Robert H. *Wer war der gemeine Mann? Der dritte Stand in der Krise des Spätmittelalters.* Vienna, 1979.

Macek, Josef. *Der Tiroler Bauernkrieg und Michael Gaismair.* Berlin, 1965.

Maron, G. "Bauernkrieg." In *Theologische Realenzyklopädie,* 5, fascicle 3/4: 321–38. Berlin and New York, 1979.

Martini, F. *Das Bauerntum im deutschen Schrifttum von den Anfängen bis zum 16. Jahrhundert.* Halle, 1944.

Maurer, Hans-Martin. "Der Bauernkrieg als Massenerhebung: Dynamik einer revolutionären

Bewegung." In *Bausteine zur geschichtlichen Landeskunde von Baden-Württemberg*, pp. 225-95. Stuttgart, 1979.

Maurer, Justus. *Prediger im Bauernkrieg*. Stuttgart, 1979.

Merx, Otto, ed. *Akten zur Geschichte des Bauernkriegs in Mitteldeutschland*. Vol. 1, sect. 1. Leipzig, 1923; reprinted, Aalen, 1964.

Michaelis, Heinz. "Die Verwendung und Bedeutung der Bibel in den Hauptschriften der Bauern von 1525/26: Unter Berücksichtigung der bedeutendsten Reformentwürfe aus der Zeit des 15. Jahrhunderts." Th.D. dissertation, Greifswald, 1953.

Moeller, Bernd. *Deutschland im Zeitalter der Reformation*. Göttingen, 1977.

Müller, Walter. *Entwicklung und Spätformen der Leibeigenschaft am Beispiel der Heiratsbeschränkungen: Die Ehegenossame im alemannisch-schweizerischen Raum*. Sigmaringen, 1974.

Nipperdey, Thomas, and Peter Melcher. "Bauernkrieg." In Wohlfeil, *Reformation oder frühbürgerliche Revolution?*, pp. 287-306.

Oberman, Heiko A. "The Gospel of Social Unrest." In Scribner and Benecke, *The German Peasant War*, pp. 39-51.

Oestreich, Gerhard. *Geist und Gestalt des frühmodernen Staates*. Berlin, 1969.

———. "Verfassungsgeschichte vom Ende des Mittelalters bis zum Ende des alten Reiches." In Bruno Gebhardt, ed., *Handbuch der deutschen Geschichte*, 2: 360-436. 9th ed. Stuttgart, 1970.

Pickl, Othmar. "Arbeitskräfte und Viehbesatz sowie Vermögensverhältnisse Steiermärkischer Bauernhöfe im 16. Jahrhundert." In *Wirtschaftliche und soziale Strukturen im säkularen Wandel: Festschrift für Wilhelm Abel zum 70. Geburtstag*, 1:143-70. 2 vols. Hanover, 1974.

Pietsch, Friedrich. "Die Artikel der Limpurger Bauern." *Zeitschrift für württembergische Landesgeschichte* 13 (1954): 120-49.

Rammstedt, Otthein. "Stadtunruhen, 1525." In Hans-Ulrich Wehler, ed., *Der Deutsche Bauernkrieg, 1524-1526*, pp. 239-76. Göttingen, 1975.

Ranke, Leopold von. *Deutsche Geschichte im Zeitalter der Reformation*. Ed. Paul Joachimson. 6 vols. Munich, 1925-26.

Rapp, Francis. "L'aristocratie paysanne du Kochersberg." *Bulletin philologique et historique: 1967* (Paris, 1969), pp. 439-50.

Rauch, Moritz von, ed. *Urkundenbuch der Stadt Heilbronn*. Vol. 4. Stuttgart, 1922.

Rejai, Mostafa. *The Strategy of Political Revolution*. Garden City, N.Y., 1973.

Ritter, Gerhard. *Die Neugestaltung Europas im 16. Jahrhundert*. Berlin, 1950.

Rosenberg, Hans. "Der deutsche Bauernkrieg in sozialgeschichtlicher Perspektive." Lecture delivered at the University of Freiburg, November 1978.

Rössler, Helmuth. "Über die Wirkungen von 1525." In H. Haushofer and W. Boelcke, eds., *Wege und Forschungen der Agrargeschichte: Festschrift zum 65. Geburtstag von Günther Franz*, pp. 104-14. Frankfurt, 1967.

Sabean, David W. "Der Bauernkrieg—ein Literaturbericht für das Jahr 1975." *Zeitschrift für Agrargeschichte und Agrarsoziologie* 24 (1976): 221-28.

———. "The Communal Basis of Pre-1800 Uprisings in Western Europe." *Comparative Politics* 8 (1976): 355-64.

———. "German Agrarian Institutions at the Beginning of the Sixteenth Century: Upper Swabia as an Example." In Janos Bak, ed., *The German Peasant War of 1525*, pp. 76-88. London, 1976.

———. *Landbesitz und Gesellschaft am Vorabend des Bauernkriegs: Eine Studie der sozialen Verhältnisse im südlichen Oberschwaben in den Jahren vor 1525*. Stuttgart, 1972.

———. "Markets, Uprisings, and Leadership in Peasant Societies: Western Europe, 1381-1789." *Peasant Studies Newsletter* 2, no. 3, (1973) 17 ff.

Schenck, E. *Simprecht Schenck: Das Lebensbild eines schwäbischen Reformators*. Darmstadt, 1938.

Schlenck, Wolfgang. *Die Reichsstadt Memmingen und die Reformation*. Memmingen, 1969.

Schnabel, Franz. *Deutschlands geschichtliche Quellen und Darstellungen in der Neuzeit.* Vol. 1. Leipzig, 1931; reprinted, 1972.

Schnyder, Werner. *Die Bevölkerung der Stadt und Landschaft Zürich vom 14. bis 17. Jahrhundert: Eine methodologische Studie.* Zurich, 1925.

Schreiber, Heinrich, ed. *Der deutsche Bauernkrieg: Gleichzeitige Urkunden.* Urkundenbuch der Stadt Freiburg N.F., 3 parts: I, 1524; II, January–July 1525; III, July–December 1525. Freiburg, 1864–66.

Schulze, Winfried. "Die veränderte Bedeutung sozialer Konflikte im16 and 17. Jahrhundert." In Hans-Ulrich Wehler, ed., *Der Deutsche Bauernkrieg, 1524–1526,* pp. 277–302. Göttingen, 1975.

Schwarze, Elisabeth. "Veränderungen der Sozial- und Besitzstruktur in ostthüringischen Ämtern und Städten am Vorabend des Bauernkrieges." *Jahrbuch für Wirtschaftsgeschichte* 3 (1976): 255–73.

Scribner, Robert W. "Is There a Social History of the Reformation?" *Social History* 4 (1977): 483–505.

_____. "The Reformation as a Social Movement." In W. J. Mommsen, ed., *Stadtbürgertum und Adel in der Reformation,* pp. 49–79. London, 1979.

_____, and Gerhard Benecke, eds. and trans. *The German Peasant War of 1525: New Viewpoints.* London, 1979.

Seibt, Ferdinand. *Utopica: Modelle totaler Sozialplanung.* Düsseldorf, 1972.

Shanin, Theodor. *The Awkward Class: Political Sociology of Peasantry in a Developing Society, Russia, 1910–1925.* Oxford, 1972.

_____. "The Nature and Logic of Peasant Economy." *Journal of Peasant Studies* 1 (1973): 63–80, 186–206.

Skalweit, Stephan. *Reich und Reformation.* Berlin, 1967.

Smirin, M. M. *Deutschland vor der Reformation: Abriss der Geschichte des politischen Kampfes in Deutschland vor der Reformation.* Berlin, 1955.

_____. *Die Volksreformation des Thomas Münzer und der grosse Bauernkrieg.* 2nd ed. Berlin, 1956.

Stalnaker, John C. "Towards a Social Interpretation of the German Peasant War." In Scribner and Benecke, *The German Peasant War,* pp. 23–38.

Steinmetz, Max. "Die frühbürgerliche Revolution in Deutschland (1476–1535): Thesen zur Vorbereitung der wissenschaftlichen Konferenz in Wernigerode vom 20. bis 24. Januar 1960." In Rainer Wohlfeil, ed., *Reformation oder frühbürgerliche Revolution?,* pp. 42–55. Munich, 1972. Translated in Scribner and Benecke, *The German Peasant War,* pp. 9–18.

Stern, A. "Das römische Recht und der deutsche Bauernkrieg von 1525." *Zeitschrift für Schweizerische Geschichte* 14 (1934): 20–29.

Straube, Manfred. "Die politischen, ökonomischen, und sozialen Verhältnisse des Amtes Allstedt in der ersten Hälfte des 16. Jahrhunderts." In *Allstedt: Wirkungsstätte Thomas Müntzers,* pp. 28–44. Allstedt, 1975.

Strickler, Johann, ed. *Die Eidgenössischen Abschiede aus dem Zeitraume von von 1521 bis 1928.* Amtliche Sammlung der älteren Eidgenössischen Abschiede, vol. 4, sec. 1a. Brugg, 1873.

Sturm, H. *Tirschenreuth: Historischer Atlas von Bayern.* Teil Altbayern, no. 21. Munich, 1970.

Tanter, Raymond, and Manus Midlarsky. "Revolutionen: Eine quantitative Analyse." In K. von Beyme, ed., *Empirische Revolutionsforschung,* pp. 135–57. Opladen, 1973.

Thomas, Ulrich. *Bibliographie zum deutschen Bauernkrieg und seiner Zeit.* 2 parts. Stuttgart, 1976–77.

Treue, Wolfgang. "Wirtschaft, Gesellschaft, und Technik in Deutschland vom 16. bis zum 18. Jahrhundert." In B. Gebhardt, ed., *Handbuch der deutschen Geschichte,* 2:437–545. 9th ed. Stuttgart, 1970.

Vasella, Oskar. "Bauernkrieg und Reformation in Graubünden, 1525-1526." *Zeitschrift für Schweizerische Geschichte* 20 (1940): 1-65.

Virck, Hans, ed. *Politische Correspondenz der Stadt Strassburg im Zeitalter der Reformation,* vol. 1, 1517-1530. Strasbourg, 1882.

Vochezer, Joseph. *Geschichte des fürstlichen Hauses Waldburg in Schwaben.* 2 vols. Kempten, 1900.

Vogler, Günter. *"Die Gewalt soll gegeben werden dem gemeinen Volk": Der deutsche Bauernkrieg, 1525.* Berlin, 1975.

————. "Marx, Engels, und die Konzeption einer frühbürgerlichen Revolution in Deutschland." In Wohlfeil, *Reformation oder frühbürgerliche Revolution?,* pp. 187-204.

————. "Der revolutionäre Gehalt und die räumliche Verbreitung der oberschwäbischen Zwölf Artikel." In Peter Blickle, ed., *Revolte und Revolution in Europa.* Historische Zeitschrift Beiheft 4 N.F. Munich, 1975.

Vogt, Wilhelm, ed. "Die Correspondenz des schwäbischen Bundeshauptmannes Ulrich Artzt von Augsburg aus den Jahren 1524-1527: Ein Beitrag zur Geschichte des schwäbischen Bundes und des Bauernkrieges." *Zeitschrift des Historischen Vereins für Schwaben und Neuburg* 6 (1879): 281-404; 7 (1880): 233-30; 9 (1882): 1-62; 10 (1883): 1-298.

Waas, Adolf. *Die Bauern im Kampf um Gerechtigkeit, 1300-1525.* Munich, 1964.

————. "Die grosse Wendung im deutschen Bauernkrieg." *Historiche Zeitschrift* 158 (1938): 457-91; 159 (1939): 22-53.

Wackernagel, Rudolf. *Humanismus und Reformation in Basel.* Basel, 1924.

Walder, Ernst. "Der politische Gehalt der Zwölf Artikel der deutschen Bauernschaft von 1525." *Schweizer Beiträge zur Allgemeinen Geschichte* 12 (1954): 5-22.

Wassmund, Hans. *Revolutionstheorien.* Munich, 1978.

Weitnauer, Alfred. *Die Bauern des Stifts Kempten, 1525/26.* Alte Allgäuer Geschlechter, 25. Kempten, 1949.

Wieacker, Franz. *Privatrechtsgeschichte der Neuzeit unter besonderer Berücksichtigung der deutschen Entwicklung.* Göttingen, 1952.

Wohlfeil, Rainer. "Der Speyrer Reichstag von 1526." *Blätter für pfälzische Kirchengeschichte und religiöse Volkskunde* 43 (1976): 5-20.

————, ed. *Der Bauernkrieg, 1524-1526: Bauernkrieg und Reformation.* Munich, 1975.

————, ed. *Reformation oder frühbürgerliche Revolution?* Munich, 1972.

Wolf, Eric. *Peasant Wars of the Twentieth Century.* New York, 1969.

————. *Peasants.* Englewood Cliffs, 1966.

Wollbrett, Alphonse, ed. *La Guerre des Paysans 1525: Etudes Alsatiques.* Saverne, 1975.

Wopfner, Hermann. *Die Lage Tirols zu Ausgang des Mittelalters.* Berlin, 1908.

————, ed. *Quellen zur Geschichte des Bauernkrieges in Deutschtirol 1525,* part 1, *Quellen zur Vorgeschichte des Bauernkrieges: Beschwerdeartikel aus den Jahren 1519-1525.* Acta Tirolensia, vol. 3. Innsbruck, 1908; reprinted, Aalen, 1973.

Wunder, Heide. "The Mentality of Rebellious Peasants: The Samland Peasant Rebellion of 1525." In Scribner and Benecke, *The German Peasant War,* pp. 144-59.

————. "Der samländische Bauernaufstand: Entwurf für eine sozialgeschichtliche Forschungsstrategie." In Wohlfeil, *Der Bauernkrieg,* pp. 143-76.

Zimmerman, Wilhelm. *Allgemeine Geschichte des grossen Bauernkrieges.* 2nd ed. Stuttgart, 1856.

Zuck, Lowell. *Christianity and Revolution: Radical Christian Testimonies, 1520-1650.* Philadelphia, 1975.

Zwingli, Ulrich. *Hauptschriften,* vol. 4, *Zwingli der Verteidiger des Glaubens: Auslegung und Begründung der Schlussreden.* Ed. Oskar Frei. Zurich, 1952.

Index of Names

Index of Places

Note: The name in parentheses following *Kr.* is the modern administrative district (*Kreis*) in which the place is located.

Index of Subjects

Note: Grievances and demands are indexed under the objects of the grievances and demands.